"As a Tibetan, I have deep empathy fo[r those] oppressed by the Communist Chinese [...] control relies on the use of force. For [...] trust nobody will be happy in any situation. In *Unbroken*, Rushan Abbas reveals the truth of the Uyghur people's plight."

— HIS HOLINESS THE DALAI LAMA

"Abbas intertwines her personal journey with powerful historical insights, including poignant excerpts from her father's memoir during China's Cultural Revolution. This book is an intimate portrayal of courage and resilience. A must-read for policymakers, advocates, and anyone committed to human dignity and religious freedom."

— MUDDASSAR AHMED, PRESIDENT, CONCORDIA FORUM

"Rushan Abbas is my gorgeous friend. We have dinner together and go shopping together like ordinary girlfriends, but I've never seen her smile from her heart. I know why: because her family and her country are being violated every single day. Rushan is a symbol of the Uyghur people. To be honest, I was afraid to turn the pages of this book. Because I should have realized my own powerlessness on the worst oppression in the history of human beings happening to my friend. But I want many people to pick up this book and read it bcause my friend's hard life clearly points to a common challenge for all of us."

— KAORI ARIMOTO, SECRETARY GENERAL, CONSERVATIVE PARTY OF JAPAN

"Rushan Abbas stands as a fierce voice against silence, exposing the human cost of China's oppression of the Uyghur people. Unbroken is a powerful testament to love, resilience, and the urgent need for moral courage in the face of tyranny."

— RT HON DAME KAREN BRADLEY, MP DBE, MEMBER OF PARLIAMENT, UNITED KINGDOM

"Rushan's story tells in graphic detail the treatment Uyghurs experience in the genocide Xi Jinping's China is inflicting on them. Her experience tells the world why we must stop China before their evil tentacles spread further. Read her story and be moved by her courage to fight back!"

— SAM BROWNBACK, FORMER U.S. SENATOR AND AMBASSADOR AT LARGE FOR INTERNATIONAL RELIGIOUS FREEDOM

"Rushan Abbas' story of relentless and steadfast commitment to promoting and protecting the rights of her fellow Uyghurs, including her unjustly detained sister Gulshan, despite the efforts of the regime in Beijing is inspiring to all of us committed to helping the Uyghur people and to advancing human rights globally."

— SCOTT BUSBY, SENIOR ADVISOR, HUMAN RIGHTS FIRST; FORMER DEPUTY ASSISTANT SECRETARY OF STATE, BUREAU OF DEMOCRACY, HUMAN RIGHTS & LABOR

"China's genocide against the Uyghurs is the greatest crime of the 21st century. Rushan Abbas will not let us forget it."

— JAMES CARAFANO, SENIOR COUNSELOR TO THE PRESIDENT AND E.W. RICHARDSON FELLOW, THE HERITAGE FOUNDATION

"As Rushan Abbas tells her story, we hear the voice of a people who cannot speak. We see a woman of faith, determination, and courage take on evil and remain unbroken. In a time of darkness, her words are points of light."

— GORDON G. CHANG, AMERICAN COLUMNIST, AUTHOR, AND LAWYER

"This riveting narrative is strewn with broken hearts but unbroken spirit and one woman's unbroken commitment never to forsake her loved ones nor forgive her tormentors, the Chinese Communist government. Rushan's narrative lays out the suffering and resilience of her family's struggles to maintain their identity and culture. Her courage serves as a voice for millions of voiceless Uyghurs."

— RABBI ABRAHAM COOPER, SIMON WIESENTHAL CENTER; FORMER CHAIR, U.S. COMMISSION ON INTERNATIONAL RELIGIOUS FREEDOM

"As the son of Soviet Dissidents, Rushan's personal story, along with the broader experience of Uyghurs in China, is powerfully resonant. But more importantly, for anyone who cares about supporting freedom around the world, it should be required reading. Rushan's account is a call-to-action reminding us that a threat to freedom anywhere is a threat to freedom everywhere."

— URIEL EPSHTEIN, CEO, RENEW DEMOCRACY INITIATIVE

"*Unbroken* is a courageous, heart-wrenching, and deeply inspiring testimony of resistance against tyranny. As a fellow survivor of the Chinese Communist Party's brutal repression, I am moved by Rushan Abbas's strength and moral clarity. Her story echoes the cries of those silenced behind prison walls and barbed wire across all the lands under CCP rule."

— ZHOU FENGSUO, TIANANMEN STUDENT LEADER; EXECUTIVE DIRECTOR, HUMAN RIGHTS IN CHINA; CO-FOUNDER, HUMANITARIAN CHINA

"*Unbroken* is far more than a memoir—it is a fierce and unrelenting indictment of the Chinese Communist Party's campaign of repression against the Uyghur people and, by extension, against all who dare to maintain an identity outside the Party's control. In this gripping and courageous narrative, Rushan Abbas emerges as one of the most powerful voices of resistance—not only for the Uyghur cause but for oppressed peoples across the vast empire of China's silence."

— ISMAIL JUMA, TUNGKAN (HUI MUSLIM) HUMAN RIGHTS ACTIVIST

"The stories that touch us the deepest are the ones told by someone who lived them. We are all pieces of the same puzzle, and we cannot hope to preserve humanity and make the world a better place if we turn a blind eye to any atrocities, wherever in the world they are being committed. Listen to Rushan Abbas' powerful voice, learn from her strength and resilience and be inspired by it because every single one of us can become an agent for change if we choose not to run from or remain indifferent to human suffering."

— EVGENIA KARA-MURZA, RUSSIAN PRO-DEMOCRACY ACTIVIST; PRESIDENT, THE 30 OCTOBER FOUNDATION

"Rushan's story shows us that no matter how different the specific circumstances of our backgrounds might be, there is a powerful common thread linking all those with the courage to face down dictators. And because courage is contagious, I am grateful to Rushan for being willing to share hers."

— GARRY KASPAROV, FORMER WORLD CHESS CHAMPION AND RUSSIAN DISSIDENT

"The terrible plight of the Uyghur people tends to be brushed aside in the context of relations with China. Unbroken brings home in very direct and personal terms how central the issue really is if we are genuinely concerned with the protection of human rights around the world."

— AFZAL KHAN, MEMBER OF PARLIAMENT, UNITED KINGDOM

"Rushan is an inspiration, not only for her fellow Uyghurs but also for human rights advocates around the world. Her leadership and unwavering advocacy have played a tremendous role in shining a much-needed light on the horrific treatment of Uyghurs by the Chinese Communist Party. Everyone should read and share Rushan's story."

— U.S. CONGRESSWOMAN YOUNG KIM, CHAIRWOMAN OF THE HOUSE FOREIGN AFFAIRS SUBCOMMITTEE ON EAST ASIA AND THE PACIFIC

"Rushan's powerful memoir takes an unwavering stand against the CCP's brutality, not only exposing systematic oppression but empowering countless others to speak truth to power. *Unbroken* is an urgent call to action for policymakers, advocates, and all those committed to defending human dignity.

— U.S. CONGRESSMAN JOHN MOOLENAAR, CHAIRMAN, HOUSE SELECT COMMITTEE ON THE CCP

"Rushan is among the foremost human rights communicators of her generation, and this book is shot through with her characteristic honesty, lucidity, and raw power. Every word is carefully weighed, as though forged in a long fire of pain and injustice.

Yet it is also a book about love. A love between sisters that transcends evil — a force so powerful that it can convert a tragedy that would immobilize most people into an unstoppable campaigning force capable of writing this book. Read it and then act."

— LUKE DE PULFORD, CO-FOUNDER AND EXECUTIVE DIRECTOR, INTER-PARLIAMENTARY ALLIANCE ON CHINA

"In this new book, Rushan Abbas shows that she, like a Uyghur poem invoked, 'will come back, flying like a falcon, with a great triumph of victory.' Abbas's book ranges widely, chronicling topics ranging from persecution across the Uyghur region during the Great Proletarian Cultural Revolution to her relentless advocacy on behalf of her sister and family. Despite extraordinary challenges, her courage and compassion will no doubt inspire readers."

— DR. SOPHIE RICHARDSON, CO-EXECUTIVE DIRECTOR, CHINESE HUMAN RIGHTS DEFENDERS

"This is a definitive, first-hand account of how the Chinese government has systematically tried to snuff out the Uyghur identity while imprisoning millions of innocent Uyghurs, including Abbas's own sister Gulshan. She also lays out how Beijing is exporting its mass repression, likely to the country you are now in. This tragic but inspiring story will open your eyes to great cruelty that is being met with even greater fortitude by Abbas and many other brave Uyghurs. Do not turn away."

— JOSH ROGIN, LEAD GLOBAL SECURITY ANALYST, *WASHINGTON POST INTELLIGENCE*; AND AUTHOR OF *CHAOS UNDER HEAVEN: TRUMP, XI, AND THE BATTLE FOR THE TWENTY-FIRST CENTURY*

"Rushan Abbas is an incredibly strong person, refusing to be silent amid tragedy and transnational repression. Her story shows the human cost of the Chinese Communist Party's campaign to erase the Uyghur people. America must confront authoritarianism with the moral leadership and courage this moment demands."

— U.S. CONGRESSMAN THOMAS R. SUOZZI

"Rushan Abbas has been a clarion and courageous voice speaking out on behalf of the persecuted Uyghur people, and her voice comes to life in every page of this moving book. You cannot read Rushan's story without coming away changed for the better, inspired by her strength and motivated by her determination to achieve justice for the Uyghurs. Her words remind us to cherish our freedom, and they call us to stand tall and speak out boldly for those whose freedom has been trampled."

— DR. KATRINA LANTOS SWETT, FORMER CHAIR, U.S. COMMISSION ON INTERNATIONAL RELIGIOUS FREEDOM; PRESIDENT, LANTOS FOUNDATION FOR HUMAN RIGHTS & JUSTICE

"Student, translator, sister, relentless advocate: perhaps as much as any single person, Rushan Abbas brought the plight of China's repressed Uyghur ethnicity into the American consciousness. This fascinating account of her journey shows that even in an age of autocrats, a single fearless voice can speak truth — and bring shame — to power."

— SABIN WILLETT, LEAD ATTORNEY FOR THE GUANTANAMO UYGHURS (2005–2013)

"Rushan Abbas's gripping memoir invites us to consider the costs of standing up to a totalitarian regime. Beijing mercilessly uses any draconian tactic at its disposal to silence the voices decrying a modern-day genocide. From state surveillance to facial recognition and DNA testing, Xi Jinping is bending technology to dystopian authoritarian ends as his regime works to perfect the repression algorithm. But Rushan, animated by the unfailing love for her imprisoned sister and the persistent hope for freedom in her Uyghur homeland, offers an inspiring counterpoint to the limits of authoritarian control. Everyone who cares about freedom and democracy should learn from Rushan and other brave Uyghurs as they demonstrate the urgency — and the necessity — of fighting for a future that values human dignity."

— DAMON WILSON, PRESIDENT AND CEO, NATIONAL ENDOWMENT FOR DEMOCRACY

"*Unbroken* is a meticulous, detailed indictment of the wholesale persecution of a people considered to be in the way of China's economic progress. Because nearly every nation on Earth stands to profit from this progress, the plight of the Uyghurs, constitutes one of the great Third Rails of global politics. Rushan Abbas, her extended family, and such heroic figures as Wu'er Kaixi, a central inspiration in the famous Tiananmen Square resistance of 1989, have now joined forces to protest and prevent China's continued efforts at suppression and eradication. *Unbroken* is the voice of a brave woman raised in the name of her people, a people for generations under the relentless thumb of a world power that brooks no nonsense."

— MICHAEL WOLFE, AUTHOR OF *ONE THOUSAND ROADS TO MECCA*

"In *Unbroken*, Rushan carries the conscience of her father and translates it into our current moment. Unimaginable pain is channeled into unstoppable advocacy. Her voice is fearless, and a powerful reminder that the fight for justice spans generations."

— SAMEER ZUBERI, MEMBER OF PARLIAMENT, CANADA

Unbroken: One Uyghur's Fight For Freedom © Ottawa, 2025 Rushan Abbas

First Edition published in Canada and United States
Published by Optimum Publishing International.

All rights reserved. No part of this publication may be reproduced in any form or by any means whatsoever or stored in a data base without permission in writing from the publisher, except by a reviewer who may quote passages of customary brevity in review.

LIBRARY AND ARCHIVES CANADA CATALOGUING IN PUBLICATION
Title: Unbroken: One Uyghur's Fight for Freedom
Rushan Abbas

Subjects: Transnational Repression, Human Rights , Religion, CCP, Chinese Hegemony, Geo-politics, Uyghur Genocide,
Description: Optimum Publishing International Canada edition

ISBN 978-0-88890-360-0 (Trade Paperback)
ISBN 978-0-88890-359-4 (Hardcover)
ISBN 978-0-88890-316-7 (ePub)

Jacket and interior design by Jess Albert

PRINTED AND BOUND IN CANADA
Marquis Printing

For information on rights or any submissions, please e-mail to Optimum: deanb@opibooks.com
Optimum Publishing International
Dean Baxendale, President & CEO
Toronto, Canada

www.optimumpublishinginternational.com
www.opibooks.com
X @opibooks | Instagram @opibooks

UNBROKEN

ONE UYGHUR'S FIGHT FOR FREEDOM

RUSHAN ABBAS

DEDICATION

To my sister, Gulshan Abbas, who has been unjustly imprisoned by the Chinese government since September 2018. Her only "crime" was being my sister, someone who spoke the truth. Gulshan *hede*, this book and everything I do is for you. Your strength, your resilience, and your spirit fuel my every step.

To my mother, Mariye Abliz, and my father, Abbas Borhan, who instilled in me the values of integrity, courage, and love for our people. Your sacrifices are the foundation upon which I stand.

To my beloved husband, Abdulhakim Idris, your love and strength have been my anchor. I'm deeply grateful to have you by my side.

To my children, Misron, Shad, Shireen, Bugrahan, and Forkan, the light in my life, who remind me every day why we fight—for a future where no child has to grow up fearing that their future and their lives are uncertain due to a totalitarian country like the CCP's China.

To Dr. and Mrs. Faulkner and their family, the reason I found a place in the land of the free and the home of the brave, and the platform that allows me to fight for freedom today.

To all the people in China who are suffering under the Chinese Communist Party's oppression. This book is for you. To all the freedom-loving people of the world. This fight is for you.

To Freedom.

CONTENTS

	Acknowledgements	x
	Preface	xii
	Foreword	xiv
	Foreword	xvii
	Introduction	xix
1.	ONE VOICE, ONE STEP	1
2.	CHINA'S LONG BLACK ARM	11
3.	YOU CAN NEVER BE A SINGER	27
4.	WHAT MY FATHER WITNESSED	32
5.	RESURRECTING THE UYGHUR IDENTITY	52
6.	THE 1980s STUDENT PROTESTS	62
7.	TENACITY	81
8.	GUANTÁNAMO	103
9.	TWO STARS DEPART FROM THE SKY	123
10.	IN SEARCH OF MY SISTER	147
11.	ECONOMIC COLONIALISM AND THE VOICE OF REGRET	161
12.	THE GENOCIDE OLYMPIC GAMES AND OUR GENOCIDE REPORT	176
13.	THE LIGHT OF HOPE	198
	A Letter to the Uyghur Diaspora	218

ACKNOWLEDGEMENTS

Writing this book has been a journey of profound reflection, pain, and hope, and I could not have done it alone.

I am deeply grateful to my family—my brother Nijat Abbas and his wife, Nuriman, for their unwavering support, and my brother Dr. Rishat Abbas, whose advocacy and resilience continue to inspire me. I also thank his wife, Hamra, for her steadfast dedication. To all of their children, my nieces and nephews, you are an invaluable part of my life, and your presence brings me strength and hope. Your care and support mean more than words can express, and I am forever grateful to walk this journey with all of you.

To my niece Ziba, a beacon of strength in her fight for her mother's freedom, and her sister Zamira, whose courage shines through hardship. And to Gulshan's granddaughters—Zelilah, Sabina, Eliza, and Amira—who carry their grandmother's spirit despite her absence.

Erika Kuenne's commitment throughout this challenging journey has been unwavering, and her constant presence, encouragement, and belief in this cause have been a powerful source of strength. Erika's kindness, compassion, and determination have made all the difference, and I am truly thankful for her help.

My anonymous friend's guidance in 2018 and 2019 was tremendously crucial. During a time of limited resources and staff support, her confidence, belief in me, and guidance shaped my advocacy. From editing my speeches and press releases to offering personal encouragement, her unwavering support transformed me into the advocate I am today. I will forever be thankful for her impact on my journey.

I owe a great debt to the countless individuals and organizations who stand in solidarity with the Uyghur people, lending their voices, their platforms, and their resources to expose the truth. To my colleagues, fellow

ACKNOWLEDGEMENTS

advocates, and the brave survivors who have made the actions in this book possible, you have reminded me that we are never alone in this struggle.

The process of bringing this book to life would not have been possible without the dedication and hard work of several individuals who were instrumental in shaping its content.

Deepest gratitude goes to Sikander Sohail, whose considerable writing and editing expertise brought these stories to life. Sikander's skill in transforming verbal and audio accounts into a cohesive and compelling narrative has been instrumental in shaping this book.

To Ekrem Hezim: I am thankful for his invaluable contribution in meticulously transcribing my father's memoirs from his handwritten notes, preserving his powerful testimony. Ekrem also helped reconstruct my own memories from Urumchi and my university years, playing a crucial role in helping me with groundwork.

To Sabrina Sohail, whose deep understanding of my work and personal journey enabled her to play a vital role in the book's development.

And to Muyesser Emin, and Abdulmuqtedir Udun, whose careful translation of my father's memoirs has ensured that his words and experiences are preserved for future generations.

I am immensely grateful to all of my friends and allies whose unwavering support and encouragement have sustained me through every challenge. Their belief in me, their strength in moments of doubt, and their willingness to stand by my side have been a source of resilience and hope. Their solidarity is a testament to the power of true friendship in the face of adversity.

PREFACE

The weight of silence is something you only truly understand when your voice is stolen from you. When speaking the truth carries a price too heavy to bear. When the person you love most—your dearest sister—is taken and locked away in a dark dungeon, simply because you dared to use your voice in a free country to expose a totalitarian regime's crimes against humanity and genocide. When the words you long to speak could cost you your freedom—or your life.

I am an Uyghur. That alone made me a target in my homeland. The language I spoke, the prayers I whispered, the stories my ancestors passed down—these were not just pieces of my identity; to the Chinese government, they were threats. But I did not fully grasp the depth of that danger until I saw my people disappear, one by one, swallowed by a ruthless system designed to erase us.

This book is not just my story. It is the story of all who refuse to be silenced, of all those who decided to stand up to the Goliath that is the Chinese government. You will see that the fight for the human rights and freedom of the Uyghur people is composed of individuals who took it upon themselves to lend their time, expertise, and compassion to our cause. People who heard our pleas for help and rose to the occasion.

Our story is a testament to the power of truth, even when the world chooses to look away. It is about resilience in the face of injustice, about hope in the shadow of despair. And above all, it is about freedom—not the kind that is given or taken by governments, but the kind that burns in the hearts of those who refuse to surrender. It is about love—the unbreakable love that sustains a people, a family, a fight.

This book also carries the voice of my late father, Abbas Borhan, through his memoir and first-hand account of the horrors he witnessed during Mao

PREFACE

Zedong's Cultural Revolution in the 1960s and 1970s. His story, intertwined with mine, serves as both a warning and a call to action. I am honored and humbled to carry on his work to uplift and protect our people.

This book is not only about the Uyghur genocide. It is also about Beijing's broad global ambitions of totalitarian control. I will direct readers to later chapters where I describe China's growing authoritarian influence, transnational repression, and encroachment on democratic institutions worldwide. The Uyghur crisis is a warning to the world, and the fight for Uyghur freedom is deeply connected to the fight for global human peace and security. As I often say to world leaders in my advocacy: if we do not use our voice to stand up for human rights today, the only voice left to us tomorrow will be the voice of regret.

Our fight is for the fundamental principles of human dignity, justice, and the future of a free world. The world will not remain free if we allow authoritarian regimes to continue to advance their systems of repression, using modern technology and our greatest achievements for evil. When silence is traded for economic gain and progress is defined by those who prioritize power over humanity, our shared principles of justice and freedom are at risk. If we fail to stand against this, we jeopardize the very foundations of a just and democratic world. This book is for all of us who are responsible for what happens next.

To those still imprisoned, still unheard: I have not forgotten you. This story is for you.

FOREWORD
By Dr. Adrian Zenz

In early 2017, the Chinese Communist Party (CCP) embarked on a campaign of detaining over a million Uyghurs and other ethnic group members in so-called "reeducation camps." This campaign, unprecedented even by Chinese standards, constituted the centerpiece of a whole set of repressive policies designed to break apart ethnic communities and remake them in the image of the CCP. Chilling words spoken by senior officials confirm that Beijing's policies in the Uyghur homeland seek to "break their roots" and eradicate their independent identity.

If that was the goal, it is clear that the CCP's genocidal campaign to break the spirit of the Uyghurs has failed. This book, aptly titled *Unbroken*, is a remarkable testimony to the life, dedication, and resilience of Rushan Abbas, an Uyghur woman and intellectual whose tireless advocacy for the plight of her people has confounded the efforts of the government of the world's largest country to cover up its atrocities in the region.

Rushan and her family suffered the CCP's persecution from early on. During the Cultural Revolution, when Rushan was an infant, her father, Abbas Borhan, was detained for political reeducation. Shortly after, her mother was arrested by Mao Zedong's Red Guards, leaving the young infant screaming in the arms of her grandmother. Throughout this fateful period, Rushan experienced the sudden disappearance of family members at the hands of a totalitarian dictatorship. Sadly, these traumatic experiences would foreshadow worse things to come for her people.

Consequently, this book not only tells Rushan's own story. Intertwined with hers are those of her father and her sister, Gulshan Abbas. Only a few days after Rushan's first prominent appearance to advocate for her people at a panel organized by the Hudson Institute in Washington, DC in September

FOREWORD

2018, her sister was detained by the Chinese authorities. Gulshan Abbas, a medical doctor who never engaged in political activism or even any act of resistance against the CCP, was later sentenced to twenty years in prison for allegedly "participating in terrorist organizations." Besides having to contend with the arbitrary detention of her sister as punishment for her advocacy, Rushan has received anonymous death threats and has been attacked by name by Chinese government entities. Rather than dissuading her from speaking out, these efforts to silence her only reinforced Rushan's tenacity.

When I first met Rushan in June 2019, I was struck by her deep passion and unbending dedication to the cause of her people. Since then, Rushan's tireless advocacy and global outreach have been an inspiration to us all. Inasmuch as her remarkable spirit and that of other Uyghur advocates and scholars is representative of the spirit of the Uyghur people, it is my belief that the CCP's desperate attempts to "break their roots" are ultimately doomed to fail. This "unbroken" resilience is succinctly summarized by the author in these words, which I would like to quote:

> The CCP wants to take our hope or make us believe there is none. They are wrong. [. . .] People in every nation are beginning to see the truth [. . .] That is why we will not stop our work, nor give up our hope for a better future.

Perhaps most importantly, the work of Rushan and other Uyghur advocates is not just about seeking justice for the plight of their own people. Their advocacy transcends ethnic and national boundaries, as it aims to "defend the free world" against forms of tyranny and oppression everywhere, making the world a better place for all of us. In short, their struggle is to challenge humanity to "never again" stand by in silence and passivity while a people face eradication at the hands of a powerful tyrant. It is this dedication and resilience that empowers Uyghurs worldwide in their crucial efforts to remain unbroken as they promote the future development of their culture in the diaspora.

All of us who work to expose evil and shine a light on human rights violations around the world can draw encouragement from what I believe to be a universal principle—that truth is more powerful than denial, deception, and disinformation. To quote a verse from the Gospel of John that has given me great encouragement during the challenges of the past few years: "The light shines in the darkness, and the darkness has not overcome it."

ADRIAN ZENZ
DIRECTOR IN CHINA STUDIES
VICTIMS OF COMMUNISM MEMORIAL FOUNDATION

FOREWORD
By Ken Weinstein

Unbroken: One Uyghur's Fight for Freedom is the inspiring story of an incredible woman, Rushan Abbas, and her determination to defend her people against the most brutal human rights violation of our time: China's genocide in the Uyghur province of Xinjiang.

Rushan is the youngest child of a noted scientific researcher and a prominent physician from Xinjiang. Having seen the devastation caused by Mao Zedong's Cultural Revolution, they raised Rushan and her siblings with a profound dedication to preserving Uyghur tradition and language in the face of growing suppression from the Chinese Communist Party (CCP).

As Rushan grew older, the party's crackdown became more severe. Clashes broke out when hundreds of thousands of Han Chinese were relocated to Xinjiang to dilute the local Muslim culture. CCP agents shot thousands of Uyghurs amid the chaos. Xi Jinping's terror escalated to include DNA tests, state surveillance, and, eventually, the internment of two million Uyghurs in concentration camps.

After immigrating to America, Rushan gave up a successful career in international program management because her passion was defending her people. For this, she has sacrificed immensely, working long hours and giving up time with her own children. But she never expected that standing up to Xi's brutality would cost two of her closest relatives their freedom.

I met Rushan at a September 2018 Hudson Institute seminar titled "China's 'War on Terrorism' and the Xinjiang Emergency," which featured policy experts and academics. She addressed the plight of numerous missing family members who were taken to concentration camps—which the Chinese government refers to as "vocational education centers."

In retribution for Rushan's remarks at Hudson, the CCP detained her sister and aunt, both non-political, non-religious, and retired. While Rushan's aunt was released after a few months, her sister, Gulshan, remains detained after nearly seven years.

As this book details, Rushan's struggle for human rights is deeply personal, as is her pain over her sister's plight. Her name, Rushan, given in the dark days of the Cultural Revolution, means "brightness." Though her parents could not have known this at her birth, her life's mission has been to shed light on the CCP's barbaric—yet far too hidden—practices and the immeasurable suffering of those like her sister rounded up for no other reason than their ethnicity.

KENNETH R. WEINSTEIN
JAPAN CHAIR AND FORMER PRESIDENT & CEO, HUDSON INSTITUTE

INTRODUCTION

"I think I can, I think I can."

— THE LITTLE ENGINE THAT COULD

An inspiration from the fight for survival of my oldest son, Misron, the second-smallest premature baby ever born in Washington state

In my capacity as Executive Director of Campaign for Uyghurs and Chairwoman of the Executive Committee of the World Uyghur Congress, my foremost mission is to raise global awareness about the ongoing genocide facing my people. I am dedicated to amplifying the voices of Uyghurs who have been silenced and mobilizing international action to confront the Chinese government's crimes against humanity. Through advocacy, education, and coalition-building, I strive to garner unwavering support from democratic countries and civil societies to uphold justice, defend human rights, and demand accountability for the plight of the Uyghurs. This is no easy task. Uyghurs are not a widely known or understood ethnicity. Our homeland, occupied by the Chinese communist party (CCP), lies in the westernmost region of China, bordering Kazakhstan, Mongolia, Kyrgyzstan, Tajikistan, Afghanistan, Pakistan, India, and Tibet. The first Uyghur empire, the Uyghur Khaganate, emerged in 744 CE under the Yaglakar Dynasty, controlling vast territories from Mongolia to Central Asia. With Ordu-Baliq as its capital, the Khaganate thrived politically, militarily, and culturally, forming alliances with the Tang Dynasty and shaping ancient Silk Road trade. The Uyghurs initially followed Manichaeism before embracing Islam in the tenth century. The last independent Uyghur kingdom, the Seyyid (Yarkent) Kingdom, was invaded by the Manchu dynasty in 1759 and annexed into their empire. Ruled as a military colony from 1759 to 1862, the Uyghurs revolted forty-two times. After briefly expelling the Manchu in 1864 and establishing the Kashgaria State, the region was re-annexed in 1884 and renamed "Xinjiang" (New Territory). Our forefathers established the short-lived East Turkistan Republic twice, in 1933 and 1944, before it was occupied by the Chinese Communist government in 1949. To many Uyghurs, the region is known as East Turkistan. To me, it is my homeland.

I am an Uyghur Muslim, born where my faith is treated as a crime, and where my people endure invasion, occupation, and genocide under the Chinese Communist regime. I came to the United States in 1989 and have been an American citizen since 1995. I am a woman and have seen the bodies of the women of my community back home become the battlefield of the genocide against us. I am the daughter of two incredible parents who endured heartbreak and horrors in the hope that there would be a path to a brighter future. I am the sister of an extraordinary woman—strong, compassionate, and brilliant—whose intellect and dedication as a medical doctor and healer shine brightly. Yet, she is unjustly imprisoned in a Chinese jail, a victim of her government's retaliation against my free speech and the pursuit of justice in the United States. I am an advocate fighting for the basic human rights and dignity that have been denied to my people for far too long. My advocacy is a voice for the silenced, a tribute to those who have endured decades of oppression, and a relentless pursuit of a future where freedom and justice prevail. It is a fight to defend the very ideals of freedom and democracy that are now under threat by China's global transnational repression.

In one form or another, it has been the work of my life to speak out against the subjugation of my people at the hands of the Chinese Communist Party. My allies and I have enjoyed some success in this. In 2020, Campaign for Uyghurs was at the forefront of the push to recognize China's crimes against humanity, which meet the internationally recognized definition of a genocide. For our efforts, Campaign for Uyghurs has been nominated twice for the Nobel Peace Prize and received the World Democracy Tribute Award. We are proud to say that our cause has allies on both sides of the aisle in United

INTRODUCTION

States Congress and the Uyghur genocide remains a bipartisan issue, a fact for which I am grateful.

As a mother, I have been fortunate to raise five kind children of great character, three of my own and two stepsons whom I proudly say that I have raised since 2010. I am deeply fortunate to receive unwavering support from my family. My eldest son, who miraculously survived his premature birth at twenty-four weeks gestation with 820 grams (one lb. thirteen oz.) of birth weight, and now lives with cerebral palsy, has taught me a never-ending lesson in perseverance and patience in the face of hardship. Giving birth to him at twenty-four years old, he and I grew up together. Like *The Little Engine That Could*, struggling to continue its journey and leaving a long path behind it, passing the high hills, striving forward with all its might, my son Misron (who goes by the nickname Ronny), knows about struggling with life and moving forward through it with the will to fight.

God arranges everything for a reason and a purpose. I always thank Ronny for fighting to survive. His life has been a lesson for me. In the process of raising him, I grew up myself. I learned from him, from his tough life journey. What I consider my own strongest personality traits, such as courage, determination, endurance, patience, contentment, and never giving up, I see in him. Ronny has taught me to work tirelessly for the goals and aspirations I have for my life, to continue in the path I have chosen, and to work untiringly for the dedication I have for my homeland and the Uyghur cause. His presence has been an important lesson and a valuable gift for me as an individual, and he has made me transform into who I am today. From him and through his life, I always gain the strength that I need to fight against the CCP's coercive, malign influence against our values, human rights, and brutal genocidal crimes against my people.

As the youngest child of my wonderful parents, I was fortunate to face very little hardship. My father was a renowned scientist, and my mother was a distinguished medical practitioner in the city of Urumchi. I was raised with every hope of having an easier life than the one my parents had experienced. As I considered how to tell the story of my life, my father's words echoed in my mind.

"You can't be a singer, my daughter, because I tried my best not to make you cry when you were a baby, so your voice and lungs weren't exercised for singing." Those words that my late father used to jokingly say, have remained with me all my life. I was born amidst the social and political upheaval of the Great Cultural Revolution in China. From an early age, I witnessed the second-class standing of the Uyghurs under the Communist Party. As a university student, I co-organized two protests alongside brilliant and talented student activists despite the iron fist of the government. In those days at Xinjiang University, I learned to find my voice.

Despite living through the worst of the Mao Zedong's Cultural Revolution, a time of fear and ostracism for many Chinese citizens, and especially for Uyghurs, my father and mother both strove to ensure that my siblings and I enjoyed a happy childhood. In the last years of his life, my father wrote his memoir of the events he had witnessed during the Cultural Revolution, a rare and powerful account of a dark period of history seen through the eyes of a Uyghur intellectual and a public figure. In telling my own life story and that of the struggle of my people under China's genocidal rule, I have included excerpts of my father's writings. They offer a perspective on the conditions endured by Uyghurs during my earliest years that viscerally illustrate that our struggle is no overnight phenomenon. This struggle did not begin during my father's times and by no means ended with them, but my father's words contain a record of the tenor of life for Uyghurs that is echoed today. This book, in no small part, carries his stories and unyielding resilience as deeply as it does mine—and I believe it is all the richer for it.

I was twenty-one years old when, with the help of a wonderful American family, I left my homeland to come to the United States. The US was a foreign country, and I had no connections to my own roots. The culture was completely different, and I did not speak much English. I left my parents, whom I loved dearly, my dear siblings and friends, and my home. I left because I was looking for something we did not have back home—freedom. There, as a citizen of the People's Republic of China, I never experienced any feeling of acceptance. Rather, I felt more like a stateless person. When I watched an American movie called *Children of a Lesser God*, I felt the title was suitable for my people. And sometimes when I think of our suffering and helpless-

INTRODUCTION

ness under Beijing's brutal oppression, it feels as though *Allah* created us as a lesser people among the Muslim population. We are mostly left alone by the Muslim *Ummah* without support.

Becoming a US citizen in 1995 and pledging allegiance to the US constitution and the flag gave me, for the first time in my life, a sense of belonging to a country. In the United States, I found freedom and democracy. Over the course of my career, there have been times when my faith in the ability of the United States to uphold these values was shaken, but I believe it continues to stand for them. Even the right to voice criticism in this country when that faith is challenged is not to be taken for granted. Such freedom of speech and conscience are not found everywhere in the world, and I am grateful for it. These are the values that our people back home can't even dream of having under the overwhelming tyranny of China.

Today, my homeland, occupied by a ferocious authoritarian regime, suffers under the weight of decades of subjugation. And in the past decade, there has been a shift from the steady drumbeat of colonial takeover to something even more sinister. Our way of life, our culture, traditions, and religion have been criminalized. We are branded as extremists for even the basic practice of Islam. Surveillance systems augmented by artificial intelligence keep a watchful eye on every individual, cataloging our movements and traditional clothing. Ubiquitous security like that of George Orwell's *1984*, a massive, high-tech police state, was a cruel reality for the entire region. Our homes are forced to be open day and night to uninvited Chinese guests who sexually abuse our women and girls while sharing our beds in the name of monitoring and supervising our daily lives. Uyghurs are rounded up by the millions and disappear into concentration camps. Under the guise of reeducation or vocational training, many are funneled into factories as slave labor. Uyghur women face forced abortion, sterilization, and rape. Those who are not arrested are shipped away as slaves and forced into marriage to Chinese men, who select them from menus curated by the government. Children are ripped from their families by the millions and sent to boarding schools or state-run orphanages, to be raised under the watch of a state that seeks to wash away their culture and language.

To silence Uyghurs in the diaspora, those of us who have fled our homeland seeking asylum and freedom elsewhere in the world, China employs tactics of transnational repression and guilt by association. Across the globe, Uyghurs are coerced and cajoled into returning to China, only to be jailed or stripped of their right to travel. Others, inundated by threats against their families back home and fearing for the safety of their loved ones, are browbeaten into compliance. In truth, there is nothing surprising about these tactics of guilt by association and collective punishment. To Uyghurs and Chinese natives alike it is a familiar part of history. As a young student during my grade school years, when I was only ten or eleven years old, I read about these practices in a work of classical Chinese literature from around the fourteenth century titled *Water Margin*. It described how a single person's mistake led to their entire family being punished, even infants. In some cases, an entire town was wiped out because one resident defied the rulers. In my lifetime, I have seen that although the methods have changed, these attitudes are still very much in effect. Since the CCP took over in 1949, Beijing has targeted our people, punishing not only dissenters but also their families through arrests, torture, and executions. Many members of my own family have faced consequences for my work as an activist speaking out against this very sort of injustice. Before their deaths, my father and mother both suffered for it. Today, my sister remains in prison, where she has been held since September 2018.

Do the actions of a few dozen Uyghurs over decades justify the mass detention of millions? While the CCP is using Uyghurs and my homeland as a testing ground, not many recognize that China's genocidal policy towards the Uyghurs is actually part of its broader dark ambition to dominate the world. Explaining this to the world isn't as easy as it may seem. Lax labor rights and policies surrounding manufacturing have long made China the darling of major consumer brands across Europe and America. In the past decade, through the Belt and Road Initiative and debt-trap diplomacy, China has secured economic footholds across great swaths of Central Asia, Southeast Asia, the Middle East, and Africa, securing leverage through billions of dollars in debt and the use of authoritarian surveillance technologies. In the United Nations, China holds significant sway as the world's second-largest economy, after the United States. By these means, China has bought the world's silence regarding the plight of the Uyghurs.

INTRODUCTION

The road to freedom is long, and rife with setbacks. For every small victory, the wall of deafening silence from many of the nations of the world remains. Those Hollywood celebrities, NBA and NFL stars, famous talk-show hosts, and the majority of the media personalities who offer their enlightened perspective on every injustice have nothing to say about this genocide. Companies standing to make millions or billions through the exploitation of Uyghur labor are content to conduct business as usual. It is easy to speak out and criticize when there are no consequences. But when the perpetrator of horrific crimes is a country with influence and power, silence is convenient—and few are willing to risk their comfort to stand on the side of justice and the truth.

On challenging days when hope is difficult to find, I draw courage from my sister's kind face and from the innocent eyes of those living in darkness. My professors. My friends and colleagues. My neighbors. My people. Those millions of innocent people who are hoping that we will continue to fight for their freedom. To make a change — to defend the free world. Giving in to frustration and losing hope is simply not an option. We have to keep trying for those people who cannot rely on help from anyone. Just like many Americans, Uyghurs believe that where there is a will, there is a way. Where there is a will, we never give up—we find a way to fight. To me, that fight is about speaking out, and raising our voices together as one voice that will not be silenced.

Our fight for freedom is a powerful testament to hope and resilience, echoing the unwavering determination of the Uyghurs in their pursuit of justice, democracy, and dignity. It stands as both a defiant cry against oppression and a relentless march towards freedom. I know that if we keep fighting, speaking out, and educating, the right conditions will emerge for someone, somewhere, to take the first step towards change.

To conclude this introduction, I want to share a reflection I posted on May 9, 2024, on social media, marking thirty-five years since my arrival in the United States. It captures my journey, not just in distance but in transformation, embodying my struggle and my commitment to my people:

> Thirty-five years ago today, I set foot in the United States for the first time with the assistance of family friends, Dr.

Lin Faulkner and his wife, Lois. I hold the greatest respect for them and their children, Jenni Gant, Ed Faulkner, and Brent Faulkner, as well as their daughters-in-law, Tammy and Terri, son in-law Laroy Gant, and grandchildren. They are my family away from home. They taught me English, taught me how to drive and gave me support and encouragement through my first years in America. Even after Dr. and Mrs. Faulkner passed away, whom I remember fondly and miss dearly, their impact continues to resonate with me. Arriving in Seattle on May 9, 1989, I remember seeing the Space Needle from the sky. . . I remember my feelings very vividly: I felt worried. Everything was foreign, I barely spoke any English. I felt incapacitated. I felt alone. I felt homesick. I missed my family. I missed my language. I missed home so much.

Two months later, my mind was made up. I went to Dr. Faulkner and told him that I was going back home. He looked at me and said, "Your father and I arranged to bring you here. Let me call him tonight and ask how we can arrange for you to travel back." After a short pause, he said very calmly: "But ask yourself this question: Do you think your family sent you halfway across the world to see you come back in a couple of months? It takes time to get used to things. But if that's your decision, I will talk to your father." I went back to my room. I started to think about the reasons why I came—the freedom and democracy that we did not have back home. Respect for human dignity and the values embraced by the people and reinforced by the law of this land. I could go back now. But to what? Back to the discrimination and constant repression by the Chinese Communist Party? The oppressive government under which my people feel tormented every living minute of every day? Should I have gone back to the wanton brutality of the crackdown against the innocent Tiananmen Square protests, which I watched on TV only twenty-five days of my arrival in the United

INTRODUCTION

States? The hours went by with these thoughts in my head. Then I went back to Dr. Faulkner and told him that I would stay and continue my studies.

Dr. Faulkner passed away in late 2004. Between 1989 and 2004, we reminisced about this conversation a number of times. "That moment you came back and told me you'd stay," he would recall, "That's when you grew up."

I am proud to call myself an American for the last thirty years; as I heard a Lady say:

> Give me your tired, your poor,
> Your huddled masses yearning to breathe free,
> The wretched refuse of your teeming shore.
> Send these, the homeless, tempest-tost to me,
> I lift my lamp beside the golden door!"
>
> — EMMA LAZARUS, "THE NEW COLOSSUS"[1]

I came to this country as a stranger but found a home. Not repression and discrimination, but freedom and equality. Treated not as a second-class being but respected as a fellow citizen. Not indoctrination, but free thought. All of these things that China's occupation took away from the Uyghurs. Ever since I came to this country that I have proudly called home for thirty years, I have found ways to use my freedom and liberty to speak for my fellow Uyghur brothers and sisters who, after seventy-five years of occupation by the CCP government, are still yearning to breathe free. Unfortunately, the CCP government continues to find cruel ways to torment people who stand up to their repression.

It's been five years and nine months since they took my sister, Gulshan, a retired doctor with no political affiliation,

---

1. These lines from the poem, "The New Colossus," written by Emma Lazarus in 1883, are inscribed on the pedestal of the Statue of Liberty.

to silence me. My crime is speaking against the CCP's genocide of my people. My sister's crime is—being my sister. The personal and emotional toll has been tremendous. But I find solace in the fact that I am but one of the many Uyghurs in the diaspora who battle with the same feelings every minute of every day. And with each voice, we grow stronger. Because we know:

> The caged bird sings
> with a fearful trill
> of things unknown
> but longed for still
> and his tune is heard
> on the distant hill
> for the caged bird
> sings of freedom.
>
> — MAYA ANGELOU, "CAGED BIRD"

CHAPTER ONE
ONE VOICE, ONE STEP

During the summer of 2016, ominous news from back home was rippling through the Uyghur diaspora. Life had never been easy for Uyghurs under China's occupation of the so-called Xinjiang Uyghur Autonomous Region. But now we started to hear that policy was being reshaped very quickly towards absolute control over the population. This came alongside new region-wide surveillance systems, using image recognition software to identify and monitor Uyghurs by cultural items and clothing, facial features, and even by the patterns of our gait.

By the end of 2016, advocacy organizations like Human Rights Watch (HRW) were reporting on DNA collection and mandatory health checks for every Uyghur. Some of the people back home were optimistic, praising the new policies, thinking they would have some sort of positive effect, possibly improving health care systems for the local people. However, my fellow Uyghur activists and I were worried. We took the violation of privacy as a warning sign of things to come. Some wondered if there were plans to develop some sort of biological weapon, or to use Uyghurs as guinea pigs. What we would eventually discover was somehow more heinous. Work on a new network of internment camps began almost immediately. We began hearing stories that in many mostly Uyghur-populated regional areas, authorities were rounding people up with quotas of up to 70 percent. When the police struggled to meet these quotas in certain villages or towns, they called Uyghurs in Urumchi or parts of China-proper, asking them to return to their hometowns. Once they arrived, they were arrested on the spot. In my circle, everyone had stories of missing family members. The most prominent targets were Uyghur intellectuals, as they had been during my father's time.

Anyone who had contributed to the educational and cultural enrichment of the Uyghur region, even at the behest of the government, was now a target for arrest for this work.

Uyghur Professor Ilham Tohti, a well-known scholar from Minzu University, was a leading voice for Uyghur rights within China's legal system. He advocated for dialogue and ethnic equality and sought justice and cultural respect for Uyghurs. Arrested in 2014, later he was sentenced to life in prison on baseless "separatism" charges, symbolizing China's broader crackdown on Uyghur intellectuals.

Yalqun Rozi, a famous literary critic and scholar, was among the first Uyghur intellectuals silenced in China's ruthless crackdown. For decades, he shaped Uyghur cultural identity through over sixty groundbreaking literary critiques and more than ninety Uyghur-language textbooks approved by the Education Ministry. His writings, exploring Uyghur heritage, history, and faith, challenged state narratives and inspired a generation. But in 2016, as Beijing escalated its assault on the Uyghur identity, Rozi was arrested without cause. Despite having followed state guidelines, his textbooks were suddenly deemed subversive. In 2018, he was sentenced to fifteen years in prison.

Rahila Dawut, a renowned Uyghur anthropologist, dedicated her life to preserving Uyghur folklore and cultural heritage. As founder of the Ethnic Minorities Folklore Research Center at Xinjiang University, she was a leading voice in safeguarding Uyghur traditions. In December 2017, she forcibly disappeared and was later sentenced to life imprisonment on false charges of "endangering state security."

When I speak of Uyghur scholars unjustly imprisoned my heart aches for their children, who now carry the weight of their parents' silenced voices. In the United States, Ilham Tohti's daughter, Jewher Ilham, turned personal tragedy into global advocacy. She fights tirelessly for her father's freedom and Uyghur rights through testimonies, international forums, leading efforts against Uyghur forced labor, and working with human rights organizations to demand justice. Yalqun Rozi's son, Kamalturk Yalqun, and daughter, Tumaris Yalqun, as well as Rahila Dawut's daughter, Akeda Pulati, all living in the United States, have been forced to step into roles no child should bear. Instead of focusing on their own lives, dreams, and careers, they shoulder the

CHAPTER ONE

immense burden of fighting tirelessly for their parents' freedom and ensuring their stories are not forgotten. Their resilience is a testament to both their love and the enduring strength of the Uyghur spirit.

As Uyghurs began to disappear into prisons, reeducation camps, and labor facilities, Chen Quanguo, who was the Party Secretary in Tibet and brought over to Xinjiang as the Party Secretary in 2016, instituted a new policy called "Pair-up and Become Family." Chinese officials from the Han ruling class were assigned to supervise and monitor Uyghur households where women and children were left while their husbands and fathers were imprisoned or interred in the camps. There, they would instruct the children to monitor their mothers' actions and report on them. At night, these men slept in the same beds as the women. This practice was rife with sexual abuse, which Uyghur women could do little to prevent or to report after the fact. In 2018, Chinese state media reported that 1.1 million Han Chinese, mostly men, have been deployed into Uyghur homes to monitor and supervise Uyghurs' daily lives. They make this claim with pride, as if they are fulfilling a patriotic duty. While most Uyghur men are sent to internment camps, prisons, or forced labor facilities, Uyghur women endure unimaginable horrors—sexual abuse in their own homes and beds, stripped of their dignity and safety under a brutal campaign of repression. Uyghur girls are forced into marriages with Han Chinese men, while the Chinese government incentivizes these unions by offering the grooms housing, jobs, and financial rewards. If a Uyghur girl refuses—whether because she is not ready, does not want to marry a particular man, or rejects the forced arrangement altogether—she, along with her parents and siblings, faces the terrifying prospect of being sent to an internment camp. They are labeled as "Islamic extremists" or "radicalized Muslims" simply for resisting forced marriage with non-Muslim men. This state-sponsored coercion is a government-orchestrated campaign of mass rape of Uyghur women.

Suppression of Uyghur birth rates continues much as it has since the first protests I co-organized at Xinjiang University in the 1980s. Now, due to overwhelming evidence obtained from leaked documents, pictures, video evidence, and first-hand testimony, we know that these practices include family separation, the aforementioned surveillance, forced abortions, and sterilization. A practice was put into place that offered Han Chinese men Uyghur women as wives, who were taken from their homes to go and live with their new husbands in the mainland. Videos can be found of the women enduring sham weddings as their futures are taken from them. The program even has its own "dating app" where Uyghur women are profiled and offered without their knowledge or consent, courtesy of the state.

The Chinese government also began to implement radical birth-control policies, forcibly sterilizing almost all the Uyghur women of child-bearing age. According to research by Dr. Adrian Zenz,[2] a well-known expert on Xinjiang for his anthropological research and director and senior fellow in China Studies at the Victims of Communism Memorial Foundation, in some parts of the Uyghur region Uyghur birth rates have dropped to 0 percent, at the time of writing. I could not construct a more apt description of the horror that is ethnic cleansing.

The Chinese Embassy in the United States publicly celebrated these efforts. They take pride in their forced sterilizations as a supposed "emancipation" of Uyghur women, making them "no longer baby-making machines." This specific phrase appeared in a 2021 tweet by the Chinese Embassy, which read in full, "Study shows that in the process of eradicating extremism, the minds of Uyghur women in Xinjiang were emancipated and gender equality and reproductive health were promoted, making them no longer baby-making machines. They are more confident and independent." Twitter (now known as X) removed the post for violation of its policy.

Forcing women to marry outside their culture and turning them into commodities for men to claim and select is not some modern virtue. It only serves to rob us of the right to choose the future we wish to build. Depriving women against their will of the ability to bear children is no progressive act. It is a deeply invasive infringement of their rights.

By April 2017, the mass detentions had reached a fever pitch. When we approached US lawmakers and the State Department with our estimates that

---

2. "Sterilizations, IUDs, and Mandatory Birth Control: The CCP's Campaign to Suppress Uyghur Birthrates in Xinjiang," Adrian Zenz. Available at: https://jamestown.org/product/sterilizations-iuds-and-mandatory-birth-control-the-ccps-campaign-to-suppress-uyghur-birthrates-in-xinjiang/

CHAPTER ONE

one million Uyghurs were already in detention in the Uyghur region, some of them said *Don't exaggerate the numbers. You can't go around saying one million people are in detention.* Yet reports of Uyghurs disappearing continued to flood into our community. By the summer of 2017, my husband Abdulhakim had lost contact with his entire family—twenty-four people, including both his parents, his brother, three sisters, their spouses, and all of their children. Leading up to this we could sense that something was wrong. He had been in constant contact with his family. He spoke to his parents in Hotan almost daily. Suddenly, on April 25, 2017, when he called his mother, she told him not to call home anymore. When he tried to contact his family again after several weeks, no one answered the home phone, and eventually, no one's cell phone was working either. Then, in July 2017, Abdulhakim heard from his distant relatives in China-proper (Inner China) that all of his immediate family members had been taken into the camps. We were both heartbroken. It was another in a slew of similar stories that were becoming more and more common among our community. Our people were disappearing. We began to hear that the streets were becoming empty, and people were being taken away in the night.

Support was difficult to find. During this time, I participated in several peaceful protests at the Chinese Embassy in Washington, DC, but the story of the camps and Uyghur atrocities were not gaining any significant traction. The mainstream media were not covering this at all. Abdulhakim and I began to see the need for a new kind of advocacy for the Uyghur cause, one that could respond quickly to events as they unfolded and work as a bridge for different segments of the Uyghur diaspora and allowing them to connect with contacts in government and the media. Though it was slow to take shape, this idea eventually resulted in the organization known as Campaign for Uyghurs (CFU). CFU was established in September 2017 and registered as a non-profit non-governmental organization on December 4, 2017 by Abdulhakim and myself. Abdulhakim is the Executive Director of the Center for Uyghur Studies, a Washington, DC-based think tank, and the author of *Menace: China's Colonization of the Islamic World & Uyghur Genocide*, published in multiple languages.

In early January 2018, Abdulhakim and I began discussing the need to organize a different type of protest, one that could get the attention of the media and governments alike. I was subsequently approached by Sureyya Kashgary, a fellow Uyghur from Virginia, about possibly mobilizing Uyghur intellectuals to take some sort of action on the issue and develop different strategies that might get us the attention we needed. I told Sureyya that Abdulhakim and I were discussing some sort of action, and I would let her know once we had decided. I went back to discuss the matter with Abdulhakim. Eventually he and I hit upon the idea of staging a global event organized and led by Uyghur women. At the time, women's voices were lacking in the Uyghur movement. We largely played a supporting role to our husbands and sons, or in the background of organizations led mostly by men. We have not yet come forward to lead. Thus, calling on women's leadership was enough to differentiate the protest and give it the resonance it needed. Uyghur women are strong, highly educated and purpose-driven. We are the bearers of our community, culture, and religion around the world, as well as strong and resilient voices for those suffering back home. It was time the world heard us. If Uyghur women around the world could mobilize their families, their husbands, children, and their local organizations in order to lead a worldwide protest of the CCP's mass detention of the Uyghurs, it could be a massive show of worldwide solidarity.

I immediately began to work on this concept, reaching out to Sureyya Kashgary, Zubeyra Shamseden, Elfidar Iltebir from Virginia, and Mukerrem Kurban from Edmonton, Alberta in Canada, along with several Uyghur women from Europe. Eventually we drew together Uyghur women from all around the world. We started with a small group chat on WhatsApp with leading voices in various countries, which grew to include activists in North America, Australia, Europe, Japan and Türkiye. After some discussion within our leadership group, I put forward a name for the protest: "One Voice, One Step." There was quite a bit of excitement for the idea, and so on January 21, 2018, we made our first public announcement on social media: Under the initiative *One Voice, One Step*, on March 15, 2018, on the same day all around the world, Uyghur women would lead a march demanding the release of more than a million innocent Uyghurs in detention camps as well as justice for

CHAPTER ONE

our people back home. In New York on that same day, the United Nations would hold its annual session on the status of women. This was the perfect time to make our voices heard.

There was interest and excitement from all corners of the diaspora, and as it grew, we needed a name. The protest was about global solidarity, all of us marching together, bringing our voices together. Together, with one voice, we would take a collective step towards accountability and closing the camps. With the name *One Voice, One Step*, that small group grew to about a hundred people as the planning continued. Then another started to bring together the participants. Eventually each area participating had its own group in fourteen different countries and eighteen different cities. We received support from most of the large Uyghur organizations globally and local organizations in each country. We also had very strong support for our campaign from Irade Kashgary, Munewwer Uyghur, Aydin Anwar, Haji Nur, and a few other young Uyghur girls from the Washington, DC area who created flyers and helped with infographics for the protest.

We made posters and signs with pictures of the camps and trifold brochures. One volunteer from Türkiye came up with the brilliant idea to make scarves in the colors of our flag, a bright sky blue with a white star and crescent moon. She had five thousand scarves made, and we sponsored the cost of printing and shipping them all around the world. Soon, "Covering the entire world in blue" became one of our slogans. On the day of the protest, everybody had that blue scarf around their neck. Women, men, children—all of us. It was truly beautiful.

In the meantime, we tried to continue our advocacy on Capitol Hill. On March 5, 2018, we organized a vibrant Uyghur cultural event in the Gold Room of the Rayburn Office Building, in collaboration with Ilshat Hasan, then-president of the Uyghur American Association and a prominent advocate for Uyghur rights. The event was made possible through the support of Jamie Staley from the Tom Lantos Human Rights Commission, and longtime supporter and friend of the Uyghur people Hans Hogrefe. The room was transformed into a celebration of Uyghur heritage, adorned with traditional cultural artifacts, musical instruments, and intricately crafted items that reflect our people's rich history. Dressed in traditional Uyghur attire, we showcased the resilience and spirit of a culture that the Chinese government seeks to erase.

On March 14 in North America, the night before the event, we began seeing photos and videos of the first protests on social media, starting in Sydney, Australia followed by Adelaide, where it was already March 15. Then it began to circle the globe. Now Japan is starting. Now it's in Türkiye. Now Belgium, France, Finland, Germany, Sweden, Switzerland, now the Netherlands, and the UK. Then, Norway. Now Toronto, New York, San Francisco, and the last, Vancouver, BC. All told, *One Voice, One Step* protests took place across eighteen different cities in fourteen countries. Collectively, the protests went on for twenty-two hours straight. From start to finish, social media was abuzz with coverage of Uyghur women leading a collective movement, demanding change and justice. I could hardly sleep watching our movement covering the world in blue.

In New York, near the United Nations, people joined us from all over America: from Washington, DC, Los Angeles, San Francisco, Houston, Chicago, and Florida. We even had participants come from Canada to join us. We chartered a bus from DC to ferry as many people as we could to New York. San Francisco and Los Angeles even had their own *One Voice, One Step* protests. Our time zone was towards the end of the wave. By the time we began, *One Voice, One Step* was being covered around the planet. It was a cold day. As I looked out at the sea of blue scarves, I turned to my friend Mukerrem Kurban, who was with me at the protest at Xinjiang University in 1985, thirty-three years before. I was reminded of the feeling I had then, seeing the cry for freedom shared by Uyghurs across the Uyghur region. Mukerrem joined us in New York with her husband, Selami Cetinkaya, and their two young children: then-twelve-year-old Mehliya Cetinkaya, who has become a prominent young activist in Canada. After receiving our organization's advocacy training in Istanbul, she joined CFU's board as a Student Liaison for Canada and has been actively working in the Canadian Parliament in MP Garnett Genuis' office since the training in Toronto. Their younger daughter, then-nine-year-old Aysu Cetinkaya, accompanied them as well. Aysu is now also a young activist in Edmonton, Alberta. Mukerrem and I talked and reminisced about how far we had come since our first protest on December

CHAPTER ONE

12, 1985, when we marched in the snow on the streets of Urumchi. In New York, there were mothers who had brought their young children in strollers. We chanted our protests and handed out fliers. We gave interviews to media outlets and talked with curious passersby. Some of the young women in our group whose English was better than those in my generation had drafted a letter to the UN based on our demands and the information we wanted to share. In the company of a few other Uyghur women, I personally delivered the letter to the UN Committee on the Status of Women.

At that time, the newly appointed UN Secretary-General, António Guterres, had not once mentioned Uyghurs. In fact, China's communist party secretary and chairman Xi Jinping, the mastermind behind the genocide of my people and the various crimes against humanity suffered by Tibetans, Hongkongers, and Southern Mongolians, is often praised at the UN for implementing gender equality and women's development. China is one of the five permanent members of the United Nations Security Council (UNSC) and sits on the United Nations Human Rights Council (UNHRC). The UN remained silent. On that day in March, there was little we could expect to achieve by delivering that letter. Still, we made our voice heard, and the world could not ignore us any longer.

By that afternoon, the media landscape had changed. We started to see headlines all over reading "One Million Uyghur People in Detention." They appeared first in the Associated Press and Reuters, then in others as the story spread on Wire News. All told, the protests led by the *One Voice, One Step* initiative were covered in more than thirty languages and by more than a hundred media outlets around the world. On that day, we could not be ignored. Looking around at the powerful women leading the movement, I felt a surge of pride. Together, we mobilized communities and organizations across continents to leave their homes and their everyday lives to come out into the streets. We have shown that if we unite together towards justice, the world listens.

As a result of Uyghur women raising their voices with courage, we shattered the world's silence. Our voices of anguish and resilience echoed across borders, forcing the international community to confront the brutal reality of the Uyghur genocide. No longer could the world turn a blind eye—our suffering was heard, our truth was acknowledged, and the fight for justice began to take root.

The impact of One Voice, One Step extended far beyond that single day of protest. It planted the seeds for new organizations and more sustainable movements within the Uyghur diaspora, empowering women and communities to take on leadership roles in advocacy. In different parts of the world, Uyghur women who had once stood in the background now stepped forward to organize, mobilize, and lead.

One such organization was the Australian Uyghur Tangritagh Women's Association (AUTWA), which emerged as a powerful voice for Uyghur and other Turkic women in Australia. AUTWA promotes multiculturalism, social cohesion, harmony, and Uyghur advocacy, ensuring that Uyghur women play an active role in both their own communities and in the broader Australian society.

In Germany, the Mihrihan Anilar ("Caring Mothers") initiative took shape, driven by the same momentum. It provided a space for Uyghur women to organize, support one another, and advocate for their people—embodying the role of mothers who care for and protect their community. Over time, this grassroots movement evolved, and in 2020, under the leadership of several Uyghur women—Peride Niyaz, Suriye Ilham, Mahire Isa, and Salamet Hashim—it formally became the Uyghur Cultural and Education Association, expanding its mission to promote Uyghur identity, heritage, and activism in Europe.

Shortly after the *One Voice One Step* protest gained global media attention for China's mass detention of Uyghurs, Chinese Canadian researcher Shawn Zhang exposed internment camps using satellite images. In May 2018, he analyzed Google Earth data, revealing the rapid expansion of these camps—documenting their locations, layouts, construction timelines, and security features such as watchtowers and fencing. His findings, published on Twitter (now X) and his blog, debunked China's claims of "vocational centers" and provided crucial evidence cited by journalists, researchers, and human rights organizations that exposed the scale of repression in East Turkistan.

CHAPTER TWO
CHINA'S LONG BLACK ARM

When the information about the camps and the detentions of over a million innocent Uyghurs first came to light, we were stunned. How could it be possible that in the twenty-first century, in today's modern world, a regime would boldly attempt to erase an entire ethnic group without hesitation? How could the world stand idly by in silence? Didn't the world pledge "Never again" after World War II, the Holocaust, and Hitler's genocide of the Jewish people? How does China commit such mass atrocities against the Uyghur people and get away with it? What conditions are our relatives enduring? Are they even alive?

Uyghur activists abroad initially relied on limited information and, beginning in 2016, made efforts to inform US officials, the United Nations Human Rights Council (UNHRC), and the European Parliament about the atrocities carried out against Uyghurs by the Chinese regime. Some international organizations and media such as the online magazine *Bitter Winter* secretly sent individuals to the Uyghur region to capture images of deserted towns and villages and even the inside of detention camps. Gradually, over a dozen former camp victims began to emerge as witnesses—individuals who were detained in the camps or had been forced to teach detainees in the camps under the direction of the Chinese authorities. Although they were Uyghurs and Kazakhs, some of them were citizens of other countries or married to citizens of other countries and so were able to leave China. This brought the issue of detention camps into the spotlight as an undeniable global concern.

On August 10, 2018, during the ninety-seventh session of the UN Committee on the Elimination of Racial Discrimination (CERD), evidence of China's oppressive policies against the Uyghurs was presented. This session was a pivotal moment in bringing the Uyghur issue onto the global political stage. China, represented by forty-nine delegates, denied the existence of reeducation centers in Xinjiang and claimed that Uyghur citizens enjoyed equal freedom and rights.

The researchers were undeterred, however. Despite opposition from the session chair, interruptions to their speeches, and microphones being cut off, they presented evidence right before the Chinese delegation, exposing China's false claims. It felt as if a battle between the accomplices of genocide and the defenders of justice was unfolding in that room. The session chair, siding with China, protected its interests by attempting to limit the researchers' statements.

Less than a month later, CERD issued a report highlighting the oppression faced by the Uyghurs. This report shifted the focus of global media attention to the atrocities in the Uyghur region. Nations and organizations that had previously ignored countless Uyghur protests and petitions began questioning China's crimes. Originally denying the existence of detention camps, the Chinese authorities hedged in late 2018 that "these are not detention camps but re-education centers."

Following the *One Voice, One Step initiative* in March 2018, my voice as an activist for the Uyghur cause began to grow. It was during this time that a life-altering event occurred for me—a monumental event that uprooted me from my normal work and thrust me into a battlefield against the monstrous entity that is the CCP.

On September 5, 2018, the Hudson Institute, a prominent Washington, DC-based think tank known for its work on international affairs and national security, held a panel on "China's 'War on Terrorism' and the Xinjiang Emergency." At the time, the Institute was led by Ken Weinstein, who served as President and CEO. The panel was moderated by then-Hudson Institute senior fellow Eric Brown, a respected expert on China and the Uyghur crisis. Brown's work at the Institute centered on Asian and Middle Eastern affairs, international security, and US diplomacy, making him a critical voice in analyzing Beijing's policies and their global ramifications. Among the panelists was Louisa Greve, the Director of Global Advocacy for the Uyghur Human Rights Project. I was invited to speak as an Uyghur.

CHAPTER TWO

In addition to the two of us, the panel featured Dr. Michael Clarke from the Australian National University, Andrew Small from the German Marshall Fund, and Dr. Sean Roberts from George Washington University. With his family vanished into camps, my husband Abdulhakim Idris struggled under the weight of uncertainty. News was impossible to obtain, and despite our efforts, the world remained largely silent. I decided to testify for my missing in-laws, unaware that this decision would change my life forever.

I arrived at Hudson that day, wearing my sky-blue scarf with a black suit with matching blue embroidery. During the panel discussion, there was much discussion of the strategic value of the region to China as part of the Belt and Road[3] initiative, as well as of the torture and medical abuse taking place within the "reeducation" camps.

I had five minutes midway through the panel to deliver my statement. I thanked Eric Brown for his leadership on this critical matter. I began my speech by saying "One million is more than the entire population of Washington, DC, and it is the number of innocent Uyghur people who have been forced into China's internment camps." I continued:

> As the United States Congressional Executive Commission on China stated, this is "the largest mass incarceration of an ethnic group after the WWII". China calls the camps "vocational training centers," but according to witnesses and news accounts, "vocational training" means armed guards, barbed wire, over-crowded rooms, malnutrition, dehydration, poor sanitation. It means being uprooted from home and family. It means stamping out culture and religion. It means forced indoctrination. It means mental and physical abuse.
>
> Since Mao's occupation of East Turkistan in 1949, the government has tried relentlessly to destroy Uyghur culture

---

3. China's Belt and Road Initiative (BRI) is a massive global infrastructure and economic development project launched by Chinese Chairman Xi Jinping in 2013. It aims to enhance global trade and investment by building a network of roads, railways, ports, and other infrastructure across Asia, Africa, Europe, and beyond.

and religion. Uyghurs have been persecuted under the label of "Nationalists," "Counter revolutionaries" and "Separatists." Following the 9-11 tragedy, Communist authorities rebranded the effort as a "War on Terrorism." Today Uyghur people have become the victims of Xi Jinping's signature project, the "One Belt, One Road" initiative. The entire region is branded. Punishment is cultural and collective. Over a million people in detention are charged with no crime. Counties, districts, and neighborhoods are filling quotas. China has characterized all political resistance as "Islamic terrorism," and on that pretext developed a surveillance state built on DNA collection, ubiquitous cameras, facial-recognition software, etc. and GPS tracking devices on vehicles.

China has sent to internment camps:

- Dr. Rahile Dawut, an internationally renowned scholar who studied in the United States;
- Ablajan Ayup, a pop star; Erfan Hazim, a professional soccer player;
- University presidents Tashpolat Teyip and Halmurat Ghopur
- Muhammad Salih Hajim, a famous scholar who translated the Kuran from Arabic to Uyghur. He was eighty-two and died in a camp.

But this isn't happening simply to famous people and expats. It happened to my family.

My in-laws from Hotan, a 69- and 71-year-old farmer and housewife, three of their daughters, a daughter-in-law, and their husbands all disappeared. My husband and I have not been able to learn their whereabouts since April 2017. We fear that they were all taken to those internment camps. We have no idea where my husband's fourteen nieces and nephews are today, aged between three and twenty-two years old. We fear that many of them were sent to orphanages in inner China. We also heard Abdurehim Idris, my brother-in-law, was sentenced to twenty years in jail.

Dilnur Enver, a mother of three, came to Istanbul in 2016 with her daughter to study for a master's degree. Two young children (ages five and seven) were left with their grandparents in Kashgar. In April 2017, the local police in Kashgar contacted her and requested her immediate return, or she would be punished otherwise. Dilnur knew the returnees from Egypt and Turkey were arrested, died, or disappeared with no trace. Thus, she did not return. Her children were taken from their grandparents. As of today, she doesn't know their whereabouts. Mamutjan Erkin, a former teacher in East Turkistan was contacted by Chinese police shortly after his arrival in Turkey in 2016. They asked him to spy on the Uyghurs in Turkey and to write articles praising the communist state; he was promised money and a fancy house in Istanbul in return. When he refused, they threatened to refer him to Interpol as a terrorist. Mamutjan went public to expose this.

There are a million stories like this. And more disturbing reports, too. Radio Free Asia Uyghur Service reports that the government is constructing massive crematoria throughout the region. It's a warning sign, but so far, the world isn't watching. Among the Uyghur diaspora, despair, helplessness, fear, and depression are growing. With the staggering power of the Communist state, your attention and interest are so important. We plead with world leaders, politicians, NGOs, and civil societies to be one voice against the Communist China's cruelty and take a step together to end the mass atrocity of today's era; act now, before it is too late.

That was the plea with which I ended my remarks.

During the question-and-answer session, I highlighted the transnational repression Uyghurs in the diaspora face. Beyond the Belt and Road economic influence silencing world leaders—even those who once called it genocide—Uyghurs across Europe and Asia, as well as in Australia, Canada, and the United States, have received demands for personal data such as bank details, license plate numbers, and identification cards, under threats to their families back home. Within the shadow of China's long black arm, the state of Uyghurs in the diaspora is one of constant stress, depression, and despair.

Retaliation for these remarks took less than a week to materialize. On September 11, 2018, six days after my remarks at the Hudson Institute were posted online, my sister, Gulshan Abbas, disappeared into the camps. Gulshan, a retired medical professional and devoted grandmother, stayed in constant contact with her daughters Ziba and Zamira in the United States. She closely monitored her youngest daughter Zamira's pregnancy, offering daily advice, while also guiding Ziba, who had given birth three months earlier. Not a day passed without a call or message. My nieces' last communication with their mother was on September 10. Gulshan had just come home after a short stay in the hospital for medical treatment. She assured them she was doing fine and made plans to check in with them the following day. It was the last any of us would hear from Gulshan for years.

The next day, Ziba tried to call her mother as they had planned. Gulshan's phone immediately went to voicemail. Ziba then tried her mother's home number. Nobody answered. That evening, Zamira did the same, with the same result. Cell phone off, no answer at home. At first, they thought nothing of it. Perhaps she simply wasn't home, or something had come up. Perhaps her cell phone was off, or out of the battery. On the second day, they thought the same. By the third day, they both had the same sinking feeling. It was very unlike her to become unreachable like this. That was when they told me they couldn't get ahold of their mother.

The news brought a sense of terror. Initially, I ran away from the thought that she had been taken as retaliation for what I had said publicly. I told myself,

CHAPTER TWO

No, that isn't possible.

I haven't been in touch with Gulshan for over a year, just to protect her.

I have been living in the United States since 1989, and I am an American citizen.

I haven't even been back home since 2005.

Whatever I do here in the United States is my right; she has nothing to do with it.

They wouldn't take her just to get to me.

I kept pushing away that thought, telling myself it must be something else. There must be another explanation. My mind rejected the idea, like a foreign entity being rejected by the body. I told my nieces to keep trying, to let me know as soon as they heard anything. I could not sleep that night. The thought continued to disturb me.

Over the next two weeks, my nieces still could not get in contact with their mother. My denial began to fade, and I began to accept that she likely had been taken to the camps. My instinct was to announce her disappearance to the public immediately, but my nieces asked that I wait. Maybe, they thought, she had merely been brought in for questioning and would be released before long. Maybe they were just trying to scare her, or us. I agreed. As much as she is my sister, she is also their mother, and they had a right to determine how we would respond. For about five weeks, we kept quiet.

During this time, we were reaching out to our relatives in Europe, Türkiye, and Central Asia. We held out hope that someone might have heard something—anything—about where she had been taken. About two weeks into this waiting period we discovered that my maternal aunt in Artush had also disappeared, on the same day as Gulshan, in an entirely different part of the region. Distant relatives in Europe informed us that September 10 had been the last time anyone had heard from either of them. These were my two closest living relatives in the region, living some 870 miles (1400 km) from each other in Artush and Urumchi, and within less than a week of my appearance going live they were both selected for "vocational training" in the same camps that over a million other Uyghurs occupied.

We had some understanding of the criteria the Chinese government was employing to determine who to incarcerate in this way: intellectuals, famous writers, professors and academics, educators and religious leaders. Pillars of the community, and especially those who had travelled to Muslim-majority countries. Neither my sister nor my aunt fitted the usual profile of individuals normally targeted for so-called "vocational training," which involved teaching Uyghurs to speak Chinese instead of our own language. My sister is a retired medical doctor, my aunt, a retired schoolteacher. Both speak fluent Chinese. Neither one had travelled to any of the Muslim-majority countries that Uyghurs are targeted for visiting. They were just two ordinary, non-political, non-religious Uyghur women, leading ordinary lives.

It was clear to me that they were targeted solely as a means of silencing me. Not only had I testified to the disappearance of my own family members, I had also detailed the conditions of the camps and the targeted harassment of Uyghurs in the diaspora around the world. This retaliatory attempt to dissuade me from speaking out was entirely in line with everything I had spoken of. It also had the opposite of the desired effect.

During that time, I prepared myself. I began writing an op-ed for *The Washington Post* and reaching out to journalists. I invited a reporter from *The New York Times* to my office for an interview but asked that we hold off on running the story until my nieces gave me the green light. Finally, after five weeks, on October 19, 2018, we were sure my sister had been taken and that no further information would be coming. My nieces told me to do what I thought was right. Immediately, I reached out to my contacts at *The Washington Post* and *The New York Times* to run the story.

I doubled down on my efforts to raise awareness of the cruelty we were facing and began dedicating myself full-time towards developing Campaign for Uyghurs as an organization. I was giving interviews every day and using social media to speak out in every way I could think of. This continued for

CHAPTER TWO

months. At every opportunity, I reiterated that the sudden detention of these two women, living so far from one another and having so little in common besides their connection to me, was a clear act of retaliation against an American citizen for exercising her freedom of speech. For a time, there was a great deal of media interest in the story from media outlets and my story was covered in mainstream media such as the Associated Press, CNN, Democracy Now!, Fox News, RT America, Al Jazeera, *The Guardian*, the BBC, NBC, National Public Radio, Reuters, *Time Magazine*, ABC News Australia, SBS News, and Canada's CBC, etc. At every opportunity, I reiterated that the sudden detention of these two women, living so far from one another and having so little in common besides their connection to me, was a clear act of retaliation against an American citizen for exercising her freedom of speech.

The second time I visited the Hudson Institute, on October 24, 2018, I met Ken Weinstein, the institute's president. There was a solemn intensity in his eyes, as if he carried the weight of what he had already learned about my sister's story. He immediately committed to helping me and provided me with platforms to raise awareness about the Uyghur crisis, including speaking with the first Trump administration and referring my name to speaking opportunities at the universities and other global stages. The photo we took that day remains pinned to his Twitter/X page, even six years later, it serves as a powerful reminder of his commitment to justice and his steadfast allyship.

As I reflect on the countless interviews I gave, I feel compelled to pay tribute to my dear friend (per her family's request, I am leaving her name out), who stood by me through my toughest times. In April 2019, despite battling cancer, she remained a pillar of strength, offering comfort and encouragement. Even while enduring her own suffering, she worked tirelessly as deputy director of Campaign for Uyghurs, compiling research and preparing materials for my interviews. On October 31, 2019, as we sat by her during her final hours, I held her hand and thanked her, and she lightly squeezed it—a silent but powerful affirmation of her spirit. I will always remember her—her beautiful voice singing Uyghur folk songs, the way she masterfully played our traditional instruments, and the unyielding fire in her soul.

I am deeply grateful to be surrounded by incredible, loving, and compassionate friends who uplift me in ways words can hardly express. True friendship is not just about standing beside you in moments of strength but holding you up when you falter. When I think about friendship and unwavering support, I cannot go without acknowledging the kindness and strength of the elegant and talented Uyghur, Ihtibar Yasin from Chantilly, VA. Since my sister's detention, the weight of my fight has often left little room for the small joys I once cherished—styling my hair, carefully choosing an outfit, or taking a moment to embrace the confidence I once carried so naturally. In those moments when I neglect myself, she gently steps in to remind me of who I am.

* * *

In February 2019, I learned that my aunt had been released the month before. There remained no word as to Gulshan's whereabouts. To me, this seemed like a calculated tactic designed to undermine my criticism and the fact that I was the clear target of these detentions. Regardless, they still had my sister, and I was not about to let up.

I am the youngest of four children. I have two older brothers who both live in the United States. My oldest brother, Nijat, was born in 1958. Rishat was born in 1960. My sister is five years older than me and was born on June 13, 1962. I was born on June 14, 1967, so we celebrated our birthdays together. She used to joke that ever since I was born, I had taken her birthday. When we were growing up, the three older siblings naturally always stuck together, as they are each only two years apart in age. They all used to baby me and take care of me, especially my sister. After my mother's death in 2004, she became like a mother figure to me.

Days passed by. Weeks and months. I missed my sister dearly. It was hard. I couldn't sleep at night, constantly thinking of her soft smile. I remembered our childhood, growing up together. I remembered saying goodbye after her visit to the United States in August 2016—her face, her eyes, our last phone conversation. Her kindness, her caring words remind me to take care of myself, to eat well, and to rest. I began to travel for speaking engagements in various countries as part of the State Department's speakers' program and through agreements with various embassies. In March 2019, I went to Taiwan

CHAPTER TWO

to attend the International Religious Freedom Summit led by Ambassador Sam Brownback, former US Ambassador-at-Large for International Religious Freedom, serving from 2018 to 2021. He is a longtime advocate for religious liberty and works extensively to combat religious persecution worldwide.

Gene Bunin created the Xinjiang Victims Database (Shahit.biz), an online archive documenting Uyghur, Kazakh, and other Turkic individuals detained or persecuted in China's crackdown. It compiles testimonies, reports, and verified data, serving as a crucial resource for researchers and advocates. Bunin, a researcher and linguist with ties to the Uyghur region, launched this project to expose China's repression, and he included an entry with my sister's information.

I continued my travels—Japan in April, Austria and the Czech Republic in May, and Denmark and Germany in June. My journey continued through Türkiye, Australia, and across North America. While some of these events and forums were sponsored by the organizers, I had to fund a great number of them from my own pocket. At the time, I was also working full time in my professional job as an international business development director while devoting another eight hours a day to writing articles and press releases, giving interviews, managing the onslaught of posts and responses on social media, and traveling to raise awareness. I was quickly becoming overwhelmed. It was around this time that it became clear to me that I needed to find a way to make this work my focus.

In April 2019 I also testified before the US Senate Committee on Foreign Relations (SFRC). I testified at ten in the morning and immediately had to catch a flight from Ronald Reagan International Airport in Washington to speak at the University of Chicago. As soon as I landed, my phone was inundated with urgent messages. My husband, board members for Campaign for Uyghurs, and members of the community had been sending me messages to check our website, telling me that it was giving error messages.

I contacted our web developer, who told me what had happened. While the flight was in the air after my testimony at the SFRC, the Campaign for Uyghurs website came under a heavy cyberattack and was destroyed. He told me nothing could be saved. Within hours of my testimony, hackers had infiltrated the website and irretrievably deleted everything on it that I had produced since September 2017. I lost everything. All my writing, posts, pictures, and press releases, information, and all the web content was simply gone. I was upset and deeply frustrated. I remember feeling again that, even living in the heart of democracy and freedom, China's long black arm was reaching across the ocean to silence me after they had ravaged my heart by holding my dear sister hostage. This was fear of the truth. More and more, I was beginning to understand just how much of a threat our voice posed to the Chinese government, and the lengths to which they were willing to go to silence it. It was the impact of our work. I was emboldened. I thought the best way to deal with intimidation is to act even more strongly to expose their crimes. That is what I did. I doubled and tripled down on my efforts.

We rebuilt the site with better security and daily backups. Campaign for Uyghurs became my focus, with my brother Rishat providing crucial emotional, mental, and financial support. I started to seek grants for Campaign for Uyghurs, leading to a successful proposal to the National Endowment for Democracy (NED), effective October 1, 2019. On September 5, exactly a year after my life-changing speech at the Hudson Institute, I left my job to become a full-time activist.

The NED has been a critical supporter of CFU, helping us to strengthen civil society efforts to amplify our fight for Uyghur human rights and religious freedom, and demand accountability for the CCP's genocidal policies.

This support has been pivotal in expanding our advocacy efforts, enabling us to expand our outreach, mobilize international campaigns, and directly engage policymakers in democratic nations worldwide. In a time when the Chinese regime relentlessly seeks to silence our voices, NED's commitment to religious freedom and democracy has been instrumental in exposing through legitimate, peaceful means China's transnational repression and forced labor practices and Beijing's vast network of overseas police stations operating worldwide. The CCP has poured billions into influencing campaigns, economic coercion, and conducting hi-tech surveillance to crush any opposition. However, through NED's continuous support of Uyghurs, Hong Kongers, Tibetans, and Chinese dissidents, we've found a powerful and effective way to push back on Beijing's malign influence and authoritarian reach globally. NED's backing has been a vital part of the global movement for freedom and justice, fighting the CCP's attempts to suppress those who dare to speak out.

CHAPTER TWO

As I write these lines, I would like to express my gratitude to CFU's supporters and community members who have stood by our organization with steadfast dedication. I extend my deepest appreciation to our advisory board members—Eric Brown, Scott Busby, Dr. Rebecca Clothey, Dr. Peter Jan Honigsberg, Dr. Sean Roberts—and our board chair, Turdi Hoja, as well as our board of directors—Dr. Maya Mitalipova, Dr. Mehmet Ali-Hafiz, Mukerrem Kurban, Mehliya Cetinkaya, and Asiya Ablet—whose commitment has been instrumental in advancing our cause. I am also thankful to our deputy directors, Dilmurat Sulayman and Tunisa Matsedik-Qira, whose efforts have strengthened our mission, and for Campaign for Uyghurs' General Secretary, Kamalturk Yalkun, the son of imprisoned Uyghur intellectual Yalkun Rozi, whose strength reflects the very essence of our struggle. When we first founded our organization, Kaiser Siyit from Northern Virginia was instrumental in guiding us through the intricate process of registration and securing our non-profit status.

Wu'er Kaixi (Orkesh Dölet in Uyghur) is a historic leading figure in the fight for democracy against the CCP and he is also someone I have known since childhood, the son of my father's close friend from their university years. I take immense pride in calling him a brother in this struggle. A fearless democracy activist, Wuer Kaixi rose to prominence as a student leader during the 1989 Tiananmen Square protests, where his defiance against the Chinese regime made him one of the most recognized figures of the movement. In exile he has remained a tireless advocate for democracy and human rights, particularly for the Uyghur people, speaking out against injustice with unwavering conviction. In 2021, I invited him to join Campaign for Uyghurs as Honorary Chairman, and he has since stood with us, strengthening our fight with his leadership and vision.

I would like to also recognize my brother Rishat's support and wisdom. My brother, Dr. Rishat Abbas, arrived in the United States around the same time I did in 1989, determined to forge a new path. In 1994, he earned his PhD in pharmaceutical sciences from Ohio State University, a testament to his dedication and intellect. Over the years, our bond deepened—not just as siblings but as partners in our shared mission. In both our personal lives and our advocacy, we have stood side by side, navigating the challenges of exile while advocating for our people. I am immensely proud of him, not only as a distinguished Uyghur scientist recognized globally, but also as a fearless and unwavering voice for Uyghur advocacy in the diaspora. His resilience and leadership continue to inspire me and countless others in our struggle for justice. Rishat has spent his life at the crossroads of science and justice. A pioneering pharmaceutical scientist, he has dedicated more than thirty years to developing life-saving medicines, leading research that has shaped modern treatments across multiple diseases, including cancer. He became a force in clinical research, guiding the development of ten groundbreaking innovative medicines. His name appears in more than one hundred and fifty scientific publications, patents, and book chapters, and his contributions have earned him prestigious honors from the US Department of Defense and the United States Air Force as well as scientific associations. While his scientific achievements broke new ground, his heart was always with his people—the Uyghurs. He witnessed firsthand the tightening grip of Chinese repression while he was growing up in Urumchi during Mao Zedong's Great Cultural Revolution. As he built his career in science in the United States, he never abandoned the Uyghurs' fight for freedom.

In 1998, he co-founded the Uyghur American Association, becoming its first elected president and laying the foundation for Uyghur advocacy in the United States. His voice reached the halls of Congress, briefing lawmakers and officials about China's brutal crackdown. When the world turned a blind eye to the 1997 Ghulja Massacre,[4] my brother took action, pushing for the creation of the Uyghur-language service at Radio Free Asia to break China's information blockade. His efforts helped to secure vital funding for Uyghur human rights initiatives, ensuring that the struggle for justice had the support it desperately needed. Rishat's influence has shaped the global fight for Uyghur rights. As an honorary chairman of the Uyghur Academy from 2015 to 2021, he helped build a worldwide network of intellectuals and activists. In 2019, after our sister Gulshan's detention, he stood before world leaders

---

4. The Ghulja Massacre was a brutal crackdown on Uyghur demonstrators in Xinjiang on February 5, 1997 by the CCP. A peaceful protest for religious freedom and human rights escalated into violent repression, making it one of the deadliest state attacks on Uyghurs before the mass internment crisis.

CHAPTER TWO

at the United Nations General Assembly, testifying on China's atrocities. He played a key role in lobbying for the *Uyghur Human Rights Policy Act* of 2020, a landmark US law that condemned those responsible for the Uyghur genocide. When the 2021 Uyghur Tribunal convened in London (UK) to expose China's crimes, my brother Rishat was at its core, compiling and coordinating critical evidence and organizing Uyghur intellectuals around the world to translate hundreds and thousands of pages of testimonies into English. Now, as the elected president of the Uyghur Academy–International and a senior adviser to Campaign for Uyghurs, and the World Uyghur Congress, he remains relentless. He has also been leading the Global Uyghur Academy, focusing on preserving the Uyghur identity, language, and culture within Uyghur diaspora communities while training the next generation of Uyghur youth leaders. He is not just a scientist or an advocate, he is a guardian of truth, a voice for the voiceless, and a tireless warrior against injustice.

Rishat's wife, my sister-in-law Hamra, is someone I feel incredibly fortunate to call my own sister. Her kindness, generosity, and unwavering support have been a constant source of strength in my life. Behind the scenes, often without recognition, she's been the quiet force that has always been there for me. She's gone out of her way, time and again, to buy outfits for me—beautiful, thoughtful clothing—when she noticed I didn't have the time or energy to shop for myself, especially when I was preparing to speak at international forums and summits, representing my people. She understood the pressure and the sacrifices and, without asking, took it upon herself to ensure that I felt confident and presentable, even when I couldn't. Hamra has also been the one to think of my well-being in ways I never would. She would get me gift cards for massages, knowing how exhausted I'd be after those long, grueling cross-Atlantic and cross-Pacific flights. I still have those cards tucked away, because I've never found time to take a break for myself. Even now, I can't bring myself to indulge in self-care, but her thoughtfulness will always resonate with me. For more than thirty years, Hamra has been my closest friend and my most understanding family in the United States.

At Campaign for Uyghurs, my husband, Abdulhakim Idris, my brother, Rishat Abbas, and I stand together in an unyielding fight to expose China's crimes and hold the CCP accountable. In response, the CCP and its proxies have relentlessly attacked us with libel, online harassment, and smear campaigns, desperate to discredit our work. But their fear only affirms the impact of our efforts. We have spearheaded critical initiatives to bring global attention to China's genocide and atrocities—efforts that have shaken the CCP to its core. Yet, the price of our advocacy has been devastating. My brother and I continue our daily fight against the CCP, knowing that our actions cost our sister Gulshan her freedom. Despite this heartbreak, we refuse to be silenced. We press forward, drawing strength from one another, from our people, and from the unwavering belief that justice will prevail. The more they try to erase us, the louder we will fight.

Despite my deep love for my family, my parents, and the homeland that shaped me, I left everything behind and came to the United States alone when I was not even twenty-two years old. I was searching for something we were denied—a life of freedom and democracy. These fundamental rights, the very essence of human dignity, are under relentless attack by the totalitarian Chinese Communist Party. Their brutality not only crushes my people but threatens the very foundation of the free world. This is not just a Uyghur struggle—it is a global fight for justice, for humanity, and for the future of all who cherish freedom.

I often find myself lost in thoughts of my family—of my grandfather, my teachers, my childhood friends, and the years spent growing up in Urumchi. I remember my parents' unwavering love and care, especially in my earliest years, and how their warmth shaped the person I am today.

My father's voice echoes in my mind, teasing that I could never be a singer because he did everything, he could to ensure that I never cried as a baby. He used to say that since I never exercised my lungs through crying or screaming, I simply wouldn't have the voice for it. It was always a joke, but behind his playful words was a truth I cherish—he tried so hard to protect me from sadness. He was nurturing in a way that few fathers are, tender in his love, unwavering in his support. He held me through life's smallest moments, always cushioning the world so I would never feel it too harshly.

And as my life progresses, I realize how blessed I have been to always have people who nurture and uplift me. Though I may not have been meant to be a singer, I was always meant to be carried forward by the kindness of those around me.

CHAPTER THREE
YOU CAN NEVER BE A SINGER

In the 1950s, Mao Zedong, Chairman of the Chinese Communist Party (CCP), initiated a "land reform" campaign in East Turkistan with the intention of stripping Uyghurs of their wealth. Then, in the early 1960s, Mao's regime targeted Uyghur intellectuals under the guise of the "Hundred Flowers Campaign," a brief political movement in China initiated by the CCP in 1956 and 1957. The campaign encouraged intellectuals, scholars, and citizens to openly express their opinions, criticisms, and suggestions about the government and its policies. The name Hundred Flowers Campaign comes from a famous slogan attributed to Mao: "Let a hundred flowers bloom, let a hundred schools of thought contend." This was ostensibly meant to promote a variety of viewpoints and foster debate to improve governance. The result was very different, as it became a means of identifying dissenting voices to be blacklisted, and a vast number of those targeted were Uyghurs.

The Great Cultural Revolution of 1966 was one of the most devastating political movements in China's recent history. While Chinese scholars claim that three million Chinese people died, some estimates go as high as ten million. Uyghur scholars suggest that at least 1.5 million Uyghurs alone perished. It was also put forward by the Uyghur elites that since the Chinese Communist Red Army first occupied East Turkistan in 1949, the Chinese government's targeting of Uyghurs through various political movements has been a regular practice and national policy.

Mao Zedong launched the Great Cultural Revolution to eliminate dissent and reassert his control over China and the CCP. The movement aimed to revive revolutionary zeal, purge traditional culture, capitalist elements, and perceived enemies, while addressing what Mao saw as the party's deviation from true communist principles.

During the Great Cultural Revolution, Mao Zedong called upon young people, including students in universities and high schools, to form paramilitary groups known as the Red Guards. These Red Guards were charged with enforcing Mao's ideology by helping to purge perceived counterrevolutionary elements within society and promote radical communist beliefs. They were encouraged to denounce authority figures, intellectuals, and anyone considered to have bourgeois or capitalist tendencies. The Red Guards conducted mass rallies, seized property, destroyed cultural artifacts, and subjected individuals to public humiliation and violence in their fervent pursuit of Maoist ideology.

I was born in Urumchi, in 1967, the year after Mao launched the Great Cultural Revolution. Amidst the turmoil of repressive policies, my father, Abbas Borhan, named me "Rushan," which means *light, brightness,* or *lucid* in Uyghur in the hope of seeing some light during this dark time. At this time, my father became a target of Mao's notorious Red Guards, joining the ranks of countless intellectuals facing persecution. As the Chairman of the Department of Biology at Xinjiang University, my father was an easy target for the Red Guards' anti-intellectual fervor, as well as the anti-Uyghur sentiment. Mao's personality was authoritarian, ruthless, and marked by a deep belief in his own ideological vision of purity, brutal pragmatism, and a utopian future. It was a propaganda-driven glorification of Mao, portraying him as an infallible leader whose thoughts were absolute truth. After a brief period of struggle, government pressure eventually resulted in my father's removal from his chairmanship.

Meanwhile, my mother, Mariye Abliz, a medical doctor at the Xinjiang University Hospital, also fell victim to the oppressive regime. Persecution during this time took many forms, and no one was free of it. At times, it was my mother who bravely confronted adversity, while at others it was my father. Even my maternal grandfather, Abliz Niyaz, was not spared; during this time, he was unjustly sentenced to three years imprisonment.

After my father lost his job, he dedicated his days to taking care of me, the youngest child and precious princess of our household. We were living in an

CHAPTER THREE

apartment at Xinjiang University. My parents used to tell me how my father established a routine when I was barely a month old. He placed a schedule on the wall by my crib that displayed times for feeding, water breaks, sleep, waking times, and diaper changes, all listed clearly and meticulously. Perhaps due to this highly structured schedule, I was notably calm as a baby. I rarely cried. I never had a chance to get frustrated due to hunger or unrest or discomfort from a wet diaper. Even in my sleep, I would stay exactly as he had laid me down and wake up the same way. Because of my father's parenting method, the teachers at Xinjiang University would call me "Abbas Borhan's experimental child." I continued to hear this label from Uyghur professors from Xinjiang University and other intellectuals in Urumchi who knew my father long after I became a parent myself.

One day when I was in elementary school, I was trying to hum a Uyghur song that I used to hear my mother sing. My father said to me, jokingly, and with his kind smile, "Rushan, you can't be a singer because I tried my best not to make you cry when you were a baby. Your lungs were not strongly exercised by screaming and crying when you were a baby, and your upper voice is underdeveloped for singing. You were always such a patient child, never crying for hunger, thirst, being wet or sleepiness. That was by design— I tried not to give you a chance to cry."

But in those dark times, dad was taken away from us to the political reeducation sessions (detailed in his memoir, Chapter Four of this book), and one day the Red Guards came and grabbed my mother to drag her to the "Red Building," a place to hold and indoctrinate targeted intellectuals in Xinjiang University. That day, I cried so hard, and my crying voice never left my mother's ears during the two weeks she was locked in the Red Building. My mother told me this story many times when I was older.

As she told it, she was sitting in the courtyard of the property my paternal grandparents owned in the residential area across from the front gate of Xinjiang University. She was holding me in her arms. The Red Guards— students loyal to Mao Zedong with red stripes on their sleeves—suddenly burst into the house to take my mother into the school and continue their oppression. When they barged into my grandparents' home, mom tried to pass me into the arms of my grandmother. However, the Red Guards couldn't tolerate my mother's defiance even for a moment. They forcefully tore me from her grasp, rudely thrusting me towards my grandmother before dragging my mother away. In that heart-wrenching moment, I, who had been raised without reason to scream and cry, suddenly burst into inconsolable sobbing. The echoes of my cries rang in my mother's ears as she was forcibly taken from our home to the Red Building.

Throughout my early childhood, the entire population of my homeland was in sorrow and despair. The Great Cultural Revolution was marked by the closure or destruction of mosques, the repurposing of religious sites as pig farms, and the long-term imprisonment of renowned Uyghur intellectuals, nationalists, wealthy individuals, writers, religious figures, and even ordinary teachers. This revolution, which also witnessed the beginning of the systematic destruction of the Uyghur culture, began in 1966 and only concluded with the death of Mao Zedong in 1976.

I only learned when I grew up that my father was labeled a "local nationalist" and a "pest," and my mother as the "Iminov group's communicator" (Iminov was described in dad's memoir, Chapter Four of this book) and a "local nationalist." Later, I learned that the targets of the Red Guards were people who were proud of their Uyghur identity, who kept certain Uyghur books with historical, national, or ethnic identity, or copies of the Holy Qur'an at home and prayed, who kept works on Uyghur history, who had even the slightest discontent with the government, who had even once mentioned the glorious Uyghurs' history, who worshipped Allah instead of Mao Zedong, or who did not salute Mao Zedong's portrait or read Mao Zedong's selected works. They were the ones who did not express loyalty to the Chinese regime. Teachers who dared to mention the long history of the Uyghurs or the roots of Uyghur identity in class were also targeted. Even those who spoke about their dreams of independence were targeted. Rightists, leftists, and anyone involved in small talk about nationalism became targets as well.

When these people were arrested and tried, two Red Guards would seize them by the shoulders to force them to bow to the ground, repent of their sins, and promise to be loyal to the party and the government. This kind of violence spread not only in China, but also to the villages. Sometimes those who were targeted by the Red Guards were killed by various nefarious means.

CHAPTER THREE

Uyghur writers have not had the opportunity to publish accounts of the hardships endured by the Uyghur people during the Cultural Revolution. More accurately, the Chinese regime has not allowed Uyghurs to publish works related to the CCP's atrocities during that tumultuous decade. China concealed its crimes against humanity during the Cultural Revolution just as it has been hiding its current genocide in the twenty-first century: the mass imprisonment of millions of Uyghurs in concentration camps and the disappearance of countless Uyghur elites. However, an unpublished memoir exists that serves as a testament to these atrocities. This document containing vital information about the grave crimes perpetrated by the Chinese Communist regime in Uyghur from the mid-1960s to the late 1970s now rests in my hands and is the memoir left to us by my father, Abbas Borhan.

Titled "What I Witnessed," my father's memoir has not yet been published. He wrote a part of it while he was in Urumchi, and the rest in the United States when he was visiting me and my brother Rishat in 2005. When he was planning to return home after staying for about five months, my father suggested that we keep the manuscript in the United States

My father wrote down the names of the Uyghur people who were subjected to mistreatment and public humiliations. I recognized some, but not all of the names. It was clear, however, that most of them were Uyghur intellectuals, lecturers, and staff of Xinjiang University. I also recognized the names of some well-known Uyghur intellectuals. The descriptions of the Great Cultural Revolution in my father's memoir and the critical information about some of the people from the era in which I was born and raised, what they were subjected to, and the cruelties they suffered, provide a rare first-hand account of our history. My father was a living witness to the darkness of that time, and his writings are evidence that our struggle is older and deeper than many people in the world, even those sympathetic to our cause, realize today.

CHAPTER FOUR
WHAT MY FATHER WITNESSED

The following chapter contains excerpts from the memoir of my father, Abbas Borhan, written in the first person by him. In his memoir "What I Witnessed," my father wrote about the fate of notable Uyghur figures such as Muhammed Imin Iminov, who were unjustly imprisoned and tortured to death. Anyone who reads his memoir can clearly understand that the Chinese regime's oppression of the Uyghurs did not start with the launch of recent concentration camps. My father's memoir highlights this point clearly.

* * *

It was the spring of 1966. The Great Proletarian Cultural Revolution (often referred to as the Cultural Revolution), started on May 16, 1966, when Mao Zedong issued a document called the "May 16th Manifesto." This chaos marked the beginning of a tumultuous era in Chinese history in which right and wrong were turned upside down and justice was buried deep in darkness. On May 16th, an official announcement from the Chinese Central Committee marked the beginning of the Cultural Revolution, sparking widespread activity and enthusiasm for the movement. In the meantime, a task force led by a Chinese individual named Guan was dispatched from the central authority to the Uyghur region. One day, a meeting was called for all the teachers and cadres. We convened in the hall located on the upper floor of the Xinjiang University School Library. The school administration notified us that the leadership of the Cultural Revolution unit had arrived.

CHAPTER FOUR

The deputy chief of that unit addressed the gathering while my wife, Mariye, and a family friend, Abdurehim Shawdun,[5] and I sat together.

The head of the unit said: "The problem at Xinjiang University is serious. If the problem at the university is solved, 80 percent of Xinjiang's problems will be solved." The people here are either 'revisionists, foreign-linked sources or local nationalists,' he said sternly. I whispered to myself, "They already have the labels, and the accusations lined up for us." The speech was a foretelling of the days that lay ahead of us. We wrote down his words one by one, feeling the mounting mental tension that often heralds the dawn of a political movement. In the middle of June, I led the Preparation Department students to harvest wheat in the Sanping Agricultural Field near Urumchi and came back a month later. I was the only teacher guiding the students throughout our journey.

The leadership of the Great Cultural Revolution unit urged the public to publish "Great Wall Newspapers." "Write even if only 1 percent of it is truth," they said. The instructions from above were delivered, "If there is a mistake, correct it, if not, be careful." The first Great Wall Newspaper about me reads "Abbas Borhan is a local nationalist." There were discussions of the content of the paper. Some persisted in declaring that "a great cultural revolution, directly initiated and guided by our great leader, has begun." Red flags began to mount. Large-print newspapers flooded the streets. The large print produced by our biology department, featuring content about me, is now being affixed to the walls in our school. My wife, Mariye Abliz, and I often discussed these things when we got home. Mariye would say, "There's always a silver lining to everything. It's alright; these days will pass too," asking me not to pay attention or care.

Mariye has a remarkably courageous and kind character. In August 1966, the people of Xinjiang University took things a step further, requiring us to wear hats resembling the long paper hats that the government forced wealthy Uyghur individuals who were branded as "local nationalists" to wear in the 1950s. One morning, seventy to eighty teachers and staff were made to wear these hats. By afternoon, numerous other cadres and teachers were

---

5. His daughter, Shadiye Abdurehim, now works as a reporter at the Radio Free Asia Uyghur Service.

also forced into wearing them. Even the university barber who worked at the barber shop took charge, leading two students to force the hats onto more than ten teachers and other Uyghur intellectuals. When I returned home at noon, I advised Mariye, "Don't go to those areas in the afternoon. Stay home." Mariye responded with, "It's okay, I have to go to work" and left after tidying up the dishes. On her way, the barber, accompanied by a few students, forcefully made Mariye wear a hat crafted from newspapers.

One day, they forced us to come to the front of the library building in the middle of the school. We were lined up on the stairs in rows. From time to time, someone would arrive and direct us to stand in one manner, only for someone else to come along and instruct us to stand differently. Suddenly, someone pushed me, and I fell down the stairs. Had it not been for the body of someone in front of me, my head would have hit the edge of the stairs, and I would have been hurt badly. The Chinese man named Wen came out from the far left and shouted loudly, "Today marks a significant revolutionary movement. Well done. Let's root out all the devils and evildoers, and let's pull out the ones behind them, the ones next to them, the ones below them, and the ones above them!" He repeated his words passionately, punctuating them with chants of "Let's eradicate the demons! Let's eliminate all the pests!" The slogans echoed around.

While we were tired, the vice principal named Yon'gang came into our ranks and asked, "Where should I stand?' A student immediately made a hat out of newspaper and put it on him. Except for Wen and Zhu, all the principals were dressed in paper hats and labeled as "pests." Abdulhakim Jappar, former President of Xinjiang University, who went to work in the countryside, returned from an educational campaign in the fall of 1965. When he was coming back, his car overturned. Two cadres traveling with him died, and Abdulhakim Jappar's hand was broken. A paper hat was also put on the head of the man with his arm still in a sling. Someone grabbed him harshly by his broken arm, and he cried out in agony. I was in the same line as Abdulhakim Jappar, and I was saddened by what I witnessed. One of the revolutionists standing behind me whispered to another, "The paper hat suits this pest, let's give him an even uglier one." So they swapped the "pretty

CHAPTER FOUR

hat" on my head with a more unsightly one. We couldn't see what our paper hats looked like on our heads.

A Chinese man named Wen, leading the revolutionists, labeled us "first-class pests, evildoers" and singled out nearly fifty of us. We were divided into three groups: school and faculty directors in the first, with the rest split into two more. Zhang Chunfa, the party's propaganda chief, oversaw the first group, while Yun Gang managed all three. As we were sorted, those already wearing the hat were told to leave it and go home. I later learned this from Mariye when I arrived home.

One day, even Borhan Shahidi[6] a Tatar politician handpicked and promoted by the CCP itself, was abruptly forced to return from Beijing, where he had been attending a meeting. All the way on the train on his return trip, he was condemned and forced to kneel on the train, causing wounds to his knees. When he was being criticized at the university courtyard, a Chinese student asked him, "Hey old man, how old are you?" When Borhan responded, "I'm 75 years old," the student yelled, "Then how come you're still alive?" "I will die when the time comes!" Borhan replied repeatedly.

Nusrat Shahidi and Suyum Shahidi (son and wife of Borhan Shahidi) were in the same group as us. A security guard at the door named Li Shiqing was in charge of us. We were forced to labor every day. We used to clean the canals in the school, level the sides with shovels, sweep and clean the roads in the school, and level the mounds by the lake. Students began wearing red sleeve badges that read "Red Guard" on their wrists. Mariye was still working at the University hospital.

On another day, while we were laboring around the creek across from the school's food factory, the southwest wind carried the factory's aromatic odors to us. Li Xing, a Chinese in charge of us, approached Suyum Shahidi and exclaimed, "You're wearing perfume to work!" She said "No, I didn't wear any perfume." After Li Xing finished yelling, another Uyghur intellectual

---

6. Borhan Shahidi was a politician of Tatar descent who held various positions of authority in East Turkistan. He served as Governor of Xinjiang, Vice Chairman of the provincial coalition government of the Second East Turkistan Republic and was President of Xinjiang.

explained to him, "It's not perfume, it's the scent of the food factory." Li Xing was taken aback and left without saying a word.

When Borhan Shahidi stood for criticism, they made Nusrat, Suyum, me, and others stand beside him. When they asked Borhan Shahidi, "Did you oppose the party and socialism?" he never said "Yes." Instead, he would reply, "I support the party and socialism." Then, a man named Rahman Arinsha boldly asked, "Are you a revolutionist?" After a moment of silence, Rahman Arinsha muttered to himself, "No! You are not." Later, he questioned, "Did you protect the party and socialism?" Rahman paused again and said, "*Yes.*" It seemed Rahman meant to say "No!" in his mind, but the word came out wrong and mistakenly said "yes" instead. This led to an uproar among the people, accusing Rahman Arinsha of defending Borhan Shahidi instead of criticizing him. Consequently, they pulled Rahman down for his one wrongly spoken word, and placed him among us, the "accused."

The criticism event taking place in the field was filled with tension. Just then, Mao Zedong's call to "Target the commanding headquarters" echoed around. Slogans urging listeners to "root out those leading towards capitalism" reverberated through the air. The Red Guards started to organize into squads, gearing up for "communication" trips to Beijing, China's capital. Red Guards from mainland China also began to arrive. Everywhere, slogans demanding the downfall of Liu Dingtao, which included the state heads Liu Shaoqi, Deng Xiaoping, and Tao Zhu, started to be heard. The school was gripped with an atmosphere of tension.

The Red Guards formed smaller groups and started collecting lunch money from the school, using it to travel to China to establish "contacts." They typically traveled in groups of three to five individuals. Along the way, they would chant slogans like "Rebellion is justified" and "Let's eradicate the demons!" Large-scale printing of "Quotations from Mao Zedong" began, and everyone had a copy in their hands. Initially, excerpts like "Yugong's Moving of the Mountain" and "Let's work for the people" were prominent.

In late September, large-print newspapers with slogans like "If the father is virtuous, the child will be good; if the father is evil, the child will rebel" flooded our school. In the afternoons, we saw many Uyghur students wearing signs that said "I'm a rebel, I'm a fool." This lasted for three days. The news-

CHAPTER FOUR

papers featured images of Mao Zedong welcoming millions of Red Guards in Tiananmen Square, with crowds holding Mao's Little Red Book, wearing badges with his image, and carrying banners promoting "Let's work for the people." Mao first welcomed Red Guard representatives in Tiananmen Square[7] on August 18, 1966. At the time, the entire society was engulfed in violence, conflict, burglary, and frequent house searches. We were *"Pests"* with labels on our backs. The Red Guards, composed of students, would beat us with ribbons and curse us as they pleased. However, despite the challenging circumstances, Mariye by my side, our family found solace and joy within our home.

In October 1966, Mariye discovered she was pregnant with Rushan. It would be our fourth child. Our oldest son Nijat was eight, Rishat was six, and Gulshan was four years old. I raised chickens and often encouraged Mariye to consume more eggs. Our household remained harmonious and cozy, providing us with a slice of serenity amid the chaos outside. Mariye used to have very strong morning sicknesses during the first few months of her pregnancy, usually lasting all day long. I started to take charge of household chores and preparing our family meals. Usually, every evening a few "Pests" would gather at our house to study politics and cook together. Gradually, however, attendance dwindled, and the learning stopped as the administration's grip on us loosened. Key figures also faced trials, and even high-ranking officials such as the Secretary of the Autonomous Region, Wang Enmao, and his deputy, Wugang, came under criticism. As the scrutiny lessened, we found ourselves dedicating more time to our family life. I would sometimes take on the responsibility of cooking entirely. Despite the upheaval, Mariye remained committed to her medical profession.

On June 14, 1967, Mariye gave birth to a healthy girl. I named her Rushan, which means "light or brightness," hoping that clarity would soon emerge from the darkness and chaos of our time when everything seemed so dark and unjust.

---

7. This time during the Cultural Revolution came to be known as "Red August." During the ensuing violence carried out by the Red Guards, 10,275 people were killed, 33,695 homes were ransacked, and 85,196 families were displaced.

It was the end of 1967. People from one rebel group came and searched our home and put all our things in a small storage room and sealed them there. Our house had two bedrooms, and there was a small dark storage closet between them. I built a small working space there, put up a lamp, made a desk and a table and made a tiny office for myself so that I could read and write there.

The rebels collected our blankets, bedding, pillows, and our clothes, leaving only two blankets for our three children and the baby, and another one for me and Mariye, and left only one set of clothes for everyone.

We were very upset about this, and Mariye and I complained to each other helplessly after they left. One day, when I went to the school courtyard, they posted some quotations of Mao Zedong: "If I fight with nature, if I fight with the earth, if I fight with people, I will feel very happy." Of course, this is supposedly also a kind of hysteria, and a description of the "anger" of the revolutionaries against the "pests." During this process, the saying "the pen is mightier than the sword" was very visible and people continued to shout that. But the struggle with "sword" was a direct order from Mao Zedong.

Newspapers often published pictures of the Red Guards targeting officials, university teachers, and intellectuals who were perceived as representing the old order or having bourgeois tendencies and attacking them physically, pulling our hair. We were subjected to public humiliation and physical abuse. Red Guards conducted "struggle sessions" where the accused were publicly denounced, criticized, and sometimes physically assaulted. We were forced to wear humiliating signs or placards around our necks, denouncing our alleged crimes against the revolution. The major Beijing newspapers with such pictures were pasted here and there on our university campus. We were sometimes ordered to "look at the major newspapers about people like you" and taken to the campus to read such articles and see the pictures.

Since the end of February 1968, the rebels have been divided among themselves. They used to call themselves the number 1 command, number 2 command, and number 3 command. They were in armed conflict with each other. The city of Urumchi was also divided into two, called the red area and white area. The "rebels" of this place would come and settle in our university as well.

CHAPTER FOUR

Teachers who lost their jobs due to the political campaign would often gather in front of our door to exchange information and chat. We discussed the large newspapers, various events, and incidents. In the evenings, when Mariye returned home from the hospital, I would recount to her everything I had heard, one by one.

The campus was full of panic, threats, and fear. Even if we walked inside the school grounds, we were afraid that someone would come to us from any direction. Those wearing Red Guard badges on their wrists were allowed to insult, condemn, humiliate, and try anyone they wanted. No one would defend us. They labeled us as "demons." This became the common name for most of the Uyghur intellectuals. Others referred to us as "revisionists" and "foreign-linked sources," and they labeled me as a "local nationalist," and hung signs on our backs. The General Assembly gathered us together and said, "You must wear these boards everywhere, even when you use the toilet."

One of the posters of Mao Zedong, saying "Now the world is chaotic. The revolution will continue in another seven to eight years. Every ten years, we will carry out movements like this" was affixed to the wall. The Red Guards flooded the whole campus. Sometimes, they'd come over to us to inspect the signs hanging on our backs, and I'd even hold the sign up for them to get a better look. The sign did not bother me. I heard one of the Red Guards say, "This guy didn't even care about wearing the sign on his back!"

They ordered all of us to gather together. We assembled at the front of the main gate. A Chinese revolutionist named Li Shiqing often berated us. "Listen!" he said to us when we gathered, and he ordered me to translate to Uyghur. Stepping forward, I translated: "You will crawl out of the houses you currently reside in and crawl back to where you came from; the revolutionary class will take those houses." When he finished, he asked if anyone had anything to say. I spoke up: "Firstly, I am from Artush, which is 1400 km (870 miles) from Urumchi. How can I crawl back there? Secondly, my wife is a doctor in this university—you have classified her position as a member of the revolutionary class. What will I do if she doesn't want to move back to Artush?" He didn't answer my question. Instead, he shouted, "Disperse!" and left. It was clear that this order abused our rights. When I came home and told Mariye, she didn't seem to care and just smiled and said, "Let's just ignore."

One time, one of my "pest" friends was passing by and he saw that I hung the criticism sign we carried on our back upon the outside door of the main gate. "Why did you hang the sign outside the door?" he asked. "They instructed us to hang it on the door," I smiled and responded jokingly "so, they didn't specify the inside or outside door, did they?" "That is right," he replied with a smile.

One day, students and rebellious teachers gathered to beat up one teacher that they deemed a "pest" and started to beat him violently. Blood flowed from his nose. The teacher exclaimed, "My nose is bleeding! Please let me clean it up!" One of the students who was beating the teacher screamed at him and yelled: "The blood from his nose is fake!" Later, other students gave her a hard time by saying "A physiology student cannot differentiate real blood from fake blood."

A student arrived at our home while leading the Red Guard high school students to search our home. Taking one of my anatomy books in hand, one of them exclaimed, "Look at this X-rated book with a picture of a naked man!" Flipping through our books, he showed the pictures to other students. "It's not an X-rated book, it's a science book on anatomy," I said. No one listened.

They tore up our books and took our personal pictures from our photo albums to the front of our apartment and burned them. Years later, Mariye always complained about how we lost all of our pictures from the times that we were young, including our wedding photos. Some deemed such erratic actions to be "revolutionary" and "expressions of courage." A few days later, several other students came and searched our home again. One student took my Russian and Chinese dictionary. I just sat and watched them speechlessly as they took our personal belongings as they pleased.

The world is both big and very small. Twelve years later, in 1980, I visited Ulughchat County to inspect and promote science and technology work in the countryside. A county chief took me to Toyan Prairie at the Torgat junction of Ulughchat. Toyan Prairie, the starting point of the Chaqmaq River, is a beautiful meadow. It is said that there are chrysanthemums on the snowy mountain above. It appears as a beautiful meadow with greenery like painted landscapes. A large spring emerges from the bottom of the valley. When one speaks of the amount of water in the basin, it is like a giant stone mill grinding

CHAPTER FOUR

four stone slabs of water. This water is a large fountain that flows from under the base of chrysanthemums, nourishing the green pastures. Many families live on the hillside below that lake.

Suddenly, a young man came out of the border office in Torgat to say hello—and introduced himself! He was the student who had searched my home and took my Russian and Chinese dictionary in 1968. We both recognized each other. While remembering what he did then, he apologized for taking the dictionary from my home during the Cultural Revolution. I hugged him and jokingly said "You have grown quite a bit!"

On a clear day in early 1968, influential Uyghur poet Tiyipjan Eliyev[8] came to our house. Since Tiyipjan's marriage with Mariye's close friend Helchem from medical college, we have become close family friends and have been visiting each other often. He was also labelled as a "pest" at that time. We talked for some time. A few days later, Tiyipjan was taken for "struggle"[9] by the Red Guards. "You are a pest yourself, why did you go to the house of that pest?" they told Tiyipjan and interrogated him for several days for visiting my house. Tiyipjan's wife, Helchem, told us about this. Later, Tiyipjan Eliyev and other Uyghur intellectuals were sent to the villages of Jimisar County to work as forced laborers.

During 1968, this revolutionary upheaval was still on. Newspapers in Beijing published articles with titles like "Rebellion Is Justified," and large-print newspapers of Mao Zedong titled "Let's hold the Silingbu (Command Headquarters) under fire!" The supporters of No. 1 and No. 2 Silingbu

---

8. The famous Tiyipjan Eliyev (1930–1989) was a modern Uyghur poet. Born into an educated family, he was inspired by folk literature and began writing poetry in 1945. He worked as an editor and later held key cultural positions, including head of the Literature and Art Department in Xinjiang and editor-in-chief of *Xinjiang Literature and Art*. From 1962, he became a professional writer and was vice chairman of the Chinese Writers' Association in 1979. Some of his poems have become beloved Uyghur folklore songs, with the most renowned being "Never-Ending Song," a timeless piece that continues to resonate deeply within the Uyghur community.
9. Struggle sessions, also sometimes called denunciation rallies, were violent public spectacles where those accused of being "class enemies" were humiliated, beaten, and tortured. They occurred throughout the Cultural Revolution.

moved out of our university and settled in the No. 8 School. We heard that a cavalry led by Chinese commander Peng Dajin had arrived from Qumul. The supporters of No. 2 Silingbu who mostly consisted of students, government servants, and staff started filling the campus, and their number quickly increased. The divide bordering Nanmin (Southern Gate) also strengthened. In the campus, the activities of the Red 3rd Division of No. 2 Silingbu, which consisted of both Chinese and ethnic students, had increased. Their large-print newspapers were plastered on the walls of the opera house. They mostly criticized Wang Enmao's[10] implementation of ethnic policies. At the end of 1968, Muhammed Emin Iminov, Qali Abaq (Kazakh), Yusuf Momin, Abdurehim Letip, Ms. Selime Talip, and many other cadres came to the university. Selime Talip came from Beijing; she and her two daughters often came to our home, and she loved Mariye as her own sister. Iminov, Selime Talip, and Abdurehim Letip were friends of my father-in-law, Mariye's father, Abliz Niyaz. At this time, the plaques reading "Pest" on our necks were removed and we could enter the campus freely.

Mariye and I went to visit Iminov, one day. He was very happy to see us and talked with us warmly. Iminov used to call me "Abbas Qari" according to the habit of referring to respected people in Ikisaq (a village in Artush where I was born and grew up). They were placed in a room on the second floor of the Faculty of Literature building. Inside Iminov's room, there were two beds, a wardrobe, and a table inside the room. Iminov's son Polat, who came to accompany him, used one bed. This day, we also visited Qali Abaq (Deputy General Secretary of the Uyghur Autonomous Region) and Yusuf Momin (husband of Zulayha, a colleague of Mariye at the hospital), who was the director of the government office. We chatted with them too. The calm and serious demeanor of Iminov's son Polat left a good impression on me. Mariye had known this family since the time when Iminov and Mariye's father, Abliz Niyaz, joined the establishment of the Second East Turkistan Republic in 1944 in Ghulja. My father-in-law, Abliz Niyaz, was the chief inspector (Bash Teptish) during these years in Ghulja. After 1949 returning

---

10. Wang Enmao (Chinese: 王恩茂) (May 19, 1913–April 12, 2001) was a People's Liberation Army lieutenant-general and a politician. He was twice the Chinese Communist Party Secretary of Xinjiang.

CHAPTER FOUR

to Kashgar together, they remained very close friends. Later, when Abliz Niyaz was head of the Joint Forces department of the Southern Xinjiang Administrative Court from 1953 to 1956, he used to dine with Iminov at the public restaurant located at the new park, near the original Semen Hotel. The former Deputy Governor Zulal, a Tajik, still lives in that park. Iminov's wife Reyhan had a heart problem, and Mariye treated her at her hospital. Reyhan would send her younger daughter, Rahile, to Mariye when she needed her medicine, and Mariye would write her prescriptions.

From 1944 to 1949, Muhammed Emin Iminov assumed several important roles during the "East Turkistan Republic" era, including as a general in the East Turkistan National Army, commander of the Northern Direction, commander of the 13th division and then after 1950, he was the head of the administrative court of Southern Xinjiang. Later, from 1955 until 1957 when my father-in-law was selected to be the Governor of Artush county, Iminov was Deputy Chairman of the Xinjiang Uyghur Autonomous Region (XUAR) in Urumchi. In 1956, frustrated by China's oppressive rule in East Turkistan, Iminov led fifty-one Uyghur and Turkic intellectuals who petitioned China's Premier Zhou Enlai, urging Beijing to uphold its promises and withdraw from East Turkistan, demanding greater autonomy and rights for the Uyghur and Kazakh ethnic peoples.

Iminov had a high and respected reputation among the Uyghurs and was a confident man. His eldest daughter, Hebibe Iminov, studied at our department at Xinjiang University. She later got married to Dolqun Yasin (became a famous poet in Kazakhstan later, after exiled to Almaty). Dolqun's father Yasin Hudaberdi was the mayor of Urumchi from 1965 to 1966. Iminov really cared about Hebibe's studies and her character. Iminov often used to call me to ask about how she was doing academically and reputation-wise. He was a responsible father and cared a lot about his children's education and future. When Hebibe graduated, we assigned her to Kashgar. Iminov either sent a letter or made a phone call to show his dissatisfaction with that decision or requested reconsideration of his daughter's job assignment to keep her in Urumchi. Hebibe quietly accepted and went to Kashgar. Later she came back to Urumchi after first working at her assigned workplace for a few years. When I think back, I realize that we didn't care about Chairman

Iminov's feelings, when we sent Hebibe to Kashgar before the Great Cultural Revolution started, based on our university's idea that "It is beneficial for cultural exchange and development if we send students from Northern Xinjiang to Southern Xinjiang, and vice versa."

In 1969, one day, I bumped into Iminov on the street. He was on his way to the staff canteen on the campus with several others. "I wrote something, maybe you and Mariye should take a look at it," he said to me. I agreed. Next day, Mariye and I went to his home. Iminov showed us two articles he wrote, "The Famine in Bay County" and "The 1962 plot of Ghulja people to abroad." Mariye and I read both of them carefully. Iminov's son Polat was seated near us, reading a book and looking at us from time to time for our reaction while we were reading.

Iminov's second article was a detailed account of the fleeing of the Uyghur population through Ghulja to the Soviet Union in 1962. In this article, Iminov clearly stated that "it is more appropriate to say they didn't flee but they were expelled by the government, with the deliberate opening of borders."

After reading the articles, I sat down with a deep breath. Mariye was silent as well.

"So, what do you think?" asked Iminov. I said: "The writing is really good, but you are openly exposing the Party Committee and the government. Although it is all true, I am afraid they (meaning the Chinese government) will retaliate and take revenge on you."

"I know, I wrote them putting my head at stake! I have to do it, now I can say that I have done my duty!" Iminov replied. Sensing the danger, we sat in silence for a while, looking at Iminov with respect, pride and worry. At that time, Aytan, the head of the Red Unit 03, Alim, and Ibray from Toqsu came in, and we left. I heard that the next day the Red Unit 03 revolutionaries made Iminov's two articles into large-print newspapers and pasted them on the walls of the opera house and the Southern Gate.

The next day, Iminov ran into me on the campus. "Abbas, does Mariye know how to make Artush-style Narin?"[11] he said to me with soft smile, "Of course!" I said. I told Mariye when I came home that Iminov missed home-style food and agreed to invite those six or seven people to our house for a

---

11. A traditional Uyghur food made with lamb and thin noodles

CHAPTER FOUR

meal. I went to buy lamb meat the next day. Lamb was sold in six parts at the time. There was no good portion left, so I went again the next day, but to no avail. The meat was very lean; we couldn't make Narin with such lean meat, as this particular dish requires fat, so I didn't buy any.

During those few days when we were looking for good lamb to treat the people we loved and respected and host them at our house, something terrible happened. At almost midnight, loud announcements started coming from the streets. "Listen to this!" I woke up Mariye. "At the order of the Zhongyang,[12] we arrested key people from the anti-revolutionary group of Iminov!" the announcement repeated. We couldn't sleep and were very sad and helpless. Selime Talip wasn't home and was saved from arrest. The next day we learned that Iminov was taken away. Mariye and I were extremely worried about Iminov and we could not do anything. I was also worried about Inimov's son Polat. The students of Red Unit 03 were displaced. "We will line up and go to the Regional Party Committee to complain," they said. Their leaders didn't agree, saying it was a "direct order from Premier Zhou Enlai over the phone." Perhaps the pressure on Red Unit 03 was intense. Talk like "The ethnic issue isn't something you can touch!" was floating around.

After being subjected to brutality and harsh physical torture when he was imprisoned in the CCP's dark dungeon, and unable to have any of his family or friends visit him, Iminov suffered a lot. Our hearts were shattered. On May 17, 1970, we heard that Iminov had been tortured to death at the No. 3 Hospital in Urumchi. Muhammed Emin Iminov was fifty-five years old. We were emotionally broken.

Later we learned that when the Chinese authorities were going to arrest Iminov's daughter, Hebibe, and son-in-law, Dolqun Yasin, someone informed and helped them escape, and they fled to the Soviet Union through Ghulja. Dolqun Yasin and Hebibe's two boys, three- and five-years old, were left with Hebibe's mother in Urumchi. They grew up in Urumchi without their parents until, in the mid-80s, almost fifteen years later, they were able to travel to Almaty to see their mother and father for the first time. A poem written by Dolqun Yasin while he and his wife Hebibe were fleeing from Ghulja became a beautiful song in later years and spread among the Uyghurs

---

12. The central government

as one of the folk songs. Mariye hummed this song at home for many years, remembering them.

I am going far away, carrying the pain of parting

(Kiter boldum yiraqlargha hijran yukini artip),

Hold on, o beloved, when you miss me, groaning.

(Chidighinsen piyaqlargha, seghinghanda uh tartip)

Do not say I am gone, I shall come back again,

(Tashlap ketti dimigin, ketsem yene kilurmen)

Let not the enemies smile with satisfaction, do not weep.

(Dushmenler soghuq kulushmisun, kozungni yashlima ghemde)

I will come back, flying like a falcon, with a great triumph of victory.

(Burkuttek uchup-egip, ghelbe bilen kilurmen)

— A POEM BY DOLQUN YASIN, IMINOV'S SON-IN-LAW

* * *

In the spring of 1969, several workers came and told me to take my blanket and pillow. "You will go to study the Mao Zedong thought!" they told me. I collected my blanket, a pad for the bed, and pillow left with them. On the street workers were stationed here and there. None of them were from the

CHAPTER FOUR

Red Rebels. All of us who gathered there sat in silence looking at each other. Ebeydullah, a Kazakh teacher, looked like a revolutionary responsible for us. "Where are you taking us?" I asked him, "Stay quiet, do not ask anything from me," he said and pointed to the military officials. Those who picked us up were mostly people who had joined the military administration in accordance with Mao's order to "End the rule of the bourgeoisie over the schools." We sat for about an hour. Meanwhile, the linguist Mirsultan Osmanof's wife, Dileysa, brought a pot of Suyqash.[13] Everyone sat down without saying a word. Mirsultan Osmanof offered us Suyqash. "You have some," he offered it to me, and I took it. They took away Mirsultan Osmanof before everyone else. We didn't see him later until he returned home eight years later in 1977; he had been imprisoned somewhere else. The rest of us were taken a few hours later to a large hall behind the People's Theatre at the Southern Gate. "You will sleep here," they told us. Two armed guards stood at the door. Fortunately, the floor we slept on was wooden, not cement.

The next day, Mariye brought food for me. We were locked there for three days. On the first day, they told us to move into the underground of that place. It was damp and very cold; it was where the catalyst and sewer system were installed. I appealed to them, "We will have incurable rheumatism for the rest of our lives if we stay here for long." We, the detainees, all insisted and did not want to come down. They didn't send us to the underground. We spent three days eating the food brought by our families. Mariye brought food to me every day. She was only allowed to meet from a distance.

I mostly talked with Abdushukur Muhammetimin, Professor at the Faculty of Literature at Xinjiang University, and Rena's husband. According to Mariye, when she was passing by the People's Theatre, she heard people screaming and moaning, being beaten and tortured harshly. Mariye was very sad, as she thought we might be tortured like that too. The third day, she quietly asked "Did they torture you?" I said "No." "Don't talk! You're not allowed to talk!" the two-armed Chinese guards shouted in Chinese.

On the fourth day, when it was almost evening, we were ordered to tie up our stuff. When we left the east-facing door of the house, around thirty to forty of us were ordered to board a bus with iron bars on the windows.

---

13.   An Uyghur soup

Our luggage was thrown into another black car. Armed soldiers surrounded the bus. It was a scene of great horror, as though they were escorting criminals. There was a military vehicle in front of us and another military vehicle behind us. No one talked. Abdushukur Muhammetimin was sitting next to me, "I hope they won't take us to the Mainland!" he whispered. "Where do you think they will take us in the Mainland?" I asked. "If they take us to Lanzhou, Xi'an we can't come back. We will disappear!" Abdushukur said. We went silent.

They took us to a military barracks near the Western train station in Western Mountain. There were no houses closer than a mile away. They placed us in a garage with double-winged doors. Among the people who joined us from the outside were Latif, a Tatar man who has a garden house across from the 8th Army office, and Abdulqadir Haji, the Imam of the Saybulaq Mosque. Abdulqadir Haji knew me and my father as well. Shireli, a composer from the Arts Institute, was also in the room with us. He didn't talk to anyone and just recited Mao Zedong Quotes. Looking at him reciting the Mao Zedong Quotes so diligently, I was angry and irritated. We had steamed buns from the prison for two days. We were given a small, steamed bun made of red sorghum and corn flour, with a hole in the middle. They also gave us vegetable scraps thrown away from the soldiers' canteen, after pouring them in hot water just once. The food was so bad that we protested and went on a hunger strike for a couple of days. This worked, and they agreed to give us wheat steamed buns from the soldiers' canteen, which we paid for ourselves. The door was opened twice a day while we had our food and used the toilet, and two armed soldiers stood outside the door.

Fifteen days later, the door opened in the afternoon. We couldn't believe our eyes. Wow, what an amazing view! About thirty to forty men and women were coming towards us, holding stuff on their hands. Among them were Sayfuddin's driver, nicknamed "Niyaz Hitay," and Niyaz's wife Goherhan was the assistant to Ayim, Saifuddin's wife. Originally, Goherhan, trying to learn our whereabouts, went to the residents near the People's Theatre, and learned that we had been taken in the direction of the Western Train Station from a woman who saw us passing by as she was standing in front of her house. When Goherhan went to the Western Train Station and asked

CHAPTER FOUR

the people there, they told her that "It has been a couple of weeks that some Uyghur detainees arrived in that place where soldiers stayed." Thus, Goherhan informed the families at Xinjiang University and brought them here.

Mariye was among them too. When Mariye became worried about our disappearance and asked around about us, Hemit and Amine, who were transferred from the military to the Working Group, told Mariye that "They have not been taken far away, they are in the military barracks near the Western Train Station. Do not tell anyone about this!"

After meeting with our families, the soldiers drove them away and brought us back to the barracks where vehicles are parked. The soldiers loosened up after this event. Later, we learned, an illiterate Chinese man named Long Shoujin, who became the commander and first secretary of Xinjiang province, was the man who ordered our detention. We were taken to the military barracks, as the prisons were full. Once, Long Shoujin boasted about his illiteracy at a meeting: "I don't know even write a few words. I joined the revolution holding a pistol, not a pen," he said proudly. "You became like an independent dukedom, why do you use Xinjiang time here, not Beijing time? The entire country should use only Beijing time!" he said. "There are so many revisionism elements linked overseas, and nationalists in Xinjiang!" he also said. He arrested twelve thousand people in a day. Later, he arrested many more people, claiming they were "members of the Inner Mongolia People's Party."

We became more and more friendly and talked to each other in detention. Shireli also put down his Mao Zedong Quotes later and joined our jokes. "A devil rode a camel, sank the camel, hid the camel, making it dumb,"[14] I joked once. We talked a lot. When we wanted to use the toilet, we usually shout "I report, commander!", and the door would open. Almost every day, people from one or two families came to visit us in this place. The days became easier to pass. After thirty-two days, we were all released from our detention. They gave us a pickup truck to go to the university campus.

---

14. This phrase metaphorically represents oppression—the way the Chinese government has suppressed Uyghur culture, identity, and voices. The "devil" is a symbol for tyranny, and the "camel" stands for the oppressed people.

In early July in 1969, my father-in-law, Abliz Niyaz, was detained in Artush where he was imprisoned for three years, subject to brutal torture. He was beaten often and, in the winter, forced to stand barefoot in the snow until he lost consciousness. When he awoke, numb and barely able to feel his feet, he found himself lying in the cold corner of his prison cell. After three harrowing years in detention, he was finally released in 1972.

After I returned to the university, the authorities sent us to forced harvest labor. All the staff and teachers at the university went. We worked for long hours every day. Mariye came with us as a doctor. When we had time, we would sit down by the stream, surrounded by clear water, and rest and talk. Although we had spent that entire month harvesting, none of us received any payment for our month-long harsh physical work in the field. The place was peaceful, breezy, and beautiful. Mariye treated the farmers there too. The farmers sent horses to call her to their home for treatment. Once, when Mariye rode a horse to go to a farmer's home, the horse ran away, and she found herself in danger but, luckily, she was safe. After we returned home, the faculty and university staff gathered to study. We learned "quotes" and went through indoctrination under the supervision of the military and other managers. In the morning, we asked for "instructions" from Mao Zedong while looking at his photo. During lunch and in the evening, we reported our daily activities in the same way. We reported four times a day to Mao.

In the 1970s, tensions began again. One midday, all my children were at home. My eldest son Nijat was preparing vegetables. My second son Rishat was trying to light the stove. A group of people came in and took me away, not even giving me a chance to say goodbye to my children. "You will report your problems; your issue is very serious!" they said. "The Strike One, Fight Three campaign has started," they told me.

That day and night, five or six people took turns to "struggle" me, beating and torturing me with sleep deprivation, taking turns in three shifts for twenty-four hours. When I asked for water, someone gave me a mug, but another man took it away. They struggled me like that all night, making me stand the whole night and day, and didn't give me any water. They only released me around eight a.m. the next morning after almost forty hours. When I got home, Mariye was waiting for me. She had made breakfast with milk

CHAPTER FOUR

and eggs. I was so happy. "I couldn't sleep all night," she said. One reason they interrogated me was that they suspected I was "a board member of an anti-revolutionary organization." They tortured me like that twelve more times, each time with sleep deprivation, long interrogation, and struggles. Every time I came home, Mariye would meet me with a warm welcome, and my children would surround me with enthusiasm and squeals.

On the day they started struggling me, they also took Mariye and locked her in a house at the General Administration. When they came to take Mariye, she was holding our daughter Rushan in her arms. Rushan clung to her mother and didn't let her go. One Chinese man took Rushan from her mother's arms, threw her into the house, and dragged Mariye away. The voice of Rushan clinging to the door and crying could be heard for a long time. Mariye often used to tell this story to Rushan, and she grew up hearing this as her early childhood story. Rushan's voice could be heard 2-3 miles away at the house she was locked up in through the night, Mariye would tell her.

The people who struggled us were from the 3015th military unit. A prison guard nicknamed "Qalighach Binam" from the prisoners' camp was responsible for our faculty. He was a very harsh, bad-tempered, and bad-mouthed man, and treated people as if he was dealing with criminals in a real prison. Sometimes he did the interrogation himself. He showed arrogance, and questioned people while putting his pistol on the table.

After almost twenty days, we were moved to a larger class after putting beds there. A dozen youngsters were assigned to watch over us. One day, they called us and asked the Party members to come out. I stood without moving, looking here and there. "Why are you not coming?" they said. "Am I still a Party member? I am anti-revolutionary!" I retorted. "Let's go!" One of them shouted, and we went together.

In late February 1972, students began to be sent to military farms for training. The students who watched us started leaving, one by one. "Anti-revolutionary" students left too. At last, I tied up my luggage and returned home. We were out of work again. Mao Zedong Quotes were often brought to us. Everyone had to read the Quotes and Red Books.

CHAPTER FIVE
RESURRECTING THE UYGHUR IDENTITY

My childhood unfolded amid the Great Cultural Revolution, exposing China's inhuman rule. In middle school, we awakened to our national identity, recognizing China as a colonial aggressor. The brave Uyghur intellectuals of the 1980s revived our crushed spirit and culture, making that era a rare time in the Uyghur homeland, when our Uyghur identity flourished. The impact of this change was reflected in the major events that took place among the Uyghur students in Urumchi's universities in the mid-80s.

We were fortunate to learn within the relatively broader national political atmosphere established after Deng Xiaoping came to power in 1978. When we entered middle school in 1979, the school textbooks had been revised. After Deng Xiaoping's policy of "correcting erroneous and unjust cases" was implemented, many Uyghur intellectuals were released from prisons, reinstated in their jobs, and returned to their original positions in schools and educational institutions. They immediately took action. With great dedication, they published many books and articles about Uyghur history, culture, and national identity, laying the groundwork for the revival of the Uyghur national spirit. Religious figures were released from prisons and mosques that had previously been closed, destroyed, or turned into pigsties were gradually restored. As a result, in 1978 my father was also appointed Chairman of the Xinjiang Science and Technology Society.

The period from 1979 (after diplomatic relations with the United States were established to the Tiananmen Square Massacre by China in 1989) was like a decade of revival, restoration, and uplift for Uyghurs. During that brief ten-year period, thousands of Uyghur works on our history, classical literature, and culture were published, providing a strong foundation for the development of a renewed Uyghur identity. Uyghurs began to live like Uyghurs once again. We were able to learn our history: that our homeland was established as the first East Turkistan Islamic Republic in 1933 with its center in Kashgar, and then again in 1944 with the East Turkistan Republic, whose center was in Ghulja. We learned that our older generations had fought for their freedom against Chinese warlords such as Yang Zengxing, Jin Shuren, and Sheng Shicai, but were unable to prevail.

The Manchurian Qing dynasty occupied our homeland and imposed the name "Xinjiang"—a derogatory term for the Uyghurs that means "New Frontier" or "New Border"—in 1884.

I remember hearing an oft-repeated refrain from the CCP as I was growing up: "The last century was the Century of Humiliation. This is the Century of Retaliation." It reflects the Chinese Communist Party's nationalist narrative of reclaiming power and global dominance after what it considers a long period of subjugation by foreign forces.

The term "Century of Humiliation" refers to the period from the First Opium War (1839–1842) to the founding of the People's Republic of China (PRC) in 1949, during which China feels it suffered military defeats, territorial losses, and foreign control over its economy and politics. The CCP exploits this historical grievance to fuel nationalism, presenting itself as the party that ended foreign humiliation and restored China's sovereignty. Dubbing the twenty-first century the Century of Retaliation suggests that China sees this time as an era in which to reclaim its rightful place as a dominant world power, pushing back against Western influence. The CCP portrays economic, military, and technological advances as part of its mission to correct past injustices. This includes military expansion, economic dominance, technology and espionage, and geopolitical aggression. This vow is both a warning and a strategic message. China aims to reshape global power dynamics in its favor, using past grievances to justify present-day ambitions. Evocations of this vow stoke China's nationalism and the legitimacy of the CCP, which fuels domestic support by portraying China as rising against past oppression. They also serve as the basis for Beijing's aggressive foreign policy and attempts to justify expansionist ambitions as "correcting historical wrongs," positioning China in direct opposition to the US-led global order.

This has already resulted in severe human rights abuses, including mass repression and genocide in occupied East Turkistan, Tibet, and Hong Kong. From an early age, China's future leaders are indoctrinated to view democracy as a threat, reinforcing a system designed to expand CCP dominance at the cost of global stability.

Under Xi Jinping, China has become increasingly aggressive, using military expansion, economic coercion, and political influence to undermine democracies. It exploits democracy's openness while maintaining an authoritarian state. For decades, the CCP has manipulated economic ties, technology transfers, and diplomacy to strengthen its grip on power while eroding global stability. Continued engagement with China only fuels its rise at the expense of freedom. The only solution is to sever all ties—economic, technological, and diplomatic—before the threat escalates further.

In 1949, the Chinese Communists invaded and occupied our homeland after several prominent Uyghur leaders mysteriously perished in a controversial plane crash while traveling to Beijing via Almaty, Kazakhstan. The alleged crash, near Lake Baikal in the Soviet Union, killed figures like Ehmetjan Qasimi, Abdulkerim Abbas, and Ishaq Beg and others who had been negotiating East Turkistan's future. Whether the crash was an accident or a political assassination, their deaths enabled Communist consolidation of the region.

China's invasion was driven by a combination of strategic, economic, and ideological motivations. Strategically, the region serves as a crucial buffer zone, bordering eight countries, including Russia, Mongolia, and Kazakhstan. Controlling East Turkistan allows China to secure its western frontier, preventing foreign influence that could threaten its territorial integrity. The Uyghur region's vast deserts and mountains make it an ideal location for military testing and nuclear experiments, which China has exploited, conducting its first nuclear test at Lop Nur in 1964.

Underneath these mountains are natural resources, including oil, natural gas, coal, and rare earth minerals, all essential to China's industrial and technological growth. The region's vast agricultural lands and cotton production are key to China's global supply chains, particularly in textiles. Additionally, East Turkistan is central to China's Belt and Road Initiative (BRI), serving as

CHAPTER FIVE

a major transit hub for trade routes linking China to Central Asia, the Middle East, and Europe. By controlling the region, China ensures uninterrupted access to these resources and secures critical trade corridors.

By 1955, China further solidified its grip on our homeland, renaming it the "Xinjiang Uyghur Autonomous Region," thereby erasing East Turkistan's sovereignty and silencing Uyghur aspirations for freedom.

During the Great Chinese Famine of 1959–1961 caused by the policies of the Great Leap Forward initiated by Mao Zedong, many parts of China suffered severe food shortages, leading to widespread hunger and death. His first article was about man-made famine that occurred in Bay County, near Aksu in the Uyghur region from 1960 to 1961. Known as the Xinjiang Famine, it was a tragic event that resulted in widespread starvation and death among the Uyghurs. He wrote about a Han Chinese man named "He Rui" who became the party secretary of Bay County in 1960-1961. He Rui even collected the grain the Uyghur farmers kept for their personal use, claiming "the farmers under-reported their grain harvest." Claiming "the farmers hid grain," he forcibly took all the grains from the farmers and left them to starve. According to the article, many people witnessed some farmers picking and eating peels of vegetables from waste at the County Party Committee kitchen. People reported this situation to the higher authorities. When the government sent Mamut Islam, the Deputy Governor of Aksu, to Bay County to investigate, he transported his relatives in a vehicle and returned them to Aksu and then made a false report to the governor's office that "nothing is wrong there." In fact, the number of Uyghur people who died of hunger in Bay County at the time was around 20,000, Iminov wrote. At that time, the total population of Bay County was 100,000 people.

According to an unpublished memoir from Saifuddin Azizi, Chairman of the Xinjiang Uyghur Autonomous Regional Revolutionary Committee between October 1955 and January 1967, more than 15,000 Uyghurs died from this man-made famine in Bay County. To this day, the Chinese government has not disclosed the exact number of people who perished in Bay County due to starvation. In fact, official historical records, statements, and government-approved publications either omit this event or attempt to downplay it. However, Saifuddin Azizi, who served as the Chairman of the XUAR from 1955 to 1977, documented the famine in his unpublished memoir "Omur Dastani" (The Epic of Life: The Sun Over Tengritagh), which he wrote in the early 1990s. The Chinese government prohibited its publication. Saifuddin documents that this catastrophic event was not due to natural disasters or unforeseen circumstances but was deliberately orchestrated by the Chinese Communist government as part of its brutal ethnic policies in the (XUAR). According to his memoir, at the time of the famine, Saifuddin Azizi was studying at the Party School in Beijing (1960–1962) and was unaware of the crisis. Bay County, ironically, was a region rich in grain production. In 1960, while famine raged across China, Bay County had a grain reserve of over 40 million jin (approximately 20,000 tons). However, in an attempt to curry favor with Mao Zedong and support famine-stricken regions in China, Wang Enmao issued a secret order to transfer these grain reserves to Urumchi. He Rui, the Communist Party Secretary of Bay County, locked the county's grain warehouses and deliberately withheld food from the local population, even as mass starvation took hold. When people began dying, Aksu Prefecture Party Secretary He Jingnian visited Bay County for a superficial investigation but did not report the severity of the crisis to higher authorities. Both He Rui and He Jingnian actively concealed the scale of the deaths from the Aksu Prefecture government and the XUAR authorities. This is from "The Epic of Life":

> In 1961, upon returning to Urumchi for a winter recess, Saifuddin Azizi attended a special meeting regarding the Bay County famine. At the meeting, He Jingnian, following Wang Enmao's orders, downplayed the situation and evaded responsibility. He even pretended to weep in front of Saifuddin, but Saifuddin, seeing through the act, lost his temper and shouted at him, saying, "In a county with only 100,000 people, the deaths of over 15,000 is no small matter! You must be held accountable!" Wang Enmao, however, intervened to protect He Jingnian. In 1963, Saifuddin Azizi personally traveled to Bay County to investigate. Even years after the famine, the people of Bay were still suffering

from its aftermath—many were visibly weak, sickly, and psychologically broken. The primary perpetrator, He Rui, received a mere five-year prison sentence, but under Wang Enmao's protection, he was soon released and reassigned to another government position. Similarly, He Jingnian was briefly demoted from First Secretary to Second Secretary but was later transferred to Urumchi and appointed head of the Grain Bureau. During Saifuddin Azizi's visit to Bay County, he met with local Uyghur farmers who, upon seeing him, collectively broke down in tears, mourning their suffering. In the village of Qizil, thousands of farmers wept as they described the horrors they had endured.

Saifuddin Azizi's memoir was not allowed to be published even after his death on 24 November 2003. This unpublished memoir was provided by Eset Sulaiman, an Uyghur journalist and editor for Radio Free Asia's (RFA) Uyghur Service and a prominent Uyghur intellectual, author of "Ego and Identity" (2006), "Uyghur Wolf -totem Culture" (2001) in the Uyghur language, and editor of "Community Still Matters: Uyghur Culture and Society in Central Asian Context" (2020), which explores cultural dialogues between Islamic and Western philosophies.

Despite the ever-looming threat of retaliation from the Chinese authorities—who repeatedly shifted policies and launched relentless purges against Uyghur intellectuals every decade—the architects of our national consciousness stood undeterred. These courageous scholars and educators, the torchbearers of Uyghur identity, remained steadfast in their mission, refusing to be silenced by the cycles of repression. They understood that each crackdown was not just an attack on individuals, but an attempt to erase an entire people's history, culture, and aspirations. Yet, with unwavering resolve, they continued to cultivate the spirit of resistance, determined to safeguard the Uyghur identity and heritage against the tides of oppression.

***

In 1983, my father visited the Abdus Salam International Centre for Theoretical Physics in Trieste, Italy, a prestigious institute founded by Nobel laureate Dr. Abdus Salam. Dad was joined by a fellow Uyghur, Mr. Ablimit Eli, President of the Xinjiang Institute of Technology and grandfather of Arfiya Eri, currently Japan's first proud Uyghur Member of Parliament, along with another Chinese scholar. Despite the language barrier, my father and Dr. Salam formed a deep bond of mutual respect. My father was inspired by Salam's brilliance and admired him as a rare Muslim Nobel laureate, while Salam was drawn to dad's intellect, sincerity, and character.

During their time in Italy, Dr. Salam expressed a keen interest in visiting Kashgar, the homeland of Mahmud al-Kashgari, the great eleventh-century Uyghur scholar and linguist. My father, deeply touched by Dr. Salam's admiration for Uyghur history, invited him to visit Kashgar and pay homage to Mahmud al-Kashgari's grave. Upon returning home, my father diligently worked to organize this visit, but due to bureaucratic hurdles, it was only in the fall of 1989 that Dr. Salam was able to travel to East Turkistan. During his visit, my parents had the honor of hosting Dr. Abdus Salam. Together, they traveled across the region, eventually reaching Kashgar and continuing to Opal, the resting place of Mahmud al-Kashgari[15]—one of the most pivotal figures in Turkic linguistic history. A millennium ago, Kashgari meticulously documented the richness of Turkic dialects, preserving the scholarly contributions of Uyghur civilization for future generations. My father continued this tradition in his own way by advocating for the education and advancement of Uyghur scholars on a global stage.

Beyond the personal bond they forged, Dr. Abdus Salam and my father became like brothers. During my father's visit to the institute in Italy in 1983, he asked Dr. Salam if Uyghur students could have the opportunity to study there. Without hesitation, Dr. Salam agreed, at first paving the way for two Uyghur scholars to be accepted as visiting researchers, then continuing the program for years. What began as a conversation in Italy blossomed into a tangible opportunity, reflecting my father's unwavering commitment to uplifting

---

15. Mahmud al-Kashgari (1005 CE - 1102 CE) was an 11th-century Kara-Khanid scholar and lexicographer of the Turkic languages from Kashgar.

CHAPTER FIVE

the Uyghur people. His vision extended beyond borders, ensuring that Uyghur scholars could contribute to and thrive in the global academic community.

I remember how important this relationship was for my father, and I never could have known that it would give me common ground with more people who later went on to be strong allies in the fight for the Uyghur people. The values Dr. Salam and my father shared, the human dignity they glorified, and the compassion and empathy they both embraced immediately bonded them. They called each other brothers. The ties formed through shared respect and academic collaboration became the foundation for alliances that continue to shape our struggle for justice and recognition today. Their fruitful friendship is a testament to how intellectual and cultural exchanges can have ripple effects beyond their initial scope, influencing movements and fostering support in unexpected yet powerful ways.

During our advocacy work in 2019, Abdulhakim and I had the profound honor of meeting Dr. Abdus Salam's daughter and son-in-law and his son Ahmad Salam at a religious gathering in London. As we reminisced over old photographs of our fathers and spoke of their shared dreams, a deep and immediate bond formed between us—one that transcended time, geography, and even personal experience.

In that moment, we were reliving the spirit of two visionaries who, despite coming from different worlds, shared an unshakable belief in the power of knowledge and the uplifting of the oppressed. It was as if our fathers' legacies had intertwined once more, this time through us, transforming strangers into brothers and sisters united by memory, purpose, and an enduring connection.

***

In September 1984, I enrolled in the Biology Department of Xinjiang University, the most prestigious institution in the Uyghur region. Biology was never my plan. Instead, I had a deep passion for literature and had won writing competitions and published poems and articles, including one featured in the *Xinjiang Daily News*. However, as the youngest in my family, my father saw me as his last chance to carry on his academic legacy. My oldest brother,

Nijat, had studied business, while my second brother, Rishat, had gone into pharmaceutical research. As my sister Gulshan had studied medicine, my mother's field, my father, with his vast library on biology, agriculture, and genetics, insisted I follow in his footsteps and study biology.

When I was filling out my university application, my father dictated that all ten of my course choices be in biology at Xinjiang University. In quiet defiance, I left one space blank and later filled it in with "literature." A literature professor, noticing the lone entry, recognized my true passion and accepted me into his department, discreetly withholding my application from the Biology Department. My father, unaware, frantically searched for my missing application until he discovered the truth. He confronted the literature professor, who eventually surrendered my file to the Biology Department, ending my brief literary rebellion. Although I had been accepted to study literature, my father overturned the decision. He explained that studying biology wasn't just his dream—it was my best chance to leave China at that time. With his connections, he could help me study abroad, something far less likely with a degree in Uyghur literature. Later, it was his connection that ultimately enabled me to study in the United States and begin my activism, an opportunity I likely wouldn't have had otherwise.

The most exciting aspect of our early days as students was the strong national spirit among us. Young people, deeply passionate about exploring their nation's historical roots, took pride in the states their ancestors had built and began fostering aspirations to advocate for their rights, creating a powerful national atmosphere at Xinjiang University. Secret conversations among those concerned about their homeland's suffering and dreaming of shaping its future would stir the soul. These discussions were fundamentally rooted in the injustices, oppression, and the cunning strategies of the Chinese authorities against the Uyghurs. The Uyghur people could never accept the imposition of family-planning policies upon them. In addition, China's continuous atomic bomb testing in Uyghur territories posed a significant environmental threat to our homeland.

In spring 1985, Chinese authorities transferred tens of thousands of criminals from Beijing and Dongbei prisons to labor camps in my homeland. Most had death sentences with suspensions or life terms for murder,

CHAPTER FIVE

rape, and violent crimes. Some escaped from the labor camps, terrorizing Uyghur civilians by murdering families and assaulting women, fueling fear and anger. Meanwhile, Han Chinese settlement in East Turkistan continued to rise.

While most Uyghurs were already struggling with unemployment, the growing presence of settlers was exacerbating poverty and intensifying ethnic discrimination. Inequalities in the education system were also a factor fueling Uyghur discontent. Ismail Amat,[16] who was the head of what the Xinjiang Uyghur Autonomous Region, had made some modest efforts to support Uyghur intellectuals and to advocate for Uyghurs' interests, such as stating that "50% of the workforce in government positions should be Uyghur." However, he was about to be transferred to Beijing under the guise of a "promotion." Similarly, Saifuddin Azizi, who had served in the East Turkistan Republic established in 1944 and later became the head of the Xinjiang Uyghur Autonomous Region, had also been transferred to Beijing with a so-called promotion, where he became a living corpse. Ismail Amat's fate would not be much different. Although he reportedly said before his transfer in 1985, "I would rather return to my homeland Hotan and become a farmer than go to Beijing," he did not have the power to refuse the orders of the Chinese authorities.

At that time, there was a popular belief among the Uyghurs that China's policy of destruction against Uyghur officials and elites took three forms: first, destruction by killing; second, destruction by assimilation; and third, destruction by promotion. Ismail Amat had become a victim of "destruction by promotion," stirring strong reactions among Uyghur intellectuals.

At Xinjiang University, Mijit Emet, a student from Hotan, sought to address Uyghur dissatisfaction by documenting issues and presenting them to the government for correction. If this failed, he planned to organize a large-scale protest in Urumchi to pressure the authorities. What actually took place had a massive guiding impact on the Uyghur cause and on the direction of my advocacy journey.

---

16. Ismail Amat (1935–2018) was a high-ranking Uyghur politician who served as Chairman of Xinjiang.

CHAPTER SIX

THE 1980s STUDENT PROTESTS

The December 12, 1985, and June 15, 1988, Uyghur student protests, which have come to be regarded as turning points in contemporary Uyghur history and the most glorious chapters in the struggle of Uyghur intellectuals, had an extraordinary political and social impact. These two student movements, which took place in my hometown of Urumchi, the capital of the Uyghur region, occurred before the student movement in Beijing in the spring of 1989 that later led to the Tiananmen Square Massacre. I took part in these movements as one of the co-organizers, which were known as the "first democratic movements" in my homeland.

Mijit Emet, a prominent Uyghur student at Xinjiang University, held key positions as president of the Students' Union and the Autonomous Regional Students' Union, as well as deputy president of the National Chinese Students' Union. In these roles, he portrayed himself as a model citizen, suppressing his true Uyghur nationalistic feelings and adhering strictly to the CCP's expectations, maintaining a blank expression and toeing the party line. Behind the scenes, Mijit Emet secretly advocated for the Uyghur people, organizing meetings where he spoke about the need for change. He boldly exposed the deep oppression the Uyghurs endured, despite the facade of autonomy, and denounced the government's hollow promises of freedom and reform. His words highlighting the relentless suppression of rights and the tightening grip of state control became the catalyst for the "epoch-making revolution" in Urumchi in 1985, igniting a movement that would forever alter the course of Uyghur resistance.

Three days before the planned action, Mijit sent a note to my friend and me, asking us to meet on December 10 at 1:00 p.m. I assumed we would have another small planning meeting. I had been avoiding him because, during our

CHAPTER SIX

previous meetings, he kept repeating his usual advice—for me to stay low for my father's safety. Having attended several secret meetings he organized with his small circle of close friends, I knew a large protest was being planned. As I was the only female and junior student, Mijit had often warned me during those meetings, saying "We don't mind the risk, but we need to protect your father, Abbas Borhan. Your involvement could jeopardize his work." Although I disagreed, he insisted, "It's not you we worry for, but your father's position."

On December 10, 1985, everything changed. When I entered the classroom, I noticed an unusual unease among my classmates. I asked a friend what happened, and she replied, "Mijit Emet passed away last night." I was stunned, as she and I were supposed to meet him in five hours. My first thought was, "Had the Chinese secret police found out his plans and killed him?" I quickly asked, "When? Where? How?"

"Last night, at Professor Abdushukur Muhammed Emin's house, he had a heart attack and passed away suddenly," she said.

We had never known Mijit to have a heart condition; he was always fit and active. Public records later confirmed no history of heart disease. According to his friend Mehmet Tohti (who now lives in Ottawa and leads the Uyghur Rights Advocacy Project in Canada), who was with him at the time, Mijit died foaming at the mouth, and his friend believed he had been poisoned. Mijit Emet's sudden death remains an unsolved mystery to this day.

He is remembered in the Uyghur community as a figure of youthful resistance and an embodiment of the struggle for Uyghur rights during a critical period in East Turkistan's history. His death is part of the larger narrative of Uyghur grievances against Beijing's policies, which has continued to shape the region's political and social dynamics.

Mijit Emet's death could not prevent the Uyghur students at Xinjiang University from expanding their plans to address the ongoing oppression and discriminatory policies of the CCP against the Uyghur people. In fact, it had the opposite effect. Mijit's ideas and plans were carried forward by his close circle of friends, including me. After paying our final respects and sending him to his hometown of Hotan for burial, we made a solemn vow to honor his legacy by completing his mission and upholding the values he stood for. We continued to plan protest actions against the Chinese authorities. In fact, his death only fueled our passion to activate students from all of the universities and institutes in and around Urumchi. Immediately after our farewell to Mijit, we held two meetings to plan how to proceed with our protest against the government's policies.

At our final gathering on the afternoon of December 11, we assigned tasks to different students in preparation for the next day's protest, scheduled for 2:00 p.m. on December 12. We thought this way we could finish our usual four hours of classes and then begin to walk towards the People's Square by the South Gate (Nanmin) in Urumchi. At our meeting, we decided to send several students from Xinjiang University to other universities and institutions to encourage students there to join us for the protest against policies that we felt marginalized our language, culture, religious and basic survival rights, as well as our concerns over the increasing Han Chinese migration to Xinjiang. We saw this as a threat to our demographic and cultural identity while our Uyghur birthrate was being suppressed by heavy implementation of birth-control policies against our people. We had chosen several critical topics to address the next day at the protest.

1. That Ismail Amat not be relocated to Beijing, and that Uyghurs must elect the head of the Uyghur Autonomous Region through democratic elections.
2. Ending inequality in education and ensuring equal treatment for both Chinese and Uyghur schools.
3. Stopping ethnic discrimination and ensuring that the number of Uyghurs in government jobs was not lower than that of Chinese.
4. Halting the relocation of Chinese settlers to Uyghur regions.
5. Stopping the transfer of Chinese prisoners to Uyghur regions to prevent Uyghur territories from becoming prison camps for China.
6. Abolishing the family-planning (birth-control) policy imposed on Uyghurs.
7. Ending nuclear tests conducted in the Uyghur region.
8. Fully implementing the autonomy rights already granted to Uyghurs.

It was an extremely cold December. Urumchi experiences the cold of Siberia, and its winter weather often drops below −4 degrees Fahrenheit. On

CHAPTER SIX

the evening of December 11, we were running around in the cold to spread the news of the planned demonstration to the Uyghur students at the various universities in Urumchi. Due to the lack of convenient transportation, the student messengers had to walk long distances and felt the full brunt of the cold. Nevertheless, all of the universities and institutes were notified that night.

By around 10:00 p.m., after our friends had returned, we gathered at the Physics Department building for our third and final planning. My cousin Gulnur's now-husband, Helil Beg, who was a senior student in the Physics Department at the time, was also with us in the small preparation group meeting that night. Some of our friends reported that the authorities had already learned about our plans. Their names have been omitted for safety reasons, as some of our friends from that night are still in prison back home today. The authorities had decided to close all university doors and place guards at them to stop students from going outside. They had also instructed teachers to keep students in their classrooms to prevent them from going to the square. We had to make a quick decision. We changed the protest time to 8:00 o'clock the next morning to avoid the universities' attempts to stop our protest. Late that night, we had to knock on the dormitories' doors to notify students of the time change, and once again we sent our friends on their bicycles to all the universities to notify them of the updated time.

On the early morning of December 12, 1985, despite the efforts of teachers and authorities to suppress us, the students at our university made a bold and defiant stand. We scaled the fences of the school grounds and flooded into the streets, hearts filled with determination and hope. We marched to the People's Square, where an overwhelming surge of students from every corner of Urumchi started to arrive. The air was charged with a sense of urgency and resolve, as more than 15,000 students from seven universities, institutes, and technical schools from Urumchi converged in the People's Square.

By mid-morning, the crowd had swelled with a powerful energy, with each passing moment bringing more people into our ranks. Standing in front of the Uyghur Autonomous Region Party Committee building, we could see the cold, impassive windows and tightly shut doors of the government building. Behind those walls, there was silence. No one came forward to meet us, to address our demands, or to even acknowledge our presence. We were met with a deliberate and deafening indifference. But that silence only fueled our resolve. We could not—and would not—be ignored. Determined and unbowed, we made a collective decision. We would no longer wait for permission, nor would we allow the suffocating walls of suppression to stand between us and justice. Without hesitation, we took to the streets, a sea of voices and fists, united in our march. The protest that had begun as a simple gathering had now become an unstoppable force—a declaration to the world that our voices would not be silenced, that our cries for dignity, rights, and freedom would echo through the streets of Urumchi and beyond, no matter what barriers they tried to impose. In a powerful display of solidarity, as the demonstrators marched forward, defying fear and oppression, ordinary people stepped forward in a silent yet profound act of defiance against injustice. They offered water to quench their thirst, bread to sustain their strength, and snacks as a gesture of unwavering support. In that moment, every gesture became a statement, every offering a symbol of unity, proving that even in the face of oppression, the spirit of a people cannot be silenced.

Through the snow and ice-covered streets, we marched as one, our footsteps echoing on the frozen ground, our voices rising in defiant slogans. The symbolism of that moment was undeniable—this was the spark of something great. The Uyghur students' procession was not merely a display of resistance, but the beginning of the first democratic movement in Uyghur history after more than thirty-five years of oppressive colonization under the Chinese Communist Party. It was a cry for justice, for freedom, and for the dignity that had been systematically stripped from our people. That day marked the first chapter of our fight for rights, recognition, and self-determination, a fight that would echo for years to come.

Historians have described it as the first student movement after the Cultural Revolution in China and its colonies in 1949, as well as one of the earliest democratic movements in the Communist bloc of Central Asia and China during the 1980s. This movement, often hailed as the "revolutionary turning point in the history of East Turkistan," even spread to the southern regions, sparking chain demonstrations in the prefectures of Kashgar and Hotan, as well as later protests by Uyghur students in universities in China-proper.

The Uyghur youth were tremendously excited, as if this one act of defiance could drive the Chinese out and bring freedom and independence back

CHAPTER SIX

to their homeland and solve all their problems in one go. But the government was alarmed by the sheer number of students and their brave slogans. They did not dare to treat the demonstration lightly or use police or the military to disperse the students, as they had never before witnessed such a massive gathering of Uyghur youth against the government in one place. Their first tactic was to ignore us. For our part, we decided to march to the streets of Urumchi while chanting our slogans. Later in the afternoon, after marching for four to five hours, we returned to the People's Square and stood there firmly awaiting a response to our demands. At that point, the government expressed their willingness to meet with student representatives, and five students, representing tens of thousands, held talks with them. The protest ended peacefully around 6:00 p.m.

As soon as the winter break ended in mid-February 1986, broad political studies criticizing the demonstration began at all the universities and technical schools across the Uyghur region. Massive teams from the Regional Party Committee, the People's Government, the Public Security Bureau, and the Education Department were dispatched to each university to individually interrogate all of the students who had organized, participated in, or supported the demonstration. As one of the planners of the protest, I was among those who were interrogated.

It must have been the end of March by the time I was called in for my interrogation. One day, our department's political supervisor came into the classroom, called me aside and said, "The working task group has some questions for you. Come with me!" I followed him to a room that had been turned into an interrogation room. Eight interrogators, all of them older men, were lined up at two long tables at the front. Among them, three were Chinese who could speak Uyghur and the rest were Uyghurs. Some I recognized from our university. Others were from the government's special task force. In the middle of the room, directly opposite the door, there was a single chair set up for the "accused." I was ordered to sit in it. I took my place facing all those men. They sat there looking at me, and occasionally reading some materials, without saying a word. Once in a while, some of them whispered to each other while giving me strange looks. The atmosphere was very tense. The faces of the interrogators were cold and stern. Finally, after fifteen or twenty minutes of silence I said, "If you have nothing to ask me, I had better get going." A man in the middle yelled "Sit still!" and then they began asking their questions. The interrogation was conducted in Uyghur:

What is your first name and last name? Rushan Abbas.

How old are you? I am 18.

Which department and class are you studying at? Biology Department, number 2, class of 1984.

Are you the daughter of Abbas Borhan? Yes.

Why did you participate in the protest? Because all the students were participating.

Did your dad know that you were participating? No, dad learned after I came back.

Did he know that the protest was happening? No, he did not.

Do you believe this demonstration was a right action? I don't know.

Do you think it was wrong? I don't know.

Tell the truth! I am!

If you don't know whether it was right or wrong, why did you participate? Out of curiosity, to see for myself.

Did you shout any slogans? No.

Why didn't you shout slogans? I don't know.

CHAPTER SIX

Were you present at the secret meeting on the night of December 11th at the Physics Department? No!

Yes, you were! We know that you were there! Speak the truth! No, I wasn't.

You knew about the meeting. Why didn't you participate? I didn't know about such a meeting!

Other students reported that you were there on the night of December 11th. Don't lie, tell the truth! I wasn't there. They didn't speak the truth!

You were there on the night of December 11th! Tell the truth! I left for home after classes that day; I had no knowledge of it! I was not even at the university campus that night!

We know everything! You can't hide. What you know is not the truth! I was not there!

Tell the truth!

The interrogation continued like this, with different men yelling at me and asking similar questions for about three hours. It was frightening and exhausting, but I also felt a sense of pride in myself. Here I was, an eighteen-year-old sophomore, and these men with their wide tables covered in notes and papers seemed scared of me. I could sense the impact that our protest four months before had created. We had done something that these people had never thought would happen in our region.

I was somewhat ready for it, as my friends had prepared me, telling me what to say and how to handle things based on their own interrogations. My friends used to say that the system requires us to keep our wits about us, and to be very careful. This was one of those times. They told me that the interrogation team knew about the evening of the December 11 Physics

Department meeting and had a list of the students who were there that night. However, they had each denied any questions about me, insisting that I wasn't there. All those who were interrogated stuck to the same story, saying that only male students were present and that no females attended the meeting. Initially, I didn't agree with this plan. I felt that if they were taking responsibility for their actions, I should do the same and show solidarity by telling the truth about my involvement in the planning. Even in the interrogation, my body was telling me to speak from my heart and declare that everything we had done was right, that our demands for Uyghur rights were just. At the same time, another part of me was telling me to think of my friends, and my father, and how an impulsive act of heroism now might cost them in the future. There was a selfish thought there as well. Remembering my father's promise to send me abroad to study, I also had to consider how it might affect my own future, and my chances of someday leaving this place.

I had also met with two senior students from the class of 1981 who had organized the December 11 meetings, after their interrogations in mid-January 1986. I told them they should not have denied that I was at the December 11 meeting and that I should also take also take responsibility. "If we go down, we should go down together!" I said. But, like the others, they told me that denying I was present was a plan they had all agreed on. All of them, they told me, had agreed to answer this way for very important and valid reasons. "This won't just end with you—they will go after your father if we confirm that you were there. If they find out you were there, it will harm your father, Abbas Borhan, as they are trying to link this protest to someone in a higher position in the government. They're looking for 'national separatists behind the scenes.' We aren't only trying to protect you; we need to protect your father as well. Abbas Borhan is an important asset for our people. We need to make sure nothing will happen to him. You must answer the same way as we all plan to do. You need to follow the order!"

Since my father was a prominent Uyghur intellectual, a high-ranking official in the field of science and technology, he had learned from some contacts that the government had decided to punish the main student leaders of this demonstration and to crack down on the teachers who had incited them, labeling them "nationalist separatist elements behind the scenes." My

CHAPTER SIX

father once said to me at the beginning of the student interrogations, which began when we returned to school after the winter break, "Rushan, they will interrogate you too. If you say that you support the demonstration, you risk being blacklisted. You're young and must think ahead. Follow your brain, not just your heart. To protect your future, be smart—just say, 'I don't know.' That way, you'll be seen as a follower, not a leader. It's the safest path."

Although I felt in my heart that it wasn't right to escape by saying "I don't know," and strongly believed that all of our demands were justified, I hesitated because of what my friends said about my father. I thought about my father and the work he was doing for the Uyghur people by using his position and power. He served the interests of Uyghur intellectuals through his position in the government and helped the Uyghur farmers through his knowledge of agriculture and biology. I shared this inner conflict with one of the teachers at the university whom I trusted, who had great respect for my father and no love for the Chinese policies. He said to me, "Yes, the interrogations have begun, even for some teachers. Though I had no involvement, they questioned me too. When asked, 'Do you think the demonstration was right?' I replied, 'No.' I had no choice—admitting support would only bring trouble. Speaking honestly, saying the students were justified and Uyghurs had the right to express themselves, would have left a permanent black mark on my record, affecting my future. The consequences would have been severe."

He also told me that he had had a secret conversation with some of the students who led the December 12 movement and confirmed that they had all denied that I was present at the December 11 meeting. "They understand that the government is looking for 'national separatist elements behind the students' to suppress Uyghur leaders," he told me. "Your friends are both smart and brave young people who are doing this not only not to harm you but most importantly, to protect your father, a public figure and prominent Uyghur scientist whom they all respect greatly. You also need to do this. This is not something to take lightly. The hard times we've endured in the past have taught us many lessons."

After much thought, I eventually concluded that it was better to give answers that went against my beliefs than to act heroically and harm my father. So, in the interrogation, with very difficult feelings within my conscience, I was forced to deny my participation in the December 11 meeting.

The interrogators gave me a long lecture about being honest, speaking the truth, and staying out of trouble, and reminded me that my father was making great contributions to society and achieving significant results in science and technology for our region, and that if I, his daughter, got involved in incidents instigated by separatists, it would tarnish the honor of the entire family. I could sense the impact of my father's reputation even in this situation.

On December 12, 2022, on the thirty-seventh anniversary of the December 12 student movement, a program aired by the Radio Free Asia Uyghur Service included the following statement:

> The month of December is the coldest time in Urumchi, and December 12, 1985, was one such freezing day when heavy snow had fallen in the streets of Urumchi. However, the harsh cold could not prevent more than 15,000 young Uyghur students from taking to the streets in protest against the Chinese government's unjust policies. Uyghurs regard the December 12th student awakening movement, which took place 37 years ago, as the starting point of a peaceful, democratic struggle in the modern history of the Uyghur region. This is because the Chinese government's intensified efforts to oppress Uyghurs in every aspect, and its discriminatory policies towards Uyghurs, had caused widespread dissatisfaction among the people. Not even the gates, barricades, or police at schools could stop the students' massive protests. In the end, this protest forced the Chinese government officials assigned to the Uyghur Autonomous Region at that time to hold discussions with student representatives.

Unfortunately, as with any Uyghur involved in protest actions, these Uyghur students were subjected to unjust punishment by the Chinese government, who accused them of various fabricated crimes. After promising the students that their demands would be met and dispersing them, the

CHAPTER SIX

authorities soon began widespread, targeted punitive actions. The Chinese labeled this democratic youth movement the "December 12th Riot Incident." During this period, student leaders were persecuted, some were imprisoned, others were expelled from school, and some had criminal records attached to their employment files.

The December 12, 1985, protest was a groundbreaking act of defiance against communist rule, one of the earliest demonstrations against oppression across the entire Eastern Bloc and the communist world. At a time when dissent was met with brutal suppression, this protest signaled a courageous challenge to totalitarianism, igniting a spark of resistance that would echo far beyond its time and place. This protest not only underscored the Uyghur community's grievances but also highlighted the broader struggles of ethnic minorities in China seeking to preserve their cultural identity and rights amidst assimilationist policies.

* * *

Although the December 12, 1985, protest brought huge political setbacks and difficulties to many students, it spurred the growing national consciousness of university students in the Uyghur region. By 1987, Dolkun Isa, Waris Ababekri, and nine or ten of us began planning to establish an open organization at Xinjiang University. We seriously expanded the recruitment of members across faculties for this organization, which we intended to name "The Hope of Tengritagh Association." After three months of effort, hundreds of students joined our ranks.

Since the authorities blocked Uyghur students from organizing independently, we sought approval from the school youth league—the Communist Party's youth wing—and even invited their collaboration. Without their consent, forming an organization was impossible. After securing their support, we met with school leaders, explaining our goal: to educate rural Uyghurs in the rural areas. During summer breaks, university students would volunteer in villages to combat illiteracy among the Uyghur farmers.

Although the school leadership initially hesitated, claiming that "eradicating illiteracy is a state responsibility," they couldn't find any reason to oppose it and eventually agreed. After overcoming these two hurdles, we intensified our recruitment activities within the school. Every evening, we gave speeches in various departments, encouraging our fellow students' national spirit and urging them to take pride in their Uyghur identity and their homeland. I would constantly tell my father about the events happening among us at our school. He shared my excitement, deeply moved by the spirit of the students. One day, I told him that the organization called "The Hope of Tengritagh Association" would soon be officially established. My father said, "That's very good," but after thinking for a moment, he added, "Tengritagh is a symbolic name for our homeland. Could this possibly attract the attention of the government? They might ask, 'What is the hope of Tengritagh? What are you all hoping for?' This name may seem political to authorities, risking the organization's formation. The work matters more than the name, and if the government sees a reason, it could shut it down early. You may want to reconsider a different name." The next day, I conveyed my father's concerns to Dolkun and Waris. They said, "It would be great if we could meet with Mr. Abbas Borhan soon and hear his thoughts. Please relay our request to him, if we could come and meet him for a discussion." When I passed their request to my father, he replied, "Sure, let them come by tomorrow evening."

Dolkun and Waris arrived at our house later that evening after classes. My mother, Mariye, was preparing dinner. This was early December 1987, just several days before the organization's formal establishment. Dolkun and Waris were very excited at the prospect of meeting my father face-to-face and engaging in direct conversation with him since he was a distinguished intellectual and a public figure whom they had heard about for a long time but had never met him before. Dolkun, Waris, and I, representing the core members of The Hope of Tengritagh Association, had the privilege of discussing critical issues concerning the future of our people with my dad for more than four hours.

> "My children, I am overjoyed to see a new generation like you, who care deeply about the fate of your homeland and nation. I

CHAPTER SIX

used to think that Uyghur nationalism had perhaps ended with us, and that there was no hope left in the next generation. But thankfully, I was wrong. You, with your glorious ideals and fresh energy and spirit, are searching for light in our homeland clouded by darkness, and for that, I am very proud of you. The sudden explosion of December 12, 1985, movement reignited our hope. And now, your rising action has further strengthened that hope. I have been hearing about your activities through Rushan. What can I do for you? If there is anything you need from me, do not hesitate to ask," he said with a warm smile, easing any sense of hesitation we may have felt.

Dolkun and Waris presented our plans and programs for The Hope of Tengritagh Association in detail. The core of our agenda was to establish the organization and then expand its branches across all the universities in my homeland, aiming to extend its reach from the north to the south of Tengritagh. My father listened patiently until they were done. He thought for a moment, and then said,

We have experienced many political hardships and turmoil. We lived through the disastrous years of the 'Cultural Revolution.' Our experiences taught us that as long as the Chinese Communist Party exists on this land, any good work done for the nation will inevitably be met with disaster. In your current state of excitement, you cannot yet perceive the storms, harm, or even imprisonment that await you. This is a very emotional time for you. If the government learns about your projects, they will not congratulate you; instead, you will be rewarded with accusations of nationalism. The burden of this accusation is heavy, and you will not be able to bear it. You may be thinking, "Isn't what we are doing a righteous cause?" Indeed, you will be punished precisely because it is a righteous cause. I don't know if there is another country in the world where loving your homeland and people is considered a crime. How much do you understand that even sharing this with you could be enough to punish me in this country? I am unsure. However, I do not want your movement to stop. Every love comes at a price, of course, but that price should not be paid unnecessarily. We have already paid enough. You must ensure that your activities are legally protected.

My father's words seemed to implant some worry in them immediately, but that was not his intention. Reality was harsher than his words. The young members of the organization, driven by both intellect and emotion, could not fully grasp what the future held for their movement.

"The name The Hope of Tengritagh Association, alone is enough to raise concerns, my father continued. "At first glance, it seems appropriate and appealing for all of us. However, to get this name approved by the government, you will have to answer many questions. Without government approval, you can't do anything or make yourselves known to the public. This name will immediately attract the attention of the Han Chinese people." My father repeated the same points he had raised with me about how the name we had chosen would be questioned and create problems for us in getting things done. He added "They may ask you, 'Why didn't you choose a name like China Hope or Xinjiang Hope instead of Tengritagh Hope?' As much as we love this name, it is filled with ethnic connotations in the government's eyes." My father told them, "Your intentions will raise their suspicions. My dear children, spending a lifetime in prison for a single word is a common occurrence in the history of this country. What we need is not a name, but practical action."

He then gave us his advice:

> The first option is that according to the approval of the central and autonomous regional authorities, there are plans to establish two types of science and cultural associations under the Science and Technology Society, of which I am the president. One is for factories and industries, and the other is for higher educational institutions. If you wish, you can change the name of your organization to the "Students Science and

CHAPTER SIX

Cultural Association" and take a seat in one of our society's compartments. In this way, your organization will have a legal foundation, and you will benefit from the protection and support of our Science and Technology Society. If any authorities attempt to take action against you, they will first have to confront us. You can first establish the Science and Cultural Association in higher educational institutions in Urumchi, and then we will take responsibility for expanding it to other cities and regions on your behalf.

This conversation with my father became the foundation for establishing the mechanism of the organization. After analyzing the situation, the leadership agreed to adopt a new name. After some discussion, they decided on the name "Students Science and Cultural Association," as my father had suggested.

Thus, a group that could alarm the Chinese authorities, which was later labeled the "cradle of counterrevolutionaries," officially came into existence on December 24, 1987, at Xinjiang University. Dolkun Isa was elected president, Waris Ababekri became the secretary-general, and I was elected as a vice-president. The organization's structure was established, and responsibilities were distributed.

Following the creation of the Students Science and Cultural Association, thirteen branch organizations were set up in the thirteen departments of Xinjiang University. Each branch had a president and vice-president. After a few months, branches were also established with grand ceremonies in other institutions, such as the Industrial Institute, the Medical Institute, and the Pedagogical University. Uyghur directors and professors in these institutions supported the movement. The leaders of the associations from each institution gathered weekly to discuss plans. This new initiative, built on the principles of solidarity and national ideals, created excitement and hope not only in the schools but also within the broader Uyghur society.

In the early months of 1988, a concert ensemble called "Students Drenched in Joy" was established under the umbrella of the Students Science and Cultural Association. I took on the responsibility for this ensemble, which prepared a variety of artistic performances rich in national characteristics and showcased them in higher education institutions and community halls, creating a stir.

The fame of the performances by the Students Drenched in Joy spread throughout all of the higher educational institutions in Urumchi. With the help of our organization, a group of students who did not wish to return home during the winter break in February organized themselves to travel to places like Turpan, Qarimay, and Ghulja, collecting many pieces of evidence that would expose the government's relationship to national inequality under the names *Aqartish* (Dissemination) and *Jemiyet Tekshürüsh* (Community Inspection).

Thirteen students visiting Ghulja became witnesses to the stunning circumstances. Heavy snowfall in Altay, Tarbaghatay, and Ili caused Uyghur and Kazakh school buildings in the Ghulja prefecture to collapse, forcing class cancellations. Meanwhile, Chinese schools continued as usual, their brick and cement structures unaffected, unlike the weaker wood and clay buildings of the Uyghur and Kazakh schools. Seeing this situation, the students documented the dilapidated state of the Uyghur schools and the grandeur of the Chinese schools. Another group of ten students investigated Chinese gold miners near Qarimay, finding severe environmental destruction—plants uprooted, trash covering the land, and water pollution. They returned with photos and videos exposing the damage.

Our organization documented the findings of injustice and submitted them to the Uyghur Autonomous Region Party Committee, the government, and the People's Congress. A request for a meeting to address these issues, signed by representatives from thirteen higher education institutions, was also submitted.

In early March, as the winter break ended and the new academic term began, a large display documenting the government's unequal policies towards Uyghurs and Chinese was set up in front of the school library. This marked the start of the June 15, 1988, protest and the confrontation between the Students Science and Cultural Association and the Uyghur Autonomous Region government and Party Committee. Compiling evidence from three

CHAPTER SIX

regions and posting it, along with photos and explanations, in front of the library was a breakthrough that sparked a strong national awakening.

The stark contrast between the crumbling Uyghur schools and the well-maintained Chinese schools was exposed to the school community and the entire city of Urumchi, revealing systemic inequalities. The association's leadership swiftly produced a short film, screening it in the conference hall of the History Department. Thousands of students were stunned by the images of Uyghur children sitting on the ground in dilapidated classrooms while Chinese students studied in well-equipped schools, and of Uyghur laborers begging while Chinese miners prospered. This blatant reality fueled national resentment among the students. Teachers, though alarmed, hesitated to intervene, knowing that acknowledging such truths could come at a heavy cost.

The impact of the short film surpassed that of the exhibition, spreading from Urumchi to all over the region. Those once viewing the Chinese as slightly superior began to compare their lives to those of their oppressors, starting with education. The situation in the Uyghur schools in the Southern region, particularly in Kashgar, Artush, and Hotan, was far worse, depicting the deep poverty caused by the Chinese invasion.

In mid-May, an incident occurred as I neared the end of my studies and was preparing my thesis in Ghulja. A Chinese student wrote derogatory phrases in ancient Chinese script on the restroom door of the Physics Department, stating, "Let us enslave the Uyghur men and make their women into prostitutes. Uyghurs and other ethnic groups are not allowed to enter this restroom!"

On June 14, furious Uyghur students stormed the university president's office, demanding that the student who wrote the insult be identified and punished. President Abdulhakim Jappar promised to address the issue, but a month later, no action had been taken. On June 15, 1988, more than three hundred members of the Students Science and Cultural Association gathered outside Jappar's office, and when no response came, about four to five thousand Uyghur students, led by Dolkun Isa and our association's leadership, marched into the streets. Despite attempts by the school authorities to stop them, the determined protesters broke through barricades. Some teachers silently supported the students, and the call for resistance against discrimination spread as they carried a door from the Physics Department restroom, covered in insults, towards Uyghur men and women, along with their banners and slogans. The government deployed thousands of police and soldiers, ordering that demonstrators gathered in the People's Square disperse quickly.

Thousands of Uyghur community members gathered, their hearts stirred by the students' powerful slogans: "Down with national discrimination! Long live equality! We need freedom!" Tears flowed as they witnessed a generation unafraid to speak out, claiming their rights and resisting colonial humiliation.

National sentiments surged as the protest remained orderly until, after a few hours, students began returning to their dormitories.

* * *

Fast forward to the present day, and the scars of past resistance still haunt the Uyghur people. Even amidst the mass detentions that began in 2016, it is well documented that Uyghurs who had once carried the "black mark" of participating in the December 12, 1985, and June 15, 1988, student protests found themselves targeted once again. These brave individuals, marked for their defiance against oppression, were forcibly rounded up and sent to the camps and prisons, as the Chinese government continues to punish those who dared to stand up for their basic human rights. Their resistance, though decades old, remains a clear and unforgivable challenge to the authorities' efforts to erase the Uyghur identity and history.

One of the leaders of the second student movement, our friend Waris Ababekri, was sent to a camp in Urumchi in January 2019 and released in mid-November 2019. Just one week later, on November 24, news of his death sparked a great outcry from the Uyghur diaspora. He was fifty-three years old.

CHAPTER SEVEN
TENACITY

In October 1985, my father, Abbas Borhan, led a research delegation on an official trip to the United States, visiting several universities as part of an experience exchange program that allowed Uyghur and Kazakh scholars to engage with American institutions. Washington State University was one of the stops, where my father met Dr. Faulkner and Dr. Walter J. Kaiser, among many other researchers and scholars.

In the summer of 1987, my father hosted three American professors from Washington State University, including Dr. Faulkner. As part of the American scholars' visit to Urumchi, there was an arrangement to host them in our home for an Uyghur dinner. They came to our home, and we had a family dinner together with them and several Chinese officials. During the light dinner conversation, one of them (Dr. Lin Faulkner), through a Chinese translator suddenly asked me if I had ever thought of learning English. I explained that, as an Uyghur studying in an Uyghur-language school, the curriculum only allowed us to learn Chinese, so that I did not have a proper opportunity to learn English.

Then Dr. Faulkner asked me:

"Do you want to go to America to study after you graduate?"

"Of course I do," I replied.

"When do you graduate?" he asked. I told him that my studies would finish in June 1988, with graduation following immediately. He smiled and said,

"My wife Lois and I have three children, Jenni, Ed and Brent. They have grown up and left home. Now it's just my wife and me living alone in Washington State. Our home is spacious. If you'd like, you could come and stay with us like one of our own children. You wouldn't have any difficulties. Lois and I would be your host family."

I thanked him and was cautiously pleased. In my mind, I thought, "Perhaps that's just something he said casually." But in May 1988, I received an invitation from Washington State University and Form IAP-66 for a J-1 visa for visiting scholars, together with a letter from Dr. and Mrs. Faulkner. They even sent a plane ticket for a flight from Hong Kong to Seattle on July 26, 1988.

I was overjoyed—studying in America was a rare opportunity for Uyghurs. The next day, I took my documents, invitation letter, and ticket to the Foreign Affairs Department of the Education Ministry. The woman there smiled and said, "You must work in the country for at least a year after graduating from the university before going abroad—that's state policy." My heart sank; my dream was slipping away.

In June, I completed my studies. Since my academic performance had been excellent—I was one of the very few students with honor recognition as "Students with the Top 3 Qualities" every year — and both my parents had long been employees at Xinjiang University, the university's Biology Department wanted to hire me as a teacher. But I wasn't interested. I wanted a change in environment, to live somewhere different.

I told my mother, "I was born, grew up, and studied here, but I want to work elsewhere." She didn't object, saying, "Find a job that suits your career." Soon after, I got an offer from the First August Agricultural Institute. The director had reviewed my records and chosen me as the top candidate. I went to the Institute, where the staff warmly welcomed me, processed me, and told me I would start teaching on September 1. I was happy to spend the year as a teacher at this institute before going abroad to study. When friends and acquaintances asked, "Where are you going to work?" I proudly replied, "I was accepted by the Agricultural Institute."

The anticipated day of September 1 finally arrived. My dad had been asked by the government to attend a political study session in Beijing for four months and left right before September.

In the morning, I put on the atlas dress I had sewn myself, dressed nicely, and went to the First August Agricultural Institute early in the morning.

CHAPTER SEVEN

I reported to the department where I was assigned. The department head reviewed my records and, after a moment, said, "I'm sorry, but we can no longer accept you for the position. We've received orders from above." I was shocked.

"What do you mean? You already processed me as an employee. I reported to you and you told me to come back in September, when the semester starts," I said, looking him straight in the eye.

"We can't accept you—it's an order from above," he said helplessly. I went to the Personnel Department, where the head stepped inside briefly before returning with the same response: "We cannot accept you based on orders from above."

"Why? Whose orders are these? Who gave the order?"

The Personnel Department did not answer my question. Sensing that there was some sort of game behind this, I returned home, downhearted. When I explained the situation to my mother, she too was left speechless in astonishment. The next day, I went to the Education Ministry Personnel Office and explained the situation to them, saying, "You assigned me to the Agricultural Institute, and they confirmed my acceptance, but now, they're refusing me. What's going on?" I asked. The officer there replied, "If they say that, we can't interfere." Defeated, I went home and told my mother. She later called an official she knew at the Agricultural institute to investigate further. That official told my mother, "Please keep this to yourself. Deputy Secretary Janabil Simahuli[17] asked about this year's new hires. The principal listed mostly Chinese graduates, except Rushan Abbas from Xinjiang University. Janabil grew upset, saying, "Don't you know who she is? She was involved in the 1985 and 1988 demonstrations! How could you hire her without checking her political background?"

The principal was afraid but gave the order to the school's Personnel Office: Rushan Abbas cannot be kept.

---

17. Chinese: 贾那布尔·司马胡里; pinyin: Jiǎnàbù'ěr · Sīmǎhúlǐ; ethnic Khazakh (April 1934–22 November 2024). He was Deputy Secretary of the Xinjiang Uyghur Autonomous Regional Party Committee responsible for education and oversaw the Education Ministry.

After my mother told me this, I became even more distressed and didn't know what to do. During those discouraging days, I ran into one of my high-school classmates, the son of an Uyghur official, who is a next-door neighbor of the Chinese Party Secretary of Xinjiang, Song Hanliang. After greeting each other, he asked about my work, so I told him about my troubles. He offered to arrange a meeting with Song Hanliang, saying, "He controls Janabil. Maybe things will turn in your favor."

Song Hanliang was the first secretary of the Xinjiang Uyghur Autonomous Regional Party Committee in 1988. Among the Chinese officials who had governed Xinjiang since 1949, he was considered a relatively educated and somewhat humanitarian figure. He gained some praise among Uyghurs when he advocated before the Chinese central government that some percentage of the petroleum extracted from Xinjiang should stay in the region to support its economy. With my classmate's help, I visited Song Hanliang, bringing my academic records, awards, certificates, my invitation from Washington State University, and my plane ticket to the United States. He greeted me warmly. "Aren't you Abbas Borhan's daughter?" he asked me. "I know your father well—he's a well-respected Uyghur scholar. Please, sit."

I told him the reason why I came, shared my achievements, and explained my current situation. "They say I must work for a year before studying abroad, but they won't let me work after they sent me to the First August Agricultural Institute. What should I do?" I asked. Song Hanliang furrowed his brows and said, "This is mishandled! I'll call Minister Zhang Yang (from the Xinjiang Education Ministry)—he'll meet you in a few days to resolve this. If you don't hear back from him within three days, call me," handing me his personal phone number.

Hopeful, I waited three days, but by the fourth, there was still no word from Zhang Yang. At 4:30 p.m., I called Song Hanliang. "I'm Rushan Abbas. You said to call if I didn't hear back in three days. It's now the fourth, and I've had no news," I said.

"Is that so?" he replied. "Give me ten minutes and call back—I'll speak with Zhang Yang now!"

Just minutes later, I got a call:

CHAPTER SEVEN

"I'm Zhang Yang's secretary. He's in a meeting at the Pedagogical University but he wants to speak to you. A car will pick you up in thirty minutes—please provide your address." I gave him my address and immediately called Song Hanliang to inform him. He was pleased and asked me to keep him informed. As expected, a car arrived within thirty minutes and took me to the Pedagogical University. Zhang Yang was in a banquet hall surrounded by a group of people. Seeing me, he forced a smile. "You must be Rushan Abbas. Please sit," he said, pointing to a chair beside him. I listened as he praised my father's scholarly work and his books, and my academic success but said nothing about my job. Losing patience, I asked, "What should I do now? What about my study abroad and my work assignment?"

"As per national regulations, you must work locally for a year after you graduate before studying abroad," he replied.

"I understand that, but the place that accepted me has already turned me away, so where do I work?" I asked. With a forced smile, Zhang Yang reassured me, "I'll look into it and get back to you soon. Don't worry and please wait."

Days passed without resolution. After more than two weeks, I had received no word from Zhang Yang or the Agricultural Institute. I realized they were avoiding a direct refusal to prevent backlash, instead passing the matter around to wear me down. As elder Uyghur intellectuals often say, "Chinese officials are cunning; don't trust their words," and I saw this firsthand. I grew disheartened, and the city I once knew felt cold and distant. I withdrew from people, staying home to help my mother, dreading encounters with others who would remind me of my unresolved issue. Dad was still in Beijing for his political study sessions.

One day, there was a knock on the door. It was the Deputy Principal of Xinjiang University, one of my dad's close friends, who had come to see if we needed anything while dad was away.

"I just returned from a funeral prayer from the mosque (Noghay Mosque was at the front of our home) and thought I'd stop by to visit you," he said with a smile. "And it seems our famous Rushan is home!" My mother welcomed him but asked what he meant by that. He answered "Rushan has become well known within the entire region! Everyone among the officials and universities are talking about her. News of her has spread throughout Xinjiang with an official document." At first I thought it was a joke. But after hearing his next words, mom and I were surprised and asked "What's going on? What news and what document?" Looking at us in astonishment, he replied:

"Wow, do you really not know? This week's 'Red Head File' from the Education Ministry was all about Rushan. A classified document titled 'Leaders of the Education Ministry Had a Conversation with Comrade Rushan Abbas' has been distributed throughout the entire Autonomous Region. Honestly, when I saw it, I did not believe most of it and I was angry. If you saw it, you'd be even more furious. It seems to contain untruth and some slander."

My mother and I looked at each other in shock. My mother, who had always overcome difficulties with pride, cautiously asked him: "Could I send my daughter with you to get a copy of this document? We would like to take a look at it ourselves."

"That's fine, but no one should know that I gave it to you," he replied. I went with the Deputy Principal to the school administration building, made a copy of the confidential document from his office, and brought it home. Seeing this Red Head File printed in Chinese, I was enraged. I couldn't believe my eyes. Everything mentioned in it was outright lies, and insults. The document stated:

> *Rushan Abbas, lacking financial resources, livelihood security, insufficient support, submitted a false application to the Education Ministry with incomplete materials, falsely claiming she wanted to study abroad, immediately after graduating from the University. The ministry staff patiently explained that she could reapply after a year of work to complete the necessary documents. However, Rushan Abbas refused to accept this, she pressured the Education Ministry through her blood-relatives at the high position in the Party Committee to exert pressure on the Ministry. When the Ministry's leaders summoned her for a discussion at Pedagogical University, they discovered that she had falsely claimed everywhere that she was going to be a lecturer at*

CHAPTER SEVEN

the First August Agricultural Institute, while her application for studying abroad was severely lacking. Based on these findings, the Education Ministry decided to handle the matter in accordance with its regulations.

At the bottom of the document was the signature and seal of the Department of External Affairs of the Education Ministry. I was boiling with anger. Carrying the Red Head File and other supporting materials, I headed straight to the Education Ministry and walked into the Office of External Affairs. The head of the office was Hu, who was also present at the Pedagogical University meeting with Zhang Yang. Upon seeing me, Hu looked startled, his eyes narrowing. There were two Englishmen sitting in his office, but I didn't care. I asked Hu in an angry tone:

"Did you issue this ridiculous document?!"

"Yes, what is the problem?" Hu replied, glancing at the document in my hand, his face flushing slightly.

"You've written many lies and slanders. Today, I demand evidence from you for your false claims. If you cannot provide proof, I will file a complaint against you all the way to Beijing!" I said, my voice loud and firm.

"What exactly are you trying to say?" Hu asked, squinting through his small, sharp eyes.

"I will ask you three questions. First, what is Rushan Abbas's ethnicity? What am I?" I yelled.

"Uyghur," he replied, glancing at me and then, after a brief pause, at the Englishmen sitting nearby.

"And what is Song Hanliang's ethnicity?" I continued my questioning.

"Han Chinese," Hu answered, still looking puzzled.

"Then, how could Uyghur Rushan Abbas and Han Chinese Song Hanliang be blood relatives? In this Red Head File, which you published, you stated, 'Rushan Abbas pressured the Education Ministry through her blood relatives at the high-level position in the Party Committee.' I have only ever spoken to the Party Secretary, Song Hanliang. You must prove the familial relationship between Rushan Abbas and Song Hanliang. If you cannot provide evidence, I will sue you all the way to the high court!"

Hu remained silent. He was trying to read his own document about me. The two Englishmen in the room were also stunned. It seemed like they understood Chinese and were staring at me in surprise. Without changing my angry tone, I continued to question Hu. I went on by saying:

"My second question to you: In your document, you stated, 'Rushan Abbas falsely claimed everywhere that she was a lecturer at the Agricultural Institute.' Xinjiang University assigned me to the Education Ministry after I graduated, and the Education Ministry assigned me to work at the First August Agricultural Institute. The institute accepted me as a lecturer when I reported back in July, and I was scheduled to start work on September 1. My registration pass is still with them although they now have refused me. Therefore, your office and this department assigned me to the Agricultural Institute, and the institute accepted me. Does that not make me a lecturer there? What part of my statement, "I was going to work at the Agricultural Institute," is false? You must provide proof that what I said was a lie!

Hu was staring at me silently, his eyes flickering, and he avoided speaking.

"My third question: In your document, you stated, 'lacking financial resources, livelihood security, insufficient support, submitted a false application to the Education Ministry with incomplete materials, falsely claiming she wanted to study abroad.' When I submitted my application to study abroad to this office back in June, I presented my IAP-66 form, flight ticket to America, a letter confirming my room and board, and proof that an American family was covering all my expenses. Additionally, I provided documents and letters from Washington State University confirming my lab work would earn me $500 a month, with all living expenses and transportation costs covered by an American family. I have their support letter. How can you claim my documents were incomplete or false? You must provide evidence of these accusations! I give you 24 hours. Tomorrow, I will return to demand proof of these lies. If you can't provide the necessary documentation, we will resolve this matter at the court!"

I stormed out of the office and went to Zhang Yang's office, but he wasn't there. His staff told me that the Deputy Head of the Education Ministry, Nur Teyip, approved the Red Head File about me. I went to Nur Teyip's office,

CHAPTER SEVEN

but they said he had gone home for lunch. I asked for his address and went to his house. When I rang the bell, his daughter, about my age, answered.

"I need to speak with Mr. Nur Teyip. I'm Rushan, daughter of Abbas Borhan. Could you please call him? It is very urgent!" I said firmly.

"My father is resting," she said uneasily. Just then, Nur Teyip appeared from another room. After greeting me, he asked what had happened.

"You have a daughter about my age. Imagine, just for a moment, if this happened to her—if she were in my place, a twenty-one-year-old girl, fresh out of university, stepping into the world. Imagine if she was slandered, her character destroyed by lies and false claims. A "Top Secret Red Head Document" gets circulated across thousands of offices, universities, institutions, research centers, and all other workplaces within the entire region, all based on nothing but lies. What would you feel as a father, knowing your daughter's future was shattered like this with lies? I'm someone's child too. My father is someone you know well. Is this the punishment I deserve just because I filed a complaint about my mishandled employment? Is this how you destroy a young woman's future and reputation? You're a father too, so think—how would you feel if this was your daughter?"

Nur Teyip sat there, shocked, repeating, "I didn't know what it said. I didn't know this was about you." My frustration grew, and I asked, "How could you sign and approve something without reading it, without understanding the consequences?" He lowered his eyes, unable to answer, then looked at me again with a guilty face, offering only sympathetic glances. But when I demanded, "How will you fix this now?" there was no response. He stood helplessly. Once again, I felt the overwhelming reality that Uyghur officials had no choice but to obey the orders of their Chinese superiors and submit to their will. I said,

"I will file another complaint with Song Hanliang. If he cannot resolve this matter, I will go to Beijing and submit my complaint there. I will never bow to this injustice!"

At this point, overcome with frustration and despair, I felt on the verge of tears. Just moments earlier, I had confronted a Chinese official with strength, but in front of this Uyghur man, who knew my family well, I was overwhelmed by his helplessness. The realization hit me that this man, who was both Uyghur and someone who knew my parents well, could offer me absolutely nothing as a solution. My legs and hands trembled, and my heart softened as I struggled to hold it together. I didn't want to cry in front of him, so I quickly said my goodbyes and left. The moment I stepped outside, the tears came, flowing uncontrollably down my cheeks as I sobbed.

Of course, I reached out to Song Hanliang and met with him again. I explained the situation to him in detail, showing him the Red Head File issued against me, which he called a "disgrace!" He assured me he would investigate the matter further and make sure that the Education Ministry would correct and reissue the document. In the end, after Song Hanliang got involved, the Chinese official Hu who had issued the document was removed from his position and transferred somewhere else. The Education Ministry kept delaying the reissuance of the document despite promising that they would and worked on it continuously for weeks. However, my employment situation remained unresolved. While students from other regions who graduated with me found jobs in Urumchi, I remained unemployed.

This was the price I paid for my small advocacy contributions to my homeland and my people while trying to defend their rights. For a young girl who was only twenty-one years old and a fresh university graduate, it was a huge burden. In my homeland, loving one's country, striving for freedom, and fighting for one's dignity as a human being came at a heavy cost.

By now it was almost October. One day, I sat down and wrote a letter to my dad who was still in Beijing, telling him that while he raised me to be healthy and had me educated, now I was facing difficulties and injustice, Not wanting him to worry about my employment or my future, I asked him to allow me to deal with my situation myself in the way that I felt was most proper. In my opinion, "I did nothing wrong, and I would not ask anyone to help me get a job. Most certainly I will not allow my parents to ask anyone for a favor to help me get a job in Urumchi," I wrote him. I asked my father's permission to let me go and try to get a job elsewhere, perhaps in the remote countryside of my homeland.

> *"I have made the decision to go to Artush, so that you will no longer need to ask anyone to secure a job for me. Please, don't allow any-*

CHAPTER SEVEN

one to diminish your dignity or tarnish your honor on my behalf. You have already done more than enough as a father. From this moment on, I take full responsibility for my own future. Do not carry the weight of guilt for not finding me a job in Urumchi—I accept whatever fate has in store for me, with no regrets. This is my path to walk, and I will face it with strength and resolve."

So, I ultimately went to Artush, a city about 900 miles away from my hometown, after leaving him that letter and telling my mother the same thing I had told him.

As the plane soared over the rugged landscapes, over the beautiful high mountains of Tengtitagh, heading towards Kashgar, and then as I boarded the bus to Artush, a heavy weight pressed down on my chest. The journey felt endless, each mile mirroring the deep sense of injustice I had just endured over the past five weeks in Urumchi. It wasn't just exhaustion, it was the raw, aching feeling of helplessness that consumed me, like I was trapped in a world that refused to acknowledge my pain. The weight of the experience, the overwhelming sense of being powerless in the face of such injustice, lingered with me, each moment more suffocating than the last.

I became a teacher at a technical-vocational school established by a group of Uyghur businessmen and merchants. These generous benefactors aimed to provide opportunities for Uyghur students who could not be accepted by the universities due to the limited quotas, despite having passed the entrance exams. Until the 1980s, the Chinese authorities had restricted Uyghurs from opening their own schools, but this was one of the very few being established.

The school offered courses in language, math, biology, and the natural and social sciences. Its teachers were a mix of young graduates like me who had struggled to find jobs. Though classes had already begun when I arrived, the official opening ceremony had yet to take place. One day, a school official approached me and said, "The opening ceremony will be held this weekend. Please prepare a speech. You will be speaking on behalf of the teachers." I agreed but forgot to ask what topic I should address.

Since it was my first time speaking publicly, I wanted to prepare carefully. My mind was filled with thoughts of the suffering my people had endured for years, our glorious history, the progress of the world today, our current hardships, and my own personal struggles. I was determined to deliver a speech that would leave a strong impact.

On the day of the ceremony, I was invited onto the stage, feeling both nervous and excited. The large hall was packed with over a thousand people—students, teachers, writers, intellectuals, members of the local community, and religious leaders. The most respected elders of the town sat in the front row. It was mid-October, and Artush was still quite warm. I stepped onto the stage dressed as I would in Urumchi—without a head covering, wearing a short-sleeved shirt and a vest with a knee-length skirt. However, the women in the audience, following their religious and cultural traditions, wore headscarves and long-sleeved ankle-length dresses. My appearance was noticeably different from theirs. Adding to my unease, religious scholars, mosque leaders, and elders were seated in the front row.

That moment became one of the most unforgettable experiences of my life. Looking at my notes, I began my speech by acknowledging the kindness, piety, and resilience of the people in the southern region and their devotion to Islam. I praised their dedication to building mosques, performing prayers on time, and living in harmony in somewhat ordinary lives. But I also emphasized that for a nation to survive and stand tall, faith alone and praying to God was not enough.

The hall fell completely silent. It was so quiet that I could hear the faintest sound, as if even a mosquito's buzz would have been audible. At one point, I lifted my head and saw everyone staring at me with puzzled, narrowed eyes, as if they were thinking, "Are you preaching to us about our religion with that appearance? Who are you to lecture us on Islam?" After all, it wasn't appropriate for someone like me—who lacked proper religious education and was not dressed properly by Islamic standards—to speak on such matters in front of highly respected religious figures. I was still only twenty-one at the time.

But my intentions were pure. Encouraging myself, I delivered my speech with the passion I had put into preparing it. I spoke about the importance of valuing education as much as faith, emphasizing that to free our people from humiliation and suffering, and to reclaim the proud legacy of our ancestors who once built great empires, we needed a generation armed with knowl-

CHAPTER SEVEN

edge, to educate ourselves and strive towards making the best for our people and our future. My core message was that the Uyghur people must rise with unwavering determination, working relentlessly and staying resilient in the face of adversity. It is through our tireless efforts and unyielding spirit that we will earn the dignity, respect, and recognition that we so rightfully deserve, I told them. Our strength lies not just in survival, but in our ability to shape our own future—by demanding respect not as a gift, but as a consequence of our relentless pursuit of excellence and justice. It is time for the world to see us for who we truly are—strong, capable, and deserving of the respect we've earned through perseverance and resolve. Though I didn't explicitly state that the Chinese government was the source of our oppression, my message subtly and clearly pointed in that direction. What I said was what many people longed to express but dared not speak aloud. I did. That, I believe, is what moved the audience.

The moment I finished speaking, the entire hall rose to its feet, applauding for a long time. Wow! I had just gotten a standing ovation. The applause lasted for a long time. As I stepped down from the stage, many people came around me to speak to me and some people shook my hand tightly, saying, "You have spoken words worthy of Abbas Borhan's daughter!" Others remarked, "This was the most powerful speech we have heard for a very long time!" Some even told me, "Well done, Rushan Abbas! Our homeland needs young people like you" and "You gave us hope. Listening to you, we felt that we have a bright future." Journalists from local newspapers and magazines eagerly approached me, asking for a copy of my speech to publish. Now, I started to worry. I was worried about my job. If anyone told the CCP officials what had happened today, I could lose my job again. I refused to give out my speech, knowing that if it were printed, it would bring serious trouble to my father.

Still, my words spread quickly from person to person and eventually reached my father in Beijing. Without planning it, I had become well known among the people of Artush. By early February, during the winter break, I set off for Urumchi, planning to return to Artush in a month. I only took a few outfits with me, leaving my summer clothes and other belongings in my dormitory at school, assuming I would be back soon.

When I arrived home, my father had just returned from Beijing. The moment I stepped inside, he embraced me tightly, tears streaming down his face. "I couldn't be there for you during the difficult days, my dear daughter," he said as tears welled up in my own eyes.

I spent the winter break at home with my parents, barely stepping outside. However, just before the break ended, an unexpected event changed my fate.

A well-known popular public figure in Urumchi had passed away, and an invitation for his funeral came to our house. It was a bitterly cold day. My father put the invitation in his pocket and headed to the house of the deceased with my oldest brother, Nijat. Just as they arrived, they ran into Janabil Simaghuli, who was leaving the home of the deceased.

"Hey, Abbas! When did you return from Beijing? How have you been?" Janabil greeted him warmly. My father knew that it had been Janabil's informal order that had left me unemployed after graduating. My father wasn't too happy to see him and was not too friendly towards him. He simply replied politely before attempting to leave.

"Your daughter Rushan graduated recently, didn't she? Where is she now? Where is she working?" asked Janabil.

My father replied coldly but somewhat sarcastically, "My daughter has found a job in our kitchen at home, and she is cooking for us," meaning to tell him that I didn't have a job.

"What do you mean, Abbas?" asked Janabil, surprised. Father responded firmly,

"Despite her excellent academic performance, certain people's obstacles and opinion of her prevented my daughter from securing a job. She was even denied the opportunity to study in the United States." With that, my father ended the conversation and entered the home of the deceased. Inside, they served food to the guests, prayed for the deceased, and shared condolences. After about half an hour, my father left the gathering. As he walked down the street after coming out of the gate, Janabil stepped out of a black car parked near the gate on the street, and called out,

"Abbas, wait a moment."

It turned out that Janabil had been waiting for my father in his car. Janabil reached out to my father, although he seemed hesitant to speak. Suddenly

CHAPTER SEVEN

pulling his pen from his pocket, he asked "Do you have a piece of paper on you?" My father searched his pockets and pulled out the white funeral invitation and turned it over. It was blank on the back. Saying "that would work," Janabil took the invitation from dad's hand and wrote:

"To the Education Ministry, Agricultural Institute, and Urumchi Police: Process Rushan Abbas's employment, issue exit visa and passport as quickly as possible for her to travel abroad for study. I will follow up on this with a call. Janabil Simaghuli." Handing the paper to my father, he said, "Have Rushan take this to the relevant offices and places. She should not have any issue obtaining her passport. If there's any problem, please contact me directly." Then he left.

So, you're trying to clean up your own mess now? my father thought. Realizing the influence my father held in the community, Janabil likely wanted to avoid a bad reputation among Uyghur intellectuals by resolving the issue he had created for me, even if only to save face.

When my father returned home, he was covered in snow. I took his coat, shook off the snow, and hung it up to dry.

"Something interesting happened today," my father said, handing me the white funeral invitation with the note on the back. He then recounted his encounter with Janabil. After reading Janabil's note, I was somewhat irritated and declared, "I won't go to that school or the education department that refused to hire me!"

"This is not the time to act on emotions, my daughter," my father advised. "Use this opportunity to secure your passport and go to America for your studies. That will be our greatest victory. Today's decision shapes tomorrow's fate. We must act quickly to resolve this matter!" Both my mother and my two brothers agreed with my father's perspective. On Monday morning, I took Janabil's signed note to the First August Agricultural Institute. I presented it to the Personnel Office, and the official asked what it was. After explaining it was the only paper available at the time, they instructed me to wait. I overheard phone conversations while waiting for more than an hour. Finally, they issued a statement on the institute's letterhead, confirming my employment and approving my travel abroad, with the Institute Party Committee seal, and instructed that my passport be issued immediately.

I went straight to the Ministry of Education, where I presented both the school's and Janabil's letters. After waiting an hour, they gave me a letter approving my request to study abroad and instructing the Urumchi city police to issue my passport. After lunch, I went to the Urumchi City Police Department and submitted my form and passport photo. They took my phone number, promising to notify me when the passport was ready.

For Uyghurs like me, obtaining a passport from Chinese authorities was typically a lengthy and complex process, often taking months or even years. However, my passport was issued in under four weeks. Once I had it, my father contacted Dr. Faulkner to update the documents for my US visa. Within a few weeks, I received the updated admission letter and other documents from Washington State University, along with a plane ticket from Hong Kong to Seattle.

When my father and I traveled to Beijing for my visa application in late April, the Tiananmen Square student protests had already begun. My father was quite anxious, knowing that if any major incident occurred, the Chinese government might close the borders. Fortunately, I received my visa very quickly from the US Embassy in Beijing. If we had stayed beyond June 4, when the Tiananmen Massacre took place, my dream of studying abroad would have been crushed.

We returned to Urumchi and began preparing for my departure. On May 5, I left Urumchi for Guangzhou, and then on May 9, 1989, traveled to Hong Kong. Later that same day, I arrived in Seattle, where my American family, Dr. Lin Faulkner and his wife Lois Faulkner, along with their grandson, Cale Freepons, who was around seven years old, welcomed me at the Sea-Tac International Airport.

The Faulkners became my family away from home. I called them "Uncle Lin and Aunt Lois." From the very beginning, they welcomed me with open arms and enveloped me with warmth, care, and respect that I had never imagined possible. They made me feel a cherished member of their family. Uncle Lin and Aunt Lois, along with their children—Jenni, Ed, and Brent—treated me with kindness and understanding, making the move to a new country feel less daunting. Jenni, with her gentle and open-hearted nature, quickly became like a sister to me, always offering a listening ear and laughter in

CHAPTER SEVEN

times of homesickness. Ed, a veteran and former U.S. Navy, with his strong patriotism, quiet wisdom and dry humor, made me feel at ease, showing me the little things that made life in the United States easier to navigate. His wife Tammy taught me how to drive. And Brent, with his boundless energy and quiet personality, brought light and joy to every moment we spent together as family. Ed and Brent took me out to shoot guns. To that point, I had only seen guns in the movies, but on that day I actually experienced shooting with real bullets in an open field.

On June 4, 1989, when I had been living with them for just three weeks, I was invited to attend a high-school graduation ceremony. This was a novelty, as in China there were no such celebrations for educational milestones, and I was glad to be able to experience it. When I returned to the house that day, I could sense something was wrong as soon as I entered the door. Lin and Lois Faulkner both met me at the door, with drawn expressions as though something terrible had happened. Aunt Lois, as I called her, rushed forward and hugged me. She was shaking. Both were saying "Oh, Rushan, we're so sorry," over and over. Seeing I had no idea what was going on, she ushered me into the house. Leading me over to the television in the living room, she said, "You need to watch this."

I was confused, experiencing some whiplash from the beautiful graduation ceremony I'd just come from, now trying to parse the news broadcast with my limited English. As I watched, and they explained what was unfolding, my happiness began to turn to dread. I still remember what I saw on the screen. The image was dark, punctuated by flashes of light and sharp cracks. It was gunfire. People were screaming. And there was blood. A lot of blood. The text along the bottom of the screen read "Breaking News, Tiananmen Square, Beijing, China." Aunt Lois and Uncle Lin were trying to explain what was happening, but my English was not fluent enough yet for me to understand. She grabbed the dictionary, showing me the words she wanted to convey. The Chinese military had opened fire on the students protesting at Tiananmen Square.

I was shocked. As the three of us watched, Aunt Lois hugged me tight. I had tears in my eyes. For over an hour, we sat and watched the coverage, most of it going by too fast for me. Using the dictionary, they tried to translate for me as best they could. After an hour, they asked if I wanted to go to bed, but I could not tear myself away. I had to keep watching. After they both went to bed, I stayed up most of the night, trying to understand what I was seeing. I saw the gunfire and the tanks rolling into the square, the dead bodies.

My emotions were a mix of fear, heartbreak, and guilt. Friends back home, including Uerkesh Devlet (Wu'erkaixi), a leader of the student protests and a family friend who is Uyghur, were in the midst of it all. Our fathers had been old friends since university, adding a personal connection to my concern. I felt guilty for being safe in America while they faced danger, knowing that if I had still been in China, I wouldn't have been able to leave after such a massacre. This harsh crackdown would have been followed by severe penalties for anyone like me who was suspected of dissent. At the same time, I realized how fortunate I was to have people here to lean on, people with whom I could openly share my grief, a freedom I would never have had back home. Even in this simple thing, I felt the powerful difference of living in a free country.

As I processed what was happening, I was struck by the sheer brutality of the regime. Over the past thirty-five years, when I have explained to people how the Chinese government treats Uyghurs, the Tiananmen Square Massacre always comes to mind. I tell them, "Remember those students in Tiananmen Square? They were children of Chinese people. If the government can shoot at students from their own culture, imagine how they treat us." These students were unarmed, simply demanding basic human dignity, yet they were shot without mercy. As Uyghurs, we face this same cruelty every day, under a government that operates with utter barbarity and no humanity.

During my first year in the United States, the Faulkner family offered me a sense of belonging. Their care went far beyond simple hospitality; it was deep, genuine, and unwavering. They made sure I felt respected, valued, and included in everything, from family dinners to heartfelt conversations about our hopes and dreams. In those early days, they didn't just give me a roof over my head; they gave me a home, a sense of family, and a bond that would last a lifetime. Jenni, Ed, and Brent embraced me with open arms, treating me like a sister. Their genuine curiosity about my culture, combined with their warmth and openness, made my transition smoother than I ever thought possible. They became my steadfast pillars, offering me laughter, and

CHAPTER SEVEN

guidance in a foreign land. It was the love and care of this family that turned my journey in the United States into a homecoming, and I will forever be grateful for their kindness.

Through this time, the Faulkners came to have a greater understanding of the situation faced by the Uyghurs. They listened as I described the conditions I had come from, and the increasing oppression Uyghurs would come to face in the years to come.

The Faulkners continued to be like family to me as I grew into my career as an activist. In later years, after marrying and welcoming our second son, Shad, we chose his middle name, "Lindsay," as a tribute to Uncle Lin. His pivotal support in bringing me to America and providing the foundation for my new life was a gift I will always cherish, and naming our son after him was a small way to honor his kindness and generosity.

When Dr. and Mrs. Faulkner passed away, I attended both of their funerals. I still keep in touch with Jenni, Ed, and Brent, whom I also consider my family. When I think back on the love and care the Faulkners showed me during my early days in the United States, their compassion and respect, I wonder what they would think if they were alive today. I know I am where I am today because of them, and though they would be heartbroken at how the plight of the Uyghurs has escalated, I believe they would be proud of the work we have done. Without their kindness and generosity, I may well have been imprisoned, wasting away in a jail cell or concentration camp back home. As much as anyone, I owe them my life.

* * *

In the summer of 1990, while I was studying at Washington State, I visited my family in Urumchi. When I arrived, it had been about three months since the Barin Massacre had happened. My father, with tears streaming down his face, recounted the horrifying events that began on April 5, 1990.

According to my father, when some of the Uyghur youth in Barin seized the weapons of Chinese police officers during an attempted arrest, it sparked an armed incident. But the Chinese authorities didn't just target the insurgents;

they unleashed a brutal military response. Heavily armed forces, equipped with heavy weaponry and countless helicopters, descended on Barin, turning it into a war zone. Innocent mothers, babies in their cradles, young children playing on the streets, and elderly grandparents nearing the end of their lives were slaughtered in this massacre. Even Tömür Dawamat, the CCP's puppet governor of the Uyghur Autonomous Region, was reportedly reduced to tears when he saw the bodies of children piled like stones during his inspection. This horrifying event left a deep, indelible mark on me.

After returning to America that year, I took it upon myself to gather and organize the information surrounding the massacre, the Barin Massacre. I presented this evidence to Congressman Sid Morrison (WA-R) in his Washington State office during my first-ever meeting with a US congressional representative. I didn't just present the facts—I voiced my complaints and passionately demanded that the American government take a stand for the Uyghur people, who were suffering under grave injustices. This pivotal moment marked the beginning of my ongoing advocacy for my people. It also launched my efforts to bring the true situation of my homeland to the attention of the American Congress and government, igniting a fire within me that has never been extinguished.

Within a year of starting my advocacy work for Uyghurs in America, and as a consequence of my activism and of my brother Rishat in the United States, my father, who had just turned fifty-eight in 1991, was removed from his position as chairman of the Science and Technology Society, isolating him from his meaningful work. At that time, the Chinese government was concerned about my father's strong influence among Uyghur intellectuals and within the Uyghur community. Rather than simply leaving him without a job, they gave him an empty title: "Member of the Political Consultative Conference of the Uyghur Autonomous Region." In the end, my father paid the price for my actions, but I know he didn't blame me. He was proud of my work, especially in speaking out for the victims in Barin. His lifelong support and the values he instilled in me gave me the strength to do what was right. It was exactly what he would have expected from me.

On February 5, 1997, thousands of Uyghurs gathered in Ghulja to protest government policies, demanding better treatment. The peaceful demonstration focused on grievances over religious and cultural restrictions and the detention of Uyghur leaders. As tensions escalated, Chinese security forces intervened with live ammunition and tear gas, resulting in indiscriminate shootings and arrests. The official government tally reported only nine dead, but estimates suggest hundreds. After the incident, the Chinese government imposed strict measures, arresting thousands and executing dozens of Uyghur youth in Ghulja. The incident sparked global condemnation, with calls for an independent investigation.

Canadian Uyghur intellectual Gulshen Abduqadir courageously documented this atrocity, capturing its harrowing details in two powerful books (volume 1 and volume 2) titled February 5th Archives. Through meticulous research and firsthand accounts, she exposes the brutal torture, mass arrests, and relentless persecution that followed. Her work stands as a testament to the resilience of the Uyghur people and serves as an unflinching record of the Chinese government's ruthless crackdown, ensuring that the voices of the victims are neither silenced nor forgotten.

Twelve years later, on July 5, 2009, while we were in Germany celebrating Mr. Erkin Alptekin's seventieth birthday, we received the heartbreaking news of another violent crackdown on Uyghur protesters in Urumchi. This was a somber moment, as it underscored the relentless oppression faced by our people even as we celebrated the life of one of our most steadfast leaders. Erkin Alptekin, born in Kashgar in 1939, is the embodiment of resilience and leadership. His journey began with the 1949 Chinese occupation, forcing his family into exile. From Kashmir to Turkey, and eventually to Germany in 1971, Alptekin's life has been marked by his unwavering dedication to the Uyghur cause. Educated in Kashmir and Istanbul, he became a powerful voice for Uyghur advocacy as he worked for Radio Free Europe/Radio Liberty, shining a light on the Uyghur struggle on the global stage.

A pioneering leader, Alptekin co-founded the Unrepresented Nations and Peoples Organization (UNPO) in 1991, uniting Uyghur exiles in a collective fight for justice. In 2004, he became the first president of the World Uyghur Congress (WUC), leading global efforts to expose China's brutal repression of the Uyghur people. Fluent in Uyghur, Turkish, English, and German, Alptekin has spoken at countless conferences, advocating for the survival and dignity of his people. Today, as a revered figure in the Uyghur diaspora, Alptekin is seen as a guiding force in the movement for freedom and human rights. His legacy is not just as a prominent leader, but as a beacon of hope for those fighting against oppression. Mr. Alptekin's commitment to the Uyghur cause remains unwavering, a testament to his indomitable spirit and dedication to his people's survival.

CHAPTER EIGHT
GUANTÁNAMO

In 1993, while working as a research technician at the Washington State University Irrigated Agricultural Research and Extension Center in Prosser, Washington, I co-founded the Tengritagh Uyghur Overseas Student and Scholars Association, the first Uyghur association in the United States, alongside one of the most prominent Uyghur scientists, and Uyghur advocate Dr. Erkin Sidik, from California. As the organization's first vice president, I helped draft a charter that would later serve as a blueprint for future Uyghur advocacy efforts. This foundational work paved the way for the establishment of the Uyghur American Association (UAA) in 1998—a community-based organization that remains central to the Uyghur diaspora's struggle for human rights and cultural preservation. My brother, Dr. Rishat Abbas, was a founding member and the first elected president of the UAA, and I had the privilege of serving as its vice president for two terms, in 2000 and again in 2006. Throughout these years, I remained committed to amplifying Uyghur voices on the international stage.

In 1998, Radio Free Asia launched its Uyghur Service in Washington, DC, breaking the information blackout imposed by the Chinese regime. That same year, I became the first Uyghur journalist to broadcast daily reports to the Uyghur region, providing uncensored news and vital information to my people. This work served as a bridge connecting Uyghurs to the outside world and marked the beginning of my lifelong commitment to defending the truth.

After resigning from my position as a reporter/broadcaster at Radio Free Asia due to family reasons, I returned to California, determined to expand my knowledge and chart a new path. In 2000, I pursued graduate studies at California State University, Fresno. By 2002, I had transitioned into the field of international business, working as an International Program Manager navigating the complexities of global business while bridging cultures across continents.

During this time, I built a life rooted in hope, resilience, and purpose. I married and became a mother to three wonderful children—each a symbol of the future I dreamed of not only for my own family but for the Uyghur people. While balancing the demands of motherhood and a successful career, my heart and mind never strayed far from my homeland. I remained an advocate for Uyghur human rights, speaking out against injustice and using every opportunity to raise awareness. My life has been shaped by the pursuit of knowledge, the strength of family, and the unwavering commitment to the struggle for freedom and dignity of my people.

* * *

On the morning of September 11, 2001, I was living in California. I had a habit of turning on the TV to listen to news first thing in the morning as I went about my morning routine. What I saw that day shocked and terrified me. The first tower in the World Trade Center had been hit, and as I watched the live coverage from my bed, I witnessed the second tower being struck. It felt like a surreal scene from some terrible movie. I had been living in the United States for more than a decade, and in that time, I had stood at the top of those towers, taking in the Manhattan skyline.

To carry out the September 11 attacks, four planes had been hijacked by nineteen al-Qaeda terrorists. They crashed two planes into the Twin Towers in New York, one into the Pentagon, and the fourth, United Airlines Flight 93, into a field in Pennsylvania after passengers fought back. Nearly three thousand people were killed, and there was widespread destruction. As a Muslim-American, I was shocked to learn that the terrorists were Muslims, as I know Islam to be a peaceful religion. I couldn't understand how they could justify such violence in the name of faith.

In March 2002, about six months after the 9/11 attacks and almost thirteen years after I arrived in America, I was again watching the morning

CHAPTER EIGHT

news when I got a call. The voice on the other end asked, "Is this Rushan Abbas?" and said they had been trying to reach me for weeks. The caller, a VP from L-3 Communications, a US defense contractor, explained they needed my help interpreting for Uyghurs sent by the United States to the Guantanamo Bay detention camp in Cuba. Surprised to hear his request, I asked the caller to confirm whether it was true that they wanted me to go to Guantánamo Bay and translate there. The caller acknowledged that this was what they wanted.

I had heard about a small number of Uyghurs detained on the Afghanistan-Pakistan border and sent to Guantánamo Bay, but I didn't know the specifics, but when I was contacted to interpret for them, I saw it as an opportunity to learn their stories—how they ended up in Afghanistan and why they were detained—and to provide language support for them. It was also a chance to serve my adopted country by answering the call when it needed my service. As one of the few Uyghur citizens in America at the time, I had the unique privilege of receiving security clearance and access to sensitive information.

When I asked the caller when I would be going there—if I agreed to go—his reply was even more interesting. "We needed you there yesterday," he said. This was indeed a strong indication of the very short preparation time and of the urgent need for an Uyghur person like myself, who had a good command of English, to provide translation. After mutual confirmation for the last time, I hung up the phone.

The most difficult part of deciding to go was my children. Knowing I would be away from them, I hesitated. I also didn't know how they would react. My eldest son, Misron, was almost eleven, Shad was nearly eight, and my daughter, Shireen, was only five. The thought of being away from my children, knowing how much they depended on me and how much I cherished my time with them, broke my heart. I could already feel the ache of longing and the emptiness that would come. In that moment, my love for them only deepened, and I resolved that no matter what the cost, I would do everything I could to stay connected to them while I was in Guantánamo. My one non-negotiable demand with the contractor was frequent visits to my family. Nothing mattered more than my children. They were my heart, and I would carry that love with me wherever I went, no matter how far away.

A few days later, after going through government background checks for security clearance and other necessary steps for my deployment, I was sent for a short training program at the Fort Benning, US Military Conus Replacement Center in a Georgia-based unit. At first, I was uneasy when we were issued camouflage military clothing, and a duffel bag full of equipment and safety gear. During the training, they even explained how to use the gas masks issued to us.

After two weeks of basic training, while we were signing out at the final release station before deployment, I was asked the question that shocked me the most:

"Who is your next of kin for your remains?"

"Excuse me?" I responded. The marine repeated his question. Shocked by the question, I was still not able to answer him.

"Who will claim your remains if something happens to you?" he reiterated. I had a hard time understanding what they meant by saying *"remains."*

"Wait! I'm not a soldier. I'm not going to the war zone. I have been told to translate in Guantánamo Bay, but not in an active war zone where there will be a question of facing such a situation. What do you mean by 'what is left of you'?" The soldier who asked the question replied in the same way without disturbing his composure.

"Who will claim your body if you die, Ma'am?" I was appalled. I was about to say, "Forget it. I am not going to go. I am not in the military thus, no one can force me to!" However, I overcame the shock at words like *body* and *remains* by remembering my sense of responsibility to serve the country when I was needed. I had taken an oath to become an American citizen and pledged myself to the country and flag. I was also dedicated to providing linguistic support to my fellow Uyghurs while they were in detention. However, this question seemed to signal the difficulty of the mission I was going to undertake. It may have been merely standard procedure, but I was left with the grim sense that, to these military personnel, my death was not outside the realm of possibility. I finally started to tell him my next of kin.

After the training and preparations were completed, I set out for Guantánamo Bay in early April 2002. The Guantánamo Bay American

CHAPTER EIGHT

Naval Base is located in an area of 116 square km (45 square miles) in the Gulf of Cuba off the Atlantic Ocean in the North American continent. The base is also known by the name "GTMO," or "Gitmo."

Guantánamo Bay, established in 1898 after the Spanish-American War, was leased to the United States in 1903 under the Platt Amendment, allowing the United States to use it for military purposes. Despite changes in Cuba's government, the United States maintained control, paying an annual rent of $2,000. Initially a naval training center, it later provided shelter for Haitian refugees in 1993. After the September 11, 2001 attacks, the United States turned Guantánamo Bay into a military prison as part of its War on Terror, the purpose for which it is most widely known today.

The camps at Guantánamo were named using the North Atlantic Treaty Organization (NATO) phonetic alphabet, such as Camp Echo or Camp X-Ray. In January 2002, three months before my arrival, detainees from Camp X-Ray were moved to Camp Delta. Over time, more detainees arrived, and Camp Delta expanded to include 612 cells. As some sections closed, new camps were built (e.g., Camps 4, 5, and 6).

In 2002, after the September 11 attacks, the United States established two military units as a part of Operation Enduring Freedom: JTF-170, which managed the Guantánamo detention facility, and JTF-160, which handled legal and administrative operations. Both units were criticized for controversial practices. I was assigned to JTF-170 and, as the only Uyghur linguist available, worked closely with JTF-160, translating for military police and the medical team.

When I arrived in Guantánamo in April 2002, only four Uyghurs had been transferred in February 2002, and none had an interpreter. They had been waiting for two months without anyone who understood their language.

The official procedures for my translation work at the base, such as determining the place where I would stay, were completed on the first day of my arrival. Since I was initially the only female civilian contractor at the base, my living quarters were in the cul-de-sac where the commander of the base, Major General Michael Dunleavy, colonels, and lieutenant colonels in charge of the intel and other camp operations were staying.

During the nine months I spent on the base, I dedicated countless hours to engaging with officers, sharing the painful truths of Beijing's relentless oppression of the Uyghur people. Each conversation became an opportunity to shed light on the suffering and injustice faced by my people. I found myself driven by a profound sense of responsibility—to not only advocate for the voiceless Uyghurs but to ensure that the world understood the full extent of the brutality and repression my community endured. These conversations were a way to humanize the tragedy and push back against the silence that had long surrounded the Uyghur plight.

* * *

I began my translation mission wearing green camouflage. I was all dressed in military uniform. The interrogators took me to the interrogation room for my first translation. The Uyghur prisoner Adel Noori, hands and feet chained, was escorted by three or four guards, creating an atmosphere of tension. As I entered the room, I was nervous, unsure of who I was about to meet—he could have been a terrorist. Adel sat in the small, metal-walled room, chained to iron rings on the floor. I sat with two Defense Department interrogators and an FBI agent, while others observed from behind a glass partition. After everyone took their places, the lead interrogator said "Hello," and made a quick introduction to the Uyghur detainee. After that, I asked the interrogators to unchain Adel. The others agreed to the removal of the chains and let him sit freely, with only shackles on his feet chained to the ring on the ground.

The interrogation began with Adel introducing himself and discussing his journey—why he left home, where he went, and his reasons for traveling to Afghanistan. They asked about his links to al-Qaeda, his activities, and weapons training. Adel, unaware of the September 11 attacks, expressed condolences upon hearing about them, as did the other Uyghur detainees. They all shared the belief that such actions contradicted Islam.

Adel shared that he was born in Aksu, in 1969, and studies in Islamic subjects after completing his education. Due to increasing pressure from

CHAPTER EIGHT

Chinese authorities on religious life,[18] he migrated to Kyrgyzstan in 1994, where he engaged in trade and teaching. His sense of security was shaken after the rise of the Shanghai Cooperation Organization (SCO).

Formed in 1996 as the Shanghai Five, the SCO became a platform for China's push to repatriate Uyghurs. Intelligence sharing led to Uyghurs being tracked and returned to China, where they faced detention or disappearance. As China's influence grew, Adel's safety in Kyrgyzstan was increasingly at risk. The only safe option for Uyghur refugees was to seek asylum in Afghanistan, where they were protected from China's extradition demands. Life was peaceful until the September 11 attacks, after which Adel fled to Pakistan, only to be betrayed and sold to American soldiers as a "foreign fighter."

After 9/11, the United States offered rewards for capturing suspected terrorists in Afghanistan and Pakistan. Villagers, eager for money, handed over people like Adel for rewards of $5,000 to $7,000. Adel was held in Lahore for forty-five days, then transferred to Kandahar for two months before being sent to Guantanamo as a "terrorist suspect."

During interrogation, it was clear Adel had fled East Turkistan to escape Chinese oppression. He preferred staying in US custody rather than being sent back to China. At the end of the session, Adel asked to speak with me, and he said, "I am so happy to see you here. You are Rushan Abbas. I used to listen to your voice on Radio Free Asia Uyghur program." The interrogators were surprised, and after a brief exchange, we left the room. The interrogators understood that many Uyghurs recognized my name and voice from my work at Radio Free Asia's Uyghur Service.

This unexpected recognition of the detainee created some concerns for my safety with the higher-ups in the chain of command. Later that day, the base commander, Major General Dunleavy, asked me if I felt safe to continue my translation work after being recognized by one of the terrorist suspects. I said, "The Uyghur detainee has nothing against America, it is allies or the

---

18. After the collapse of the Soviet Union in 1991, the Chinese Communist Party (CCP) began labeling anyone with a strong Uyghur ethnic or national identity as a "separatist" and intensified restrictions on religious studies in the Uyghur region.

Americans. He is in this position today due to the persecution of the Chinese regime. I am here with the US military and as an American citizen. I don't fear any danger from him or his recognition."

That evening, I experienced a deep sense of sadness. I could not sleep for hours; The suffering of the Uyghur people, the massacres at Barin in 1990 and Ghulja in 1997, and the troubles that my family had gone through during the Cultural Revolution when I was born ran through my head like a film strip.

By June 2002, I was told that the remainder of the Uyghur detainees had been brought to the camp. When I got there to see the new arrivals all I saw was fifty or sixty men in identical orange jumpsuits. There was one way I knew I could find them, though. I began to yell and shout in the Uyghur language, "Are there any Uyghurs here? Anybody who's Uyghur? Can anybody hear me who's Uyghur?" Eventually I began hearing responses, first from one corner, then another:

> I am Uyghur!
> I am Uyghur!
> I am Uyghur!

I was the only Uyghur interpreter for the twenty-two Uyghurs at Guantánamo, handling both interrogations and daily tasks. Unlike those dealing with other languages, which had separate interpreters for different needs, I was called in day and night for emergencies, medical issues, and military police matters and working for interrogations, medical staff, and guards, even on weekends.

For nearly two months, I worked non-stop, without taking a day off, assisting Uyghur detainees with health concerns, guard interactions, and daily life. I became a mother figure to them and was respected by both detainees and the military police. I built connections with the guards, sharing meals and small gestures of kindness. Once they moved to Camp 4 and more interpreters arrived, my workload eased.

During my time at the camp, the detainees' basic needs were met, including halal meat and fresh fruit with meals. Long interrogation sessions often made me miss meals at the chow hall, and by day's end, only McDonald's

CHAPTER EIGHT

from the Naval Exchange was available, which I didn't prefer. I used to joke with the Uyghur detainees that the food prepared for them by the Afghan chef was much better than my MREs[19] (Meals Ready-to-Eat), which were already a couple of years old.

One day, I was called to the hospital section instead of the interrogation room. I met Uyghur detainee Abu Bakr Qasim, who was being treated for malaria. I greeted him in Uyghur, "*Salamelleykum, yahshimusiz?*" How are you? Still groggy from medication, he recognized my voice and, relieved, replied, "I am fine, thanks. Why am I here?"

Abu Bakr's eyes were blurry and tired from blood tests. Nearly a year after 9/11, he still hadn't heard the details of the attacks. We explained that he and twenty-one other Uyghurs were also brought to Guantánamo. He explained his situation and said that his only conflict was with China, which had forced him to flee Ghulja. He expressed relief at being in US custody rather than facing repatriation to China. Three days later, I returned to escort Abu Bakr to the detention camp.

In a 2006 interview after his release, he reflected on his difficult childhood in Ghulja. Forced to leave school in eighth grade due to financial struggles, he worked in a leather factory until it closed in 1990. Seeking opportunities, he moved to Guangzhou to trade goods but found it hard to earn a living. Returning to Ghulja in 1997, he was deeply affected by the aftermath of the Ghulja Massacre and the crackdown on Uyghur religious practices. Though his faith was basic, he saw religion as resistance. Inspired by young Uyghurs advocating for faith and identity, he began studying Islam while supporting himself by selling strawberries. A year later, on his way to work, Abu Bakr was arrested and accused of "separatism." He endured a week of brutal interrogation, including electric baton torture, and was forced to confess to false charges. After seven months of abuse in prison, he was released due to lack of evidence but remained under constant surveillance. Realizing he had to escape, he struggled to obtain a passport but eventually secured a one-year business visa. In June 2000, he left for Kyrgyzstan, hoping to trade

---

19. MREs are designed to sustain soldiers in combat or field conditions where traditional cooking is not possible, MREs come in sealed pouches, require no refrigeration, and have a long shelf life of three to five years.

and stay close to his family. However, due to Kyrgyzstan's ties with China through the Shanghai Cooperation Organization, Uyghurs were monitored. As his passport neared expiration, he felt trapped and sought another way out.

In July 2001, Abu Bakr crossed into Afghanistan, reaching an Uyghur neighborhood in a village near Tora Bora with about thirty Uyghur refugees. Welcomed with shelter, Abu Bakr spent his days reading the Quran, and repairing houses. The remote village had no electricity and was cut off from the world, with residents taking turns guarding against bandits. Despite China's pressure, the Taliban allowed Uyghurs to stay without questioning their documents. Two months later, the border closed unexpectedly. With no radio, Abu Bakr and the others remained unaware that the September 11 attacks had changed their fate.

On October 8, 2001, the United States launched airstrikes in Afghanistan, targeting Taliban and al-Qaeda sites, including the Tora Bora mountains. That same day, the Uyghur village was bombed. Amid the chaos, someone shouted, "Run to the cave!" Abu Bakr and others fled, staying hidden until the bombing stopped. Returning briefly, they salvaged some dates and bread from the ruins before escaping back to the cave. However, monkeys in the cave harassed them, competing for food and lodging. They endured over a month in the mountains, but as winter set in, survival became impossible. An elder advised them to flee to Pakistan, a neighboring Muslim country. The eighteen Uyghurs, struggling with severe cold and snow, traveled through remote areas to avoid airstrikes. After days of travel, they reached the Pakistani border and found refuge in the first village they encountered. Fearing deportation to China, they introduced themselves as "Uzbeks" from Afghanistan. The locals welcomed them warmly, saying, "Oh, our brothers are here. Welcome." The villagers' warm welcome quickly turned to betrayal when their leader warned of soldiers searching for foreigners. Abu Bakr and the others were taken to a mosque-like building, which was actually a prison. There, they realized they had been sold. Pakistani soldiers soon arrived, and the villagers admitted to selling the Uyghurs for $5,000 each as "foreign fighters" under the US bounty program. Shackled again, Abu Bakr and eighteen others spent two weeks in a Pakistani prison before being handed to US forces. In Kandahar, they endured harsh treatment but felt relieved to reveal their true identities as Uyghurs. After

CHAPTER EIGHT

interrogation, the US military realized the Uyghurs were in the wrong place at the wrong time. They were told they weren't enemies of the United States and would be released soon. However, despite these promises, Abu Bakr remained a prisoner in Kandahar for almost six months without proper language support, before being transferred to Guantánamo in June 2002.

In 2002, as the United States sought UN approval for a war in Iraq, it agreed to label the East Turkistan Islamic Movement as a terrorist group per Beijing's request, to secure China's support. Dr. Sean Roberts, professor of the Practice of International Affairs at the Elliott School of George Washington University, prominent scholar specializing in Uyghur issues, and the author of *The War on the Uyghurs: China's Internal Campaign Against a Muslim Minority*, has critically examined the Chinese government's claims about the East Turkistan Islamic Movement (ETIM). He questions the actual existence of ETIM. Overall, Dr. Roberts argues that the ETIM label has been instrumentalized by Beijing to frame its policies in Xinjiang as counterterrorism rather than ethnic persecution. ETIM was removed from the US Department of State's list of designated Foreign Terrorist Organizations (FTOs) and Specially Designated Global Terrorists (SDGTs) in 2020, during the first Trump administration.

In September 2002, a Chinese intelligence team came to Guantánamo by permission of the US government. Chinese interrogators subjected Uyghur detainees to extreme cold, forcing them to sit in freezing rooms for hours or days. During my time at GTMO, this was the only instance of intentional mistreatment of the Uyghur detainees. The United States handed over all twenty-two Uyghur detainee files to the Chinese. They were also allowed to take Uyghur detainees' pictures.

During my time as an interpreter, from April to December 2002, the interrogators from all the agencies were telling the Uyghur detainees that they were in the wrong place at the wrong time. When I returned home for my daughter's birthday on November 1, 2002, I signed divorce papers with my children's father. Then I returned to the base. By then, I had been working with the joint task force in Guantánamo for nine months. The interrogators were losing interest in meeting with Uyghurs, and I felt that my responsibility in GTMO was ending. I gave notice to my commanding officer, Colonel

Cummings, telling him that I was returning home to my children as soon as possible and left the base in mid-December 2002.

***

Despite the United States receiving no support from China for the Iraq war, Uyghur detainees remained at Guantánamo Bay due to Beijing's interference with their resettlement. The US government had no plans to continue holding them, but the detainees, as non-US citizens held outside the United States, lacked the right to appeal in federal court. In 2004, the Supreme Court ruled to grant *habeas corpus* rights to Guantánamo detainees, allowing them to petition for release. Abu Bakr Qasim was among the first Uyghurs to request counsel from the Center for Constitutional Rights. Sabin Willett of the Bingham McCutchen law firm took them on as clients in early 2005, as part of the firm's pro bono cases.

Sabin Willett, an accomplished attorney, played a pivotal role in representing former Uyghur detainees at Guantánamo Bay, fiercely advocating for their release after they were wrongfully detained. With unwavering commitment, he challenged their indefinite detention, securing the freedom of many and facilitating their relocation to third countries to escape the threat of torture and persecution by China. His tireless legal efforts have been instrumental in advancing the broader human rights campaign for Uyghurs, ensuring their voices and rights were heard.

While preparing for their cases, Sabin Willett began studying the Uyghurs, but before he received clearance to enter Guantánamo, the military tribunal (commission) ruled on five Uyghurs' cases, including those of Abu Bakr clearing them as "non-enemy combatant[s]" and promising their release. Sabin met Abu Bakr in July 2005, finding him shackled despite being declared innocent. Shocked, Sabin said, "Under American law, innocent people are not shackled!" This sparked media attention and led to their case being heard in the DC District Court. However, Judge James Robertson dismissed the case, claiming he lacked the authority to order their release. While the ruling was under appeal by Sabin Willett and his team, five Uyghurs were sent to

CHAPTER EIGHT

Albania in May 2006. The following day, Beijing protested, calling them terrorists and demanding their repatriation from Albania.

Seventeen Uyghur detainees remained in Guantánamo, where lawyers struggled with a lack of proper Uyghur translators. Sabin avoided government interpreters due to trust issues, using scattered Arabic phrases and an Arabic translator. Eventually, the detainees requested me by name: "Get Rushan."

In spring 2006, Sabin Willett and I connected, and I returned to Guantánamo as a freelance interpreter. Between then and 2009, before moving to Virginia, I made nearly thirty short trips from California to Guantánamo to assist with the cases. When I left Guantánamo in 2002, my work felt unfinished, leaving me unsure if the Uyghurs would find safety. I felt I had the chance to help secure their resettlement.

On June 12, 2008, the US Supreme Court ruled in favor of the Center for Constitutional Rights in the case regarding Guantánamo detainees' right to challenge their detention in US courts. This meant the case would now come before judge Ricardo M. Urbina in the Washington, DC Federal Court. When he asked if the Uyghurs were enemy combatants, government representatives said no. Judge Urbina asked them to tell him what danger the Uyghurs posed to the United States or its allies. Again, the government representatives said they had absolutely no evidence. However, when the judge asked what the government was going to do about releasing the Uyghur detainees, they said they could not, for a variety of reasons. The main one was of course that the Uyghurs would have to be placed in other countries due to the Chinese government's oppression, and the arrangements had not yet been made. He then asked them if they planned to hold the Uyghurs indefinitely. After some hesitation, the representatives replied "yes." Judge Urbina was offended by this and responded by ordering that the Uyghurs be brought to the United States to appear before him in his courtroom.

I was back at Guantánamo that morning, meeting the Uyghurs with the rest of their attorneys. We were standing on one side of the chain link fence in Camp Iguana. On the other side, the seventeen Uyghurs were lined up in front of me. "The district court heard your case this morning," I told them, "and Judge Urbina has delivered his decision." Then, I found I couldn't continue. My voice shook. At that moment, I could hear a pin drop. They were all just looking at me. All we could hear were the waves of the ocean on the shore nearby, somewhere beyond the camps. Finally, I found my voice again. "Judge Urbina has ordered the government to bring you all to his courtroom in Washington."

The silence continued. They remained standing before me on the other side of the fence, speechless. But I could sense the joy and the feeling of hope gripping them. The next day, as I was leaving the base, I saw that there was a plane at Guantánamo Airport waiting to take them. I was relieved as I boarded my flight. As I landed in Fort Lauderdale, however, I turned on my phone and saw an email from Sabin. The government had gone to the Court of Appeals and put a stop to Judge Urbina's order. Before the Uyghurs boarded the plane, the decision was delivered to the base. I just sat there, staring at my phone, filled with a sense of dread. In limbo, the Uyghurs at Guantánamo were no longer prisoners but had nowhere to go. Eventually, they were moved to a "better place," as one Uyghur detainee told an interviewer at National Public Radio (NPR) after his release, where they could exercise freely and were treated differently. He noted, "The guards knew we were innocent and should be free, but no country would take us because of China."

Working with President Barack Obama's attorney, Greg Craig, we secured a deal to bring four Uyghur detainees to Virginia, where the community had even rented an apartment for them. But when the plan was leaked, Congress swiftly banned detainee transfers to US soil, and Obama signed the bill, derailing the effort. China continued blocking resettlement, falsely labeling the Uyghurs as terrorists. Despite their ordeal, the detainees preferred US custody over the risk of being sent to China. Though declared innocent, their frustration mounted as their cases stalled and no country would take them. In June 2009, after negotiations between Sabin Willett's team and President Obama's legal counsel, Bermuda agreed to take four Uyghur detainees to aid in closing Guantánamo. With less than an hour's notice (to prevent leaks), the chosen four Uyghurs said quick goodbyes, exchanging prayers with those left behind. I got on the bus at the airport to accompany them to the State Department's private plane with Sabin and other attorneys. There was excitement in the air. I could not hide my joy from them. I had the privilege of telling them there was a plane there for them, and we were here to get them

CHAPTER EIGHT

out. I was finally able to tell them, "You will be free." Thirteen Uyghurs were left in Guantánamo.

When we were descending to Bermuda, the former Uyghur prisoners contacted their families. In fact, they had started as soon as the plane had begun its approach to the shore, and my phone had only a few bars of signal left. They called their mothers and sisters to tell them they were finally free. When Khalil asked Sabin if any Uyghur had been in Bermuda before, he replied, "Whomever among you steps on Bermuda's soil first is the first Uyghur here!"

President Obama's personal attorney, Greg Craig, and Ambassador Daniel Fried, who was appointed Ambassador-at-Large to oversee the resettlement or closure of Guantánamo Bay, played a crucial role in the negotiations. They handled the process of relocating the Uyghurs to Bermuda with extreme secrecy, concerned that if the Chinese government found out it would interfere and obstruct the transfer. Even within Bermuda, the plan was kept under wraps—only Premier Ewart Brown and his immigration minister were aware. Not even the premier's cabinet, MPs from his own party, or other government officials were informed.

We arrived in Bermuda at around 6:30 a.m., on June 11, 2009, accompanied by Sabin Willett, Greg Craig, and other government representatives. At 8:00 a.m., Premier Brown went live on television to announce the arrival of four Uyghurs from Guantánamo Bay. The revelation sent shockwaves through Bermuda. Government ministers were furious, the public was outraged, and protests erupted on the streets. Demonstrators accused the premier of making a unilateral decision without consulting the government, cabinet members, people in Bermuda or the UK government, which still held administrative oversight over Bermuda. The slogans were loud and clear: "Brown needs to go. The terrorists need to go. Take Slayton (US Consulate General in Bermuda, Gregory Slayton) and the terrorists and get out of Bermuda."

Initially, I had planned to stay only a few days, escorting the men to Bermuda and assisting with their settlement before departing. I had packed just a small carry-on with clothes for three or four days. But as the protests grew and tensions escalated, Premier Brown asked me to stay. He was worried—without me, who would communicate with the Uyghurs? They spoke no English, and the hostility in the streets needed to be countered with direct engagement and telling their stories and the Uyghurs' story, as back then, no one in Bermuda knew who the Uyghurs were.

So, we embarked on a mission per the Bermuda government's request. Every day, I took the four Uyghurs out to the streets, into the community, visiting shops, restaurants, and ice cream vendors. We spoke with ordinary Bermudians, explaining who the Uyghurs were and why they had been at Guantánamo. I told them about our people, about the persecution we faced in China, and why these men could not return home. The goal was simple: humanize them. In the evenings, we appeared on live television and radio programs taking questions, sharing our stories, and dispelling the fear-mongering narrative that had initially gripped the island.

Slowly, the mood began to shift. The protesters' chants and written slogans changed from "The Uyghurs must go" to "The Uyghurs can stay, but Brown must go." The anger was no longer directed at the men themselves but at Premier Brown's decision-making process, comparing him to a dictator and insinuating that Brown undermined democracy. After we spent days and days on the streets speaking to the general public, giving interviews and being in the media persistently, many now saw the Uyghurs not as terrorists but as victims of an unjust system. The public perception had transformed in a matter of days.

What was supposed to be a short trip stretched into seventeen days. I was still wearing the same set of clothes I had packed for a much shorter stay. Meanwhile, the controversy had reached the UK government, which had been blindsided by Bermuda's decision. Tensions ran high, and debates raged in Parliament. Legislators deliberated through the night in a heated session, arguing over whether Premier Brown had overstepped his authority. The vote finally took place in the early morning hours, after nearly fourteen hours of debate. The premier survived the motion by a single vote, narrowly avoiding a government collapse. I left Bermuda after the vote.

Ultimately, despite the political chaos, the Uyghurs remained in Bermuda and, over time, integrated into society. But their arrival had nearly dismantled an entire government, and for me, it was yet another chapter in the long, winding struggle to secure their freedom.

CHAPTER EIGHT

Almost four weeks after their arrival in Bermuda (by July 5, 2009), one Uyghur there was unable to reach his brother in Urumchi, despite making ten to fifteen attempts per day. At that time, Urumchi was under a communications blackout, and there were fears that large groups of Uyghurs were being rounded up by the government. The media blackout made it difficult for journalists to report accurately. It was later reported that a protest in Urumchi had quickly escalated into a violent massacre.

The incident began in a toy factory in Shaoguan, Guangdong, where more than eight hundred Uyghurs had been transferred from Kashgar under a labor program. On June 26, 2009, tensions between Han Chinese and Uyghur workers escalated into a violent attack. Later that night, thousands of Han Chinese, armed with iron clubs, stormed the factory, beating Uyghur workers outside their dorms and in the streets. The exact number of Uyghur deaths remains unclear, but at least thirty were reported killed, with some estimates suggesting a higher toll. Police did not intervene for hours, and bodies were left in the streets. Families in Kashgar who received the remains were threatened with eviction, land seizure, and imprisonment if they spoke out. On July 5, 2009, a protest in Urumchi was organized by Uyghurs to express their dissatisfaction with the government's downplaying of the incident. The protest was sparked by frustration over the government's handling of the situation, as well as their attempt to downplay or cover up the deaths of Uyghurs in the Shaoguan attack. The Uyghur protesters demanded justice, calling for accountability and an end to ethnic discrimination. The Chinese authorities responded with a heavy crackdown, using armed force to disperse the crowds. As in Tiananmen Square in 1989, the military responded to what began as a peaceful demonstration with machine guns and armored vehicles.

The death toll was estimated to be between eight hundred and one thousand, mostly Uyghurs, and those who mourned the fallen were detained. Bodies were buried in the desert to erase evidence. The event became known as the Urumchi Massacre. The Chinese government declared martial law and deployed thousands of troops to restore order. Two days later, Han Chinese immigrants attacked Uyghurs with machetes, clubs, and shovels, destroying shops and mosques, while police did nothing. Some suspect military personnel were involved, given the efficiency of the violence. Human Rights Watch later documented more than forty thousand Uyghurs who disappeared.

* * *

Meanwhile, back in Guantánamo, President Johnson Toribiong of Palau had offered in 2009 to resettle a group of Uyghur prisoners from Guantánamo. After months of negotiation, six Uyghurs were freed and welcomed to Palau in October 2009. I traveled there with Professor Jan Honigsberg and Mary Louise Zernicke from California for their Witness to Guantánamo project. The Uyghur men greeted us with smiles, though they faced challenges as stateless individuals without citizenship or proper documents. President Toribiong spent more than two hours with us, discussing politics and Uyghur culture and said that he enjoyed picnics with the Uyghur men. When Beijing pressured Palau to hand them over to China, the president boldly responded, "Take it up with the United States."

Eventually, two Uyghurs were accepted by Switzerland and two by El Salvador, while the last three were released to Slovakia on December 31, 2013, after eleven years in detention, all because Beijing blocked their resettlement to third countries.

During this time there was great interest in the plight of these men, and I was approached by several journalists to tell their story. I was approached, by a Canadian filmmaker named Patricio Henríquez. He had emigrated to Canada from Chile in 1974 to escape the political conditions of the dictatorship in his country, and I was able to connect with him immediately. He wanted to make a documentary film about the Uyghurs through the National Film Board of Canada. His own history as a refugee and the indignation he felt at the plight of the Uyghurs of Guantánamo told me he could be trusted to tell the story well. It was enough to help me convince the ex-Guantanamo detainees who he interviewed for the film to participate as well. His film was titled *Uyghurs: Prisoners of the Absurd*, and was released in 2014, and I was one of the main characters interviewed for the film, as well as Sabin Willett, Ambassador Daniel Fried, Judge Urbina, and some people from

CHAPTER EIGHT

the US State Department. The film was part human drama, part political thriller, and both thought-provoking and moving. In an interview, Patricio Henriquez said this about the Uyghurs' situation, "They were innocent. Not only innocent, but they were also people who were pro-America because they lived what they lived in China."

As an Uyghur-American, I deeply value free speech—a right many take for granted, but one denied to people in my homeland. In China, speaking out can lead to unimaginable consequences, with criticism met by brutal reprisals. In the United States, it's protected by law, offering a beacon of hope. In China, it's a risk that leads to disappearance. I am disappointed by the US government's failure to act against China's interference in the resettlement of Uyghur men, but despite the setbacks, I believe this long journey has ultimately bent towards justice, restoring freedom and dignity to the prisoners.

When the first five Uyghur detainees were released to Albania in 2006, my connection to my homeland was abruptly severed. Beijing branded them as "terrorists," and because I had served as their translator, I was blacklisted, accused of "providing material support for terrorism." Overnight, I became an enemy of the state, and my return to my homeland was permanently barred. My last visit home was in 2005, twenty years ago, when I traveled with Shad and Shireen to mark the one-year anniversary of my mother's passing. I did not know then that it would be my final goodbye—that the land of my ancestors would become a place I could never return to.

And today, the same Chinese government that banned me because of my translation work at Guantánamo is now weaponizing that very work against me—branding me a "Guantánamo torturer" and a "CIA agent," as CCP official Zhao Lijuan publicly tweeted alongside my photo after he blocked me on Twitter (now X) first. I wear these libelous attacks from the CCP and its officials as a badge of honor—proof that my work has had real impact. But what wounds me most is not Beijing's lies and propaganda; it is the criticism and sometime attacks that I face from some of my fellow Americans who are against the detention center in Guantánamo, who accuse me of "supporting the US operation in Guantánamo" simply because I played a critical role in securing the freedom of twenty-two Uyghurs who had been wrongfully detained.

UNBROKEN

CHAPTER NINE
TWO STARS DEPART FROM THE SKY

In his memoir "What I Witnessed," my father Abbas Borhan dedicated a section to my late mother, Mariye, who passed away on July 17, 2004. He wrote the following passage.

***

A star has departed from the sky of charity, kindness, and compassion. My children have lost their loving mother, and I lost my dear wife. Death is cruel. The doctors could not do anything for Mariye, who suddenly fell ill, had trouble breathing, and became unable to speak within a few hours. Her heart was failing. In the morning of the day, we lost her, she was walking around and hosting a few of my friends for lunch. Mariye passed away in the emergency department from sudden cardiac arrhythmia. From the time she felt sick to the time that we lost her was less than six hours. She was only sixty-six years old. We were left behind crying.

The late Mariye Abliz was born on March 18, 1938, in Kattaylaq Village in Artush County as the first child of Abliz Niyaz (born in 1915), who was a knowledge-loving man, and his wife Merejehan. She spent her childhood in that village and moved to Artush in the early 1940s. In 1946, her father, Niyaz, went to Urumchi to attend the coalition government election with the delegates of Southern Xinjiang, according to the 11-Point Treaty. The council, formation of government, and election were not realized. Abliz Niyaz, who was among the delegates who supported the Independent East Turkistan government, left for Ghulja with Ehmetjan Qasim,[20] where he became a chief inspector for the East Turkistan government. Three years after he left Artush, Abliz Niyaz joined Iminov and his division, and traveled to Kashgar through Muzdawan (Ice Mountain Pass). He then became County Governor and Chief Judge (*Hakim*) of Artush. In 1952, Mariye undertook a short-term medical course and worked at a hospital in Artush.

For four years, from 1952 to 1956, Mariye attended and graduated from the Xinjiang Medical Institute in Urumchi. She graduated at the top of her class, earning distinction for her exceptional academic achievements throughout medical school and became a doctor. She was then assigned to the Artush District Hospital. Mariye was highly respected among her teachers, classmates, and co-workers while attending school and working at the hospital.

In 1957, I came to Artush for a family visit after graduating from the Beijing Pedagogical University, and Mariye was working at the hospital. We met there and got married shortly after. We spent our entire lives with love and respect for each other. Together, we raised two sons, Nijat and Rishat, and two daughters, Gulshan and Rushan.

Our forty-seven years together passed in what felt like a single day, a lifetime of mutual respect, understanding, honesty, trust, and a deep, profound love. Mariye was the epitome of grace, gentleness, generosity, kindness, and forgiveness. In every aspect of life she was a beacon of hard work and dedication, never missing a beat—whether it was in the home, raising our children, or helping them with their studies. Her work ethic was unparalleled, yet she never failed to treat everyone in the family with sincerity, respect, and honesty.

Even in the midst of the harshest times brought by the Cultural Revolution, when the world seemed to be crumbling around us, Mariye remained calm and strong. She was my friend, my most trusted advisor, and my greatest supporter. My academic achievements and teaching success at the university would have been unattainable without her dedication, support, and sharp

---

20. President of the East Turkistan Republic, founded in Ghulja in 1944. Among the Uyghurs and other Turkic people of East Turkistan, Ehmetjan Qasim is remembered as a national hero and fighter who died defending the independence of East Turkistan.

CHAPTER NINE

insights. She made it possible for me to focus on my work while she quietly managed the household, our children's upbringing, and their education.

Her devotion to our children was unmatched. Mariye poured her heart and soul into nurturing them, ensuring they had every opportunity to succeed. She was deeply invested in their lives, particularly their studies, and it was through her guidance that all four of our children graduated from universities—one even earned a PhD, and another a master's degree. Her influence on their lives was immeasurable, and her effort was the foundation of their success.

Mariye's professional journey was equally remarkable. In January 1957, she was transferred to the People's Hospital in Urumchi, and by February 1959, she began working at Xinjiang University Hospital as a primary care physician. She worked there for thirty years, from 1959 to 1989, until she retired due to her health. There are many medical doctors that have spent their lives seeing and treating patients. But doctors such as Mariye who are serious, responsible, kind, and gentle to patients, and respected and trusted by everyone including professors, students, and other university staff, are not too common. She treated her patients with compassion. She not only saw patients at the hospital, but she also visited the patients at their homes to attend to their illnesses. She responded to every call seeking help, whether it was during holidays, breaks, early days, or late nights.

At home, Mariye's devotion to our children shaped them intellectually, emotionally, and physically with love and care. She is focused on their academic education and also instilled in them a deep sense of responsibility and of the value of hard work. Her nurturing spirit extended far beyond traditional lessons—Mariye was a mother in every sense of the word, fully immersed in the lives of our children. She took enormous pride in helping them with their schoolwork, preparing their meals with love, sewing their clothes with her own hands, and teaching them the importance of thrift and frugality, values that would stay with them for a lifetime.

Even in the face of challenges, Mariye created a home filled with warmth and security, where our children could grow and thrive. She knew the importance of family and insisted that everyone contribute to the household. She taught them that chores weren't burdens, but valuable lessons in responsibility and teamwork. Our two sons sat beside her, learning the art of laundry, while our eldest daughter took responsibility for washing the dishes. Mariye also imparted her knowledge to Rushan, teaching her to cross-stitch, knit, and sew from a young age, instilling in her a sense of creativity and craftsmanship by the age of twelve or thirteen.

Mariye was a firm believer in hands-on learning, and she made sure our children learned essential life skills. She often arranged for them to bake and cook, to nurture their independence. Each lesson was for their growth, shaping them into responsible, caring individuals. Through every gesture, every moment spent teaching them with patience and love, Mariye provided our children with the tools to navigate the world, both practically and with integrity.

But it was her heart, her unshakable belief in kindness, that truly shaped them. One day, when our eldest son, Nijat, was less than fifteen years old, he saw an elderly man struggling to carry a heavy bag. Without hesitation, he offered his help, carrying the heavy bag all the way to the man's home which was almost two-and-a-half miles (4 km) away. The man came to our house later to express his gratitude, praising Nijat for being "a very good boy." This simple act of kindness was a reflection of Mariye's guidance: she taught our children to always be ready to lend a helping hand to those in need.

Even during the hardest years, Mariye's calm composure remained. She always had an eye out for the well-being of her loved ones, attending to their sicknesses, offering help with their work, and providing support in any way she could. She also loved her siblings and her nieces and nephews dearly, and her compassion was felt by all those who knew her.

As a mother, she had high expectations for our children's studies and their character. She taught them discipline, responsibility, and respect. Beyond that, she was always observant of their mental state, ensuring they were emotionally supported and encouraged. She created an environment that fostered peace and cooperation, teaching them to care for one another. Her influence shaped their hearts. It was through her influence that they grew into the successful, compassionate individuals they are today.

Mariye had a special place in her heart for the students at the university, particularly those from poor, rural backgrounds. She went above and beyond

CHAPTER NINE

to support them, taking the time to attend to their health needs and offering a compassionate ear. She opened our home to them, inviting students over and cooking for them, providing nourishment, encouragement and emotional support. She instilled confidence in them, reminding them that they had the ability to succeed.

Her medical expertise was widely respected at Xinjiang University, and people came from all over to seek her care. Even during the Cultural Revolution, when the country was in turmoil and her own family was being persecuted, Mariye did not stop seeing patients even as her own heart carried the weight of suffering. She was a constant source of healing, an angel of salvation for many. She was remembered fondly as a doctor who made a lasting impact on the lives of those she treated.

After retirement, when we visited our children in America or traveled to Canada, Türkiye, and Saudi Arabia, her former students would seek her out to express their gratitude and pay their respects. Mariye possessed an extraordinary ability to make sound, thoughtful judgments on both social and personal matters. She believed in the transformative power of patience and tolerance, often saying, "Forgiveness is the best virtue in the world." She instilled this philosophy in our children, teaching them that strength lay in grace. She was like a flourishing orchard, offering shade, nourishment, and warmth to everyone she encountered.

A couple of years after retiring from the hospital, Mariye embarked on a groundbreaking journey to empower countless Uyghur women and leave an indelible mark on her community. She opened a bakery called *Shireen Sweet*s, the first Uyghur pastry business in the Uyghur region, introducing traditional Uyghur desserts to the market and creating vital business and employment opportunities for Uyghur women. Mariye's vision extended far beyond her own bakery. She actively sought out women and girls from rural villages across both the southern and northern regions, bringing them to Urumchi to train them in the art of Uyghur pastry-making. With remarkable generosity, she provided this training for free, equipping them with the skills and confidence to return to their hometowns and open bakeries of their own. In doing so, she pioneered an industry that allowed thousands of retired and unemployed Uyghur women to carve out a sustainable livelihood, transforming their lives and their families' futures with a new business. The ripple effects of her efforts were profound. Over the years, hundreds of bakeries—both large and small—sprang up across the Uyghur homeland, thanks to Mariye's dedication and foresight. Through her work, Mariye preserved Uyghur culinary traditions and alleviated the economic and emotional burdens of families, offering dignity and economic independence to countless Uyghur women.

Yet, despite her success as an entrepreneur, Mariye never lost her deep sense of compassion. She remained a pillar of support for orphans, the sick, and the impoverished. On her frequent travels to the southern regions and rural countryside, she extended financial and emotional aid to those in need. Even in Urumchi she sought out strangers—people who had come for medical treatment but, due to financial hardship, had been forced to abandon their care—and ensured they received the help they needed.

Mariye's name, her legacy of unwavering kindness and generosity, lives on in the hearts of the Uyghur people as a symbol of resilience, empowerment, and the boundless impact of one woman's dedication to her community.

Mariye's impact reached the vast Uyghur community, but it was within our home that her love shone brightest. She felt profound pride and joy when our son Rishat earned his doctorate in pharmaceutical science from the Ohio State University, knowing that her sacrifices and guidance contributed to their success. Her love was the foundation upon which our family stood, and even now, her memory continues to inspire us.

Her resilience was unparalleled. During the dark and brutal years of the Cultural Revolution, when both her beloved father, Abliz Niyaz, and I were persecuted, she held our family together. When I was dragged away for endless "struggle sessions," she never once showed resentment or fear; instead, she welcomed me home each evening with beautiful smile and comforting words. For me it was "even if it's a stormy day outside, it's spring at home."

But the cruelty did not spare her. In 1972, she was forcibly removed from her medical practice and sent for supervised physical labor, falsely accused of being a "Local Nationalist" and a "Black Communicator of the Iminov Group." A year later, in 1973, when the government finally admitted its mistake and restored her name, offering a hollow apology: "We made a mistake, we wrongly punished Mariye"—the damage had already been done. The

CHAPTER NINE

injustice, the humiliation, and the unbearable pain of seeing her father and husband persecuted had left deep scars. It was in those times that her heart started to have atrial fibrillation, and from the age of thirty-five she battled heart problems, a silent wound inflicted by injustice.

That wound finally took her from us on the night of July 17, 2004, at 10:30 p.m. She left without a final word to her four children, without a farewell to the husband who had stood by her side for forty-seven years. She bore so much in silence, giving more than she ever received, and in the end, it was not just heart disease that took her: it was the burden of a life spent enduring, fighting, and sacrificing for those she loved.

Mariye was more than a wife, a mother, or a healer. She was the quiet strength that carried us all. And though she is gone, her love, her wisdom, and her spirit remain with us, guiding us forward.

This memoir included my father's poem dedicated to my mother when she passed away and carved in her gravestone (original in Uyghur):

> Your youth was gone with hardship (*Yashlighing otti japaliq ejir bilen*),
>
> Your noble character will never die (*Xisliting ochmes el ichide mihir bilen*).
>
> You'd give up everything for me and children (*Jan-pida iding men we ballar uchun*),
>
> I am bound to you forever my beloved (*Rishtim menggu birge sen qedirlik hemra bilen*).

* * *

In 1975, my mother went to Shanghai for medical treatment for her heart. She brought home with her a bouquet of white plastic calla lilies. That was the first time I had ever seen calla lilies, and I was just fascinated with their beauty and uniqueness. They were so different than any other flower I had ever seen. I used to take one in my hand and look at it with curiosity. To this day, I love calla lilies. To me, the calla lily stands alone, a single petal unfolding with effortless grace. It does not need layers of petals or colors to be beautiful; its simplicity is its power. Tall and proud, it rises with quiet elegance, untouched by the chaos of the world around it. In its pure form, it is noble, refined, and unwavering. Calla lilies do not boast. They do not demand attention. And yet, they captivate. Their beauty is in their unwavering poise, their ability to endure, unshaken by the wind or rain. My mother's presence was the same—regal, steadfast, and always composed, no matter how fierce the storm.

My mother was a calla lily. She carried herself with a dignity that needed no embellishment. Through every storm, every hardship, she never bent—never let the weight of suffering steal her composure. Like the calla lily, she stood tall, rooted in patience and resilience, facing every trial with quiet strength. When I think of her, I see the calla lily: a singular bloom, standing alone yet complete, embodying grace and strength in its purest form. She was the unbroken pillar of our family, a symbol of patience and resilience. And just like the calla lily, her elegance was in how she carried herself—in the way she faced the world with quiet power, always standing tall.

When I think about the incredible woman my mother was, I also reflect on my own experience of being a mother. I have been blessed with three amazing children. Misron, my first, was born when I was twenty-four years old. He arrived one hundred days prematurely. He weighed only one pound and thirteen ounces (820 grams). Soon after his birth when he was in an incubator and fighting for survival, he dropped to one pound eight ounces. Today, Ronny lives with cerebral palsy, with all its challenges. He has never let it limit him. He has always been curious about this world, asking questions about everything around him and seeking to learn all he can. Ronny is an absolute sweetheart, intelligent and patient. In him, I see the best qualities of his own family, my parents and siblings, and all the wonderful people in my life. Raising him at such a young age taught me many lessons about life and motherhood. Until then, I had been the baby of my family, spoiled by everyone and always getting my way. All of a sudden, I had this tiny life to

CHAPTER NINE

look after. Coming to the hospital Neonatal Intensive Care Unit (NICU) every day to sit by his incubator in a surgical mask and gown, unable to hold him, I watched him struggle to keep living. All I could do was talk to him. Over the first three months of his life, he fought to grow ounce by ounce. When Ronny's weight rose to just over two pounds (a kilogram), we celebrated with a big "one-kilo" party with the doctors and nurses at the NICU at the Kadlec Hospital in Richland, Washington. It wasn't until a few weeks after he was born that I was able to hold him for the first time. I was extremely grateful that he had made it through.

Three years later, I had my second child. We named him Shadman (Shad), which means *happy one*. He was born eleven days after my brother Rishat's first son, Tilman. Shad weighed eight pounds at birth and only continued to grow from there by doubling his birth weight in two months. I used to say that I did not have regular babies—Ronny was so small and grew so slowly and Shad was growing so fast and getting so big. The neighbors used to call him "Buddha Baby" because of how chubby he was, with fat rings around his wrists. Within three months, he was already sitting up and looking around. My brother couldn't believe it. By four months, he was trying to crawl. With surprise, my brother would jokingly say, "What did you have, a human baby or . . . something else?"

Two-and-a-half years after Shad's birth, my daughter Shireen arrived, bringing with her a different kind of amazing joy. My mother picked her name, which means *sweet* in my language. This time I had someone from my family with me for the delivery. Gulshan was there. She came for Shireen's birth, bringing the love and comfort of my family, I had missed with my first two children. When Shireen arrived, Gulshan held her alongside Shireen's father, her face full of tenderness. Shireen was an elegant and beautiful little soul from the very start, delicate yet full of quiet strength.

During their childhood, as our children were growing, shaping into the people they would become, I was navigating a life split between duty and motherhood. As the first Uyghur correspondent for the Radio Free Asia Uyghur Service in 1998 and later as an interpreter in Guantánamo Bay in 2002, my work was a mission, a responsibility I could not turn away from. But even as I poured myself into it, I fought to be present for my children, to do all the things a mother is meant to do. And yet, my deepest regret is that no matter how hard I tried, it was never enough in my mind.

With my family on the West Coast and my work on the East—sometimes even further—I was constantly in motion, crisscrossing the country, battling time zones that stole hours from me. Early mornings became routine, rising at 4 a.m. to meet 9 a.m. deadlines in Washington, DC while the rest of the house slept. And then, during those long nine months stationed at Guantánamo, the distance widened unbearably. I could only return to them every two or three months, missing moments I could never reclaim.

I wish I had been there more. I wish I could have read each and every book that Ronny wanted to hear. I wish I had driven Shad to every soccer practice, not just a few. I wish I had watched Shireen twirl through every ballet lesson, not just the ones I could fit in. No matter how much I tried, and I attended, the school projects, recitals, little everyday victories—all slipped through my fingers like sand. I was doing everything I could, but as a mother, it never felt like enough. And that is the ache I carry with me still and I regret the most.

After I left Guantánamo, I received an offer from a contractor in New York. It was a tempting offer, more than double what I could expect to make in California. The job came with great benefits and accommodation. As I was considering it, eight-year-old Shad found the offer I had left on my desk. He never said anything. I ended up turning down the offer and worked at Pelco, later Schneider Electric, in Fresno, to be with my children. The money was decent but did not come close to half of what the New York job might have paid. One day, Shad asked me off-handedly how much I was making at Pelco. I told him. He looked thoughtful for a moment before saying, "Thank you, mom, for turning down that high-paying job in New York, so you could stay with us." I leapt out of my seat to hug him as I told him there was nothing, no amount of money, no offer that could take me from them. I explained to him that the only reason I had been away was not because of the money or the job prospects. It was something I had to do for my people.

Years later, when the Urumchi Massacre unfolded on July 5, 2009, my world felt like it was unraveling. I was struggling to keep my head above water, balancing the weight of a full-time job with the fight to raise aware-

CHAPTER NINE

ness, to reach anyone who might listen, who might help, contacting reporters, lawmakers' offices in Washington, and the US State Department, as well as Human Rights Watch, Amnesty International, and other human rights organizations. Each night, after the workday ended, resting was not an option—I stayed up, writing letters, drafting statements, trying to make the world see what was happening to my people.

By 2009, Ronny was eighteen, Shad was fifteen, and Shireen was twelve. Our lives had already been reshaped by divorce since the end of 2002, and the rhythm of our new normal was still settling in. Under our custody arrangement, Shireen lived with me, while the two boys stayed with their father and their stepmother. Every weekend, the three children were together, shifting between our two homes. Wednesdays became sacred—my one-on-one time with Shad and spending the nights with me, while Shireen spent the night with her dad and stepmom. The rest of the weekdays belonged to Shireen and me—just the two of us. In those moments, she was my companion; she was the heartbeat of my world, the light that anchored me in the midst of all the chaos. These were the fragments of time I held onto. The moments I tried to stretch and make enough. But even then, with the weight of my work and the world pressing down on me, I often wondered—was I giving them enough? Was I present enough? Was I still the mother they needed me to be?

One thing I must acknowledge with deep gratitude is the love and care my children's stepmother, Kathy, has shown to my children—especially my son Ronny, who has special needs. Kathy embraced him as her own, tending to his every need with patience and compassion. To this day, she continues to provide him with the essential care and daily support he requires. Because of Kathy's care—together with that of his father—I have the peace of mind to continue my fight for justice and freedom, knowing that Ronny is in the hands of people who love him and devote themselves to his care. For that, I am grateful.

My children have always been my greatest source of strength. None of them ever went through a rebellious phase; there were no slammed doors, no angry outbursts. Even as toddlers, they seemed to bypass the infamous "terrible twos." As teenagers, they never fell into the moody defiance that so many parents brace themselves for. Instead, they were kind, understanding, patient and unfailingly thoughtful, qualities that deepened our already unbreakable bond.

Ronny graduated from high school in 2010 in a regular mainstream class, and two years later, in 2012, Shad followed with high honors and as valedictorian. He had tackled multiple AP classes, balancing the weight of rigorous academics with the quiet diligence that had always defined him. When the college acceptance letters arrived, they carried names of some of the most prestigious universities. He had choices, incredible choices.

But then came the moment that tested both of us.

Shad had his heart set on a smaller liberal arts university in Washington State, but I wanted him to attend one of the top ten larger public universities. At first, I simply encouraged him to consider the public university. But as I realized he was leaning towards the smaller liberal arts school, my encouragement turned into persuasion, then into pressure. I even arranged for Sabin Willett, one of the lead *habeas* attorneys for the former Guantánamo Uyghurs (his work is listed in chapter eight), to call Shad and persuade him. Shad already knew Willett's name from resettlement efforts for the GTMO detainees, and I hoped that hearing from someone he respected might sway him. I tried every argument, every appeal, and though he listened patiently, I could sense his struggle—the weight of his own dreams against the expectations of his mother. He waited until the very last day and last hours—just before the deadline—to make his decision. When he finally called to tell me what he decided, his voice was steady, but there was an unmistakable firmness in his words.

"Mom," he said, "I'm going to the public university. But I want you to know . . . you pressured me a lot. And you can't do this to me again—not with my future decisions."

His honesty cut through me, in realization. He had made the choice I had wanted, but he had also drawn a boundary. And in that moment, I saw a young man stepping into his own life, determined to shape his own path.

I took a deep breath, holding back the wave of emotions rising in my chest.

"You're right," I told him. "I promise—I won't do this again."

CHAPTER NINE

And as much as I thanked him for his choice, I silently thanked him even more for teaching me something far greater: that a mother's love must also include the courage to let go.

And so, with that, Shad began the next chapter of his life at the university and as a young man carving his own destiny. After four years at university, Shad graduated with a double Bachelor of Science degrees with honors.

The summer before his senior year of university, in 2015, Shad came to visit us in Northern Virginia. He was interning at the US Congress, working closely with lawmakers. During his time there, he helped organize several congressional hearings, including one featuring American movie star Richard Gere, a passionate advocate for the Tibetan people and a vocal critic of the CCP's human rights abuses. Shad also met with human rights defenders, including the Uyghur advocates such as Omer Kanat, during the representatives' meetings with them. Watching my son step into this world filled me with immeasurable pride.

But amid the whirlwind of my work, my advocacy, and my responsibilities, there was always one constant in my life—Shireen. She has always been kind, caring, smart and beautiful.

She was my friend. My anchor. My light, then and now. Shireen's kindness radiated effortlessly, her serenity a calming presence in every storm. Her elegance and beauty—both inside and out—continue to fuel me with boundless love and unshakable strength. Always, no matter where I am, her light burns within me, guiding me forward every day.

We had a closeness that words can never fully capture. But as much as I loved her with every fiber of my being, and as much as I tried to be present, my career often pulled me away. We had settled in Herndon, Virginia with Shireen. But my work was in Washington, DC, and every day, I commuted 50 miles around trip, back and forth—five days a week. On top of that, my role as International Program Manager, and later International Director, at Leo A Daly demanded frequent international travel.

I did everything I could to balance it all while trying to give her all the time and attention that I was able to. But when I look back now—when I let myself truly feel the weight of it—I can't help but wonder:

Did she ever feel alone?
Did she ever wish I had been there more?
Did she ever long for a mother who wasn't always running, always fighting, always working?

The thought breaks my heart in ways that can never be mended. I feel an ache, a sorrow, a deep regret that no amount of love can undo. These are among the few moments in my life when I have shed tears of regret.

And yet, Shireen never once resented me for it.

She was always so kind, so compassionate, so understanding, far beyond her years. She had grown up witnessing my fight, seeing first-hand the sacrifices that came with advocacy. But instead of turning away from it, instead of resenting the cause that so often took me away, she embraced it.

When she graduated from high school and went on to attend university in 2016, she stepped into her own power. She ran for a student union leadership position, choosing to become an advocate for human rights. During her campaign speech, she spoke about how she was born into activism and about growing up as the daughter of an activist. She spoke about watching me fight for our people's cause since the day she was born. She spoke about the sacrifices, the struggles, the late nights spent writing statements, the endless battles against injustice. And yet, there was no bitterness in her words. No pain. No regret. Only purpose. She was elected for the position she wanted.

I am incredibly proud of Shireen, for her outstanding academic achievements and the remarkable success she has built in her career. Her dedication, resilience, and commitment to excellence have set her apart. From the very beginning, she approached her education with passion and determination, never shying away from challenges. Now, as she thrives in her career, she continues to inspire with her intelligence, hard work, and grace. Shireen's journey is a testament to her strength and perseverance, and I have no doubt that she will continue to achieve greatness and make a meaningful impact on the world.

My children had every reason to feel neglected, to feel burdened by the weight of my activism and my fight. But instead, they had turned it into their own strength. They had transformed it into a legacy of courage, of tenacity, of never backing down.

Unbroken.

And as I see my daughter claim her place in the world, as I watched my children becoming adults, my heart swells with something greater than pride.

Gratitude.

For all the ways they had understood me.

For all the ways they had supported me.

For all the ways they had turned pain into purpose.

I am, and will always be, incredibly proud of my children. Of Ronny. Of Shad. Of Shireen. They are not just my children. They are my greatest legacy.

In 2004, after my mother, Mariye, passed away, my father came to the United States and visited my brother Rishat's family and my home for about five months. During this time, my father was seventy-two years old. He was so happy when he heard that we were making every effort for the freedom of the Uyghur people. "I am proud of you, my children. Most importantly, it is your work to bring happiness to the people and freedom to the homeland. I am very grateful to you for these efforts," my father said.

My father had an American green card. He should have been able to travel back and forth to America as he wished. However, after he returned to his homeland in the spring of 2005, the Chinese Communist government confiscated his passport, and he could not come to America again. My father passed away in May 2010. I was unable to see him during his final five years of life; the last time I saw him was during my final visit to the homeland in 2005. After his death, I could neither attend his funeral nor visit his grave.

Speaking of my father, Abbas Borhan, and his contributions may seem like personal praise of my own family, but his legacy is widely recognized and respected by Uyghur academics worldwide. His scientific achievements left an indelible mark, and his dedication to knowledge and his people earned him profound admiration. After his passing, many Uyghur intellectuals honored him with writings that celebrated his life's work. His name was enshrined in the Uyghur book *100 Influential Uyghurs*, a collection spanning two thousand years of Uyghur history. The book acknowledges his achievements and his dedication to science, education, and the advancement of his people.

As the first Uyghur biologist in our homeland, my father was revered by his peers as the "Scholar for Life Science." His passion for his people was met with equal love and respect in return. Though many books and articles were written about his tireless efforts for the welfare of the Uyghur people, his suffering during the Cultural Revolution was scarcely documented. The CCP ensured that its crimes during this dark era remain untold, silencing the pain endured by Uyghur intellectuals like my father.

Despite those hardships, my father remained unwavering in his pursuit of knowledge. In the relatively open political atmosphere following the end of the Cultural Revolution in 1976, he contributed significantly to popularizing science in Uyghur region. He authored and published twelve books related to biology, agriculture, and general science, ensuring that future generations would benefit from his work. His legacy is not merely in the pages of history but in the minds he enlightened and the future he helped shape. He published nearly four hundred articles on the popularization of science, edited around five hundred books, and translated and published more than thirty scientific books. There are many more achievements that I may not even be aware of.

After my father's passing, Uyghur intellectuals living abroad wrote articles about him; for example, Ekrem Hezim one of the Uyghur intellectuals who lives in Munich, wrote in one of his pieces:

> The late Abbas Borhan was a beloved figure among our people. During his lifetime, he not only was a good father to capable children but also the first natural science scholar of the Uyghurs, a writer of popularizing science, a cherished son of the Uyghur people, and an advocate of Uyghur farmers living in poverty. He gained significant fame in our homeland. After founding the "Science and Technology Society," he established hundreds of branches of this society across the homeland, from the north to the south, tirelessly working to develop the situation for the millions of oppressed Uyghur farmers as much as he could and won a deep place in the hearts of our farmers and most of the Uyghur nation.

CHAPTER NINE

One of the most esteemed Uyghur intellectuals in the diaspora, author, poet, the late Ablikim Baki Iltebir, was a lifelong champion of Uyghur rights, a scholar, and a mentor to generations. He was the beloved father of Elfidar Iltebir, the president of the Uyghur American Association, a tireless advocate for the Uyghurs in the United States, and her sister, Dr. Elnigar Iltebir, who served as the China Director of the US National Security Council during the first Trump administration. Ablikim Baki Iltebir dedicated all his life to the preservation of Uyghur identity, culture, and freedom in the Uyghur homeland and abroad. While he was serving as the editor-in-chief of Radio Free Asia's Uyghur Service, his work was instrumental in exposing the truth about China's oppression. Beyond his role as a journalist, editor and advocate, he was also my teacher during my middle- and high-school years in Urumchi, shaping my understanding of our history, our struggle, and the responsibility we all bear to fight for justice. His writings, teachings, and dedication to the Uyghur cause remain an enduring source of inspiration. He left behind books and articles that continue to resonate—a legacy of truth, defiance, and the unyielding spirit of our people. In one of his articles, he describes my father like this: "In those years, the late Abbas Borhan was a role model for youth in our homeland." Ablikim Baki Iltebir continued,

> Uyghur intellectuals sensitively estimated the space in China's new political situation and started a campaign to win Uyghur rights in all fields, from education to science and technology. In the late 1970s after the Cultural Revolution ended, the Chinese Communists implemented a series of artificially liberal policies. These policies, and the relative freedom in social sciences, literature, and arts, gave new opportunities to Abbas Borhan to mobilize Uyghur intellectuals. Under the shadow of China's laws and regulations, the movement to achieve and protect national interests, fight for educational rights, and awaken the people through the media became a widespread sentiment.

In such circumstances, Abbas Borhan was first sent to Kuyton Agricultural University, which later became Shihezi Agricultural University, in 1977, as the President of the University and became one of the foremost leaders of Uyghur education. Then, he was appointed as the Chairman of the newly established "Science and Technology Society" in the Uyghur Autonomous Region. He founded the "Popular Science Publishing House" and initiated and published scientific journals such as *Knowledge Is Power* (*Bilim-Kuch* in Uyghur) and *Science and Life* (*Pen we Turmush* in Uyghur) He constructed the Science and Technology Tower of the Uyghur Autonomous Region. He also established the Science and Technology Writers Association and the Scientific Publishing House. Abbas Borhan brought together a group of talented, conscientious Uyghur and Kazakh intellectuals from various parts of the Uyghur region as well as senior natural science workers who had been marginalized by the CCP during and after Mao's Great Cultural Revolution and deprived of the opportunity to utilize their talents fully. The prime of Abbas Borhan's life was dedicated to enhancing the Uyghur nation's welfare, defending ethnic interests, and training Uyghur and Kazakh successors for the future freedom struggle. Another way of writing this is: Mr. Abbas Borhan's tenure was spent raising the quality of his nation, searching for ways to protect national interests, and training successors for future generations.

In the encyclopedic work for the Uyghurs back home, named *Pride* (*Ghururname* in Uyghur) an Uyghur book by Erkin Abduqadir, the deputy editor of the National Publishing House in Beijing, the statements related to my father's biography are given a lot of space. It contains the following information:

CHAPTER NINE

For many years, we have been left in ignorance, and our education, science and technology have not only been ignored but have been purposefully turned aside. Appreciation is an inalienable obligation.

During his tenure as the president of the Scientific and Technology Society, Abbas Borhan made significant contributions to popularizing science among Uyghurs through his diligent efforts and undeniable achievements. His unwavering commitment to maintaining and protecting the nation's unity was reflected throughout his life. His admirable character was marked by kindness, humility, modesty, and a constant willingness to help others. He exhibited no trace of narrow-mindedness, sectarianism, or regionalism.

Abbas Borhan was born on October 19, 1932, in Iksak village of Üstün Artush. From 1939 to 1947, he attended primary and secondary schools and the Qazan Madrasa in Kashgar. In September 1951, he enrolled in the Xinjiang Institute (now Xinjiang University). In 1952, he was admitted to the Biology Department of Beijing Normal University, graduating with high honors in 1957, and was assigned to teach at Xinjiang University, where he soon became the department chair of the Biology Department in the early 1960s, teaching physiology, zoology, and genetics. He also held administrative positions, such as head of the university's teaching and research department.

Abbas Borhan significantly influenced Xinjiang and national scientific and technological societies. He was recognized throughout China as a prominent figure in the field of science and technology. In 1978, he was appointed chairman of the Autonomous Regional Scientific and Technical Society. He was re-elected unanimously as the chairman of the Science and Technical Society at the second and third congresses in 1981 and 1986.

Since 1978, Abbas Borhan also served as a permanent member of the first, second, and third congresses of the Chinese Writers' Association. He was elected as the director of the first and second boards of the Xinjiang Uyghur Autonomous Region Writers' Association. Additionally, he was director, deputy director, honorary director, and adviser in various other academic societies, including the Genetics Society, Zoological Research Society, Wildlife Conservation Society, Environmental Protection Society, Future Studies Society, and Urban Construction Society. He also contributed to the journal *Arid Zone Geography*.

In addition to creating and reestablishing the Science and Technology Society, Abbas Borhan founded the Xinjiang Uyghur and Kazakh Branch Publishing House and Printing Press of the China Popular Science Press on his own initiative in early 1980. He established and became the chief editor of the journals *Knowledge Is Power* and *Science and Life*. In 1986, the Autonomous Regional Title Evaluation Committee awarded Abbas Borhan the academic title of "Chief Editor."

Among Abbas Borhan's books are *The Secret of Life, Birds Are Friends of Humans, On Plant Protection, Measures to Improve Crops, Microorganisms and Agriculture, Agriculture and Insects, Genetics and Genetic Engineering, Scientific and Technological Progress and Modern Science and Technology, Life and Environment, The New Direction of Humanity,* and *The Structure of Life.*

My father's life-long journey to uplift the Uyghur people through knowledge and empowerment is something that fills me with immense purpose. I am grateful for all that he has achieved and everything that he has done for our people, so that I may stand on his shoulders and carry his legacy forward. To protect all that was built and help keep it from extinction.

CHAPTER NINE

In March 2020, more than one hundred Uyghur researchers at the Uyghur Academy under my brother Rishat's leadership as the president of the Uyghur Academy International, founded the "Qutadghu Bilig Institute." At the same time, more than fifty Uyghur researchers in the Natural Science Department revived the *Knowledge Is Power* journal in the diaspora, aiming to promote the use of the Uyghur language in science, advance the nation's progress, and preserve its identity.

Rishat's introductory remarks include the following:

> The term "knowledge is power" holds deep meaning for me, as it reminds me of my late father, Abbas Borhan, who believed that "our nation can rise through science and technology." He founded the journal *Knowledge Is Power* in 1980 and dedicated his life to popularizing science to empower our nation and the *Knowledge Is Power* journal in our homeland inspired Uyghur youth interest in science and nurtured many Uyghur scholars. Published in more than four hundred volumes, it was forcibly discontinued by the Chinese government in 2017. Unable to bear this injustice, intellectuals in exile decided to collaborate and continue the journal abroad. The republication of the *Knowledge Is Power* journal abroad reflects Uyghur intellectuals' responsibility to our people's future and continues the legacy of ancestors like my father, who envisioned our nation's strength through science and technology. This effort aims to guide our nation towards progress and development. The republication of the *Knowledge Is Power* journal in the Uyghur diaspora will inspire our people abroad and bring us closer to our goals. I congratulate this effort and urge Uyghur scholars worldwide to unite, protect our national existence, and accelerate our path to independence. To our suffering brothers and sisters back home, stay hopeful—we are committed to your dreams. History shows that when people apply scientific and technological innovations to improve their lives, it leads to

significant changes in quality of life. While the realization of science's power spread widely, its impact varied greatly across countries and cultures in terms of time, speed, and scale.

Our national existence is under threat. In these critical times, empowering our youth through science and technology is essential to strengthening our people and is one of our urgent tasks.

In 2021, Dr. Kaiser Mijit, an economist who attended graduate school at Harvard University, writing in his foreword to the first diaspora-published edition of *Knowledge Is Power*, described my father as follows:

> Uyghur intellectuals have long been seen as torchbearers. Abbas Borhan, the first Uyghur natural scientist and science writer, played a key role in advancing our scientific progress. Featured in *100 Influential Uyghurs* (Sutuk Bugrakhan Publishing, Türkiye), he was a popular scholar and a well-respected model of human being. I was privileged to meet him, and I admired his wisdom, compassion, and dedication to his people. His books, *The Secret of Life* and *Birds Are Friends of Humans*, deeply inspired me when I was a high school student. His leadership also brought us the Uyghur-language journal *Knowledge Is Power*, each volume of which I eagerly followed when I was at university.

When my father passed away, I was deeply touched by a tribute from Uyghur poet Medinay Bawudun, whose legacy is rooted in literature and resistance. As the daughter of Bawudun Niyaz, my high school principal and a prominent poet and author, Medinay understood the weight of my father's loss for both our family and the Uyghur people. While she used to work at Radio Free Asia, she honored him with a news segment that highlighted his intellectual brilliance, integrity, and kindness, painting a lasting portrait of his impact.

***

CHAPTER NINE

On March 13, 2010, just two months before my father's passing, I married my husband, Abdulhakim Idris. Our backgrounds were worlds apart—I was a city girl from Urumchi, raised in relative comfort, while he grew up in the rural landscapes of Hotan, nearly 1300 miles (2000 km) to the south. Despite China's suppression of religious practice, he pursued Islamic studies in underground schools (*Madrissa*), defying the state's efforts to erase our faith. His journey took him from Hotan to Cairo in 1986, where he deepened his studies at Al-Ez'har University, and eventually in 1990, he sought asylum in Munich, Germany, where he later studied Industrial Management and became a cornerstone of the Uyghur diaspora movement.

A visionary and an advocate, Abdulhakim helped lay the foundation for Uyghur solidarity and organizations worldwide. He was instrumental in establishing the East Turkistan Union, the first Uyghur organization in Europe, and played a pivotal role in the formation of the World Uyghur Youth Congress, the East Turkistan National Congress, and ultimately, the World Uyghur Congress, where he has served tirelessly in numerous leadership roles. Among our people, he is known as a scholar and a steadfast champion of our rights.

He is a trailblazer, collaborator, and a friend. Through every trial, every heartache, and every battle we have fought for our people, we have stood together, a source of strength and solace for one another. With all that we have endured and continue to face, I remain profoundly grateful for the bond we share—a bond forged in affection, resilience, and an unyielding love for our people and our cause.

In October 2010, just six months after our marriage, Abdulhakim's two sons, Bugrahan (then thirteen) and Forkan (then twelve), came and joined us from Munich, Germany. With their arrival, our blended family grew to five children, ranging from twelve to eighteen years old. Bugrahan and Forkan, born in Germany, now became an important part of our home with Shireen, while Ronny and Shad remained in California.

As Abdulhakim and I balanced the responsibility of raising Shireen, Bugrahan, and Forkan, providing all they needed, we also dedicated ourselves to our work and advocacy for our people. Each day was a delicate struggle—ensuring our children felt loved, supported, and secure while fighting for justice and making an affordable living. The weight of our mission was great, but so was our commitment—to our family, to our cause, and to a future where our children could grow up in a world shaped by freedom, dignity, and hope.

Bugrahan and Forkan have grown into kind, compassionate young men, each with a strong and unique personality, yet both deeply understanding and supporting the work to which we dedicated our lives. Their empathy and support have been a source of strength, reminding us that our sacrifices were not in vain.

Bugrahan's hard work and determination led him to graduate with honors in Computer Science from the University of Virginia. Forkan, after briefly returning to Munich in 2023, has since found his professional path and built a new life in Houston, Texas, where he married a wonderful Uyghur woman who grew up there.

Both of my stepsons have not only excelled academically and professionally but have also made their mark through their passion for soccer. Their talent and skill on the field have earned them respect and admiration from both the Virginia Uyghur soccer team and the Houston Uyghur soccer team, where they are recognized as invaluable players.

Watching them carve their own futures while upholding the values we cherish has been one of the greatest rewards of our journey. Their strength and support for our work remind us that the sacrifices we made were not in vain, and our hearts swell with immense pride and gratitude.

CHAPTER TEN

IN SEARCH OF MY SISTER:

KIN PUNISHMENT AND THE CCP'S TRANSNATIONAL REPRESSION

Growing up, Gulshan had always been a kind and caring older sister. While I had followed in our father's footsteps in the study of biology, she had followed in our mother's. She devoted her life to helping those in need as a doctor. In her retirement, she suffers from a number of health concerns that require monitoring, and for which we cannot be sure she receives any of the necessary treatment. She lives with severe high blood pressure, back pain which often leaves her immobilized, osteoporosis, and recurring migraines. She has had multiple surgeries in both her eyes as well, which require regular attention and monitoring.

On December 23, 2019, the China *Global Times* published an article that tried to discredit me by claiming that:

"Rushan Abbas, leader of the so-called Campaign for Uyghurs, and Halmurat Harri, who started the 'MeTooUyghur' activity, are found to be members of 'East Turkistan' separatist groups. They first stole some Uyghurs' photos and information, claimed these people to be 'missing' relatives in Xinjiang, spread rumors on overseas media and had interactions with certain media."

In December 2020 we learned that Gulshan had been sentenced to twenty years in prison in a secret trial in March of 2019, and was not scheduled for release until 2038. We immediately called for a press conference with the US Congressional-Executive Commission on China (CECC). Several lawmakers, including Rep. Tom Suozzi, Rep. Chris Smith, and others, called for my sister's immediate release. The next day it was reported on several major media outlets. During China's Ministry of Foreign Affairs' press conference, my sister's case was specifically mentioned:

REUTERS: The United States has called for the release of a Uyghur named Gulshan Abbas. Do you have any comment on this?

WANG WENBIN (CHINESE REPRESENTATIVE): Gulshan Abbas was sentenced to jail by Chinese judicial authorities for crimes of participating in a terrorist organization, aiding terrorist activities and assembling crowds to disrupt social order. China is a country with rule of law, where criminals must be held accountable.

We urge some American politicians to respect facts, stop making lies to smear China, and stop interfering in China's internal affairs under the pretext of Xinjiang-related issues.

The same government that once used its state media to deny my sister's very existence and accused me of fabricating her story was now branding her a criminal, twisting reality to suit their agenda. They cannot even keep track of their own lies. Their contradictions expose the truth: this is not justice, but a brutal regime desperate to erase those who dare to speak out.

Not only were the charges they ruthlessly brought against my sister false and totally out of character for Gulshan, but they were also presented without any evidence to support them. My sister has never been a political person. When experts from the United Nations made a formal request for disclosure of detailed information regarding her health, the court judgment enabling her conviction, and the evidence used, China failed to respond.

My restlessness continued to grow. Without any news of my sister's fate, but certain that her disappearance was kin punishment for her association with me and my advocacy, I felt there was no choice but to double down on my efforts to win the attention of those political actors willing to help. If I was sure of anything, it was that my parents would not have wished this blatant attempt to silence me to succeed. Though I have been robbed of the chance to ask her, I believe Gulshan would not want it either.

Over the course of 2019, my husband Abdulhakim began writing letters to his own missing mother to process the grief he and the rest of his family

CHAPTER TEN

felt at losing contact with her. He wrote over and over again, and as the third anniversary of their final conversation approached in April 2020, he published these sentiments as an open letter. His letter was published on Bitterwinter.org, as well as on the Campaign for Uyghurs' website, and then it went viral. It was translated and published in more than ten languages, including English, Chinese, Arabic, Italian, French, Spanish, Turkish and Japanese. When his book, *Menace: China's Colonization of the Islamic World & Uyghur Genocide*, was published later that year, he included the letter among the appendices as well. With his words he captured the feelings of many of our people grappling with the uncertainty of their families' fates and mourning their inability to say goodbye as China holds them hostage. Below is an excerpt from his letter detailing my own part in our struggle.

> On September 5, 2018, nearly five hundred days after our last phone conversation, Rushan participated in a panel discussion at the Hudson Institute, one of America's prestigious think tanks. She talked about the disappearance of our family while pointing out the horrific conditions of the camps and the Orwellian-style complete police state that the Uyghur region had become. She called on the United States government and the international community to act. Six days later, the Chinese government abducted her sister Gulshan Abbas, who is a retired medical doctor in Urumchi. They also abducted her sixty-year-old aunt in Artush to retaliate for Rushan's activism. During these difficult times, my devoted, courageous wife Rushan was by my side. She has been not merely a soulmate to me; she has also become a best friend and companion in the journey of activism. We, as husband and wife, have continued to explore the path of salvation for our people while we try to be a voice for the voiceless and advocate for the defenseless, innocent Uyghurs. However, at the point when I lost contact with you, millions of people were being thrown into prisons and concentration camps, and the international community in this free world was mute,

while the press was not reporting on it. It seemed as if it had all been swept under the rug. Rushan has been busy sitting in front of a computer day and night sending messages to reporters. She has been trying to bring attention to these unprecedented atrocities and has been advocating for you and millions of others. The "One Voice, One Step" women's initiative generated simultaneous global protests in all four corners of the world, lasting for twenty-two hours, When I would tell people around me who are not Uyghur that China was not allowing me to have any contact or information from my parents and my family, it was so difficult for them to believe. How could such a thing happen in this information era of the 21st century?

Mother, if you could have only witnessed my wife, with a personality in many ways like yours: the same hatred and love that is as clearly defined as can be. She is never unfair to anyone, she is never afraid of anything, and she will never give up her rights. If only you could have known how she has been constantly confronting the Chinese government using every platform of social media. She constantly grants interviews with journalists and is constantly asking: "Where is my sister? Where are my in-laws? Where are my relatives? Where are millions of my people?" I can imagine how proud you would be, and the love and respect and praise you would have for her as you would encourage her to work harder and be stronger.

Rushan and I, as a couple, will spend our entire lives advocating for you and the Uyghur people. In every opportunity, in every waking hour, we are working hard. We will continue to be a voice for you, Uyghurs, and all the people of the Uyghur region in every place that we can reach—in forums, in Islamic organizations, mosques, and universities. We must reach audiences and platforms from Japan to Australia, from Türkiye to Canada, from Europe to the different states in America, and we must continue to raise awareness.

CHAPTER TEN

In April 2019, Abdulhakim and I met with several members of Congress on Capitol Hill to tell my story. Within a year, meetings like this would allow for the formation of the first bipartisan Uyghur Congressional Caucus with Tom Suozzi of New York and Chris Smith of New Jersey. Many Uyghur-American and Uyghur organizations in the United States tried hard to raise awareness and educate the general public. The many days, weeks, and months of our advocacy and continuous effort enabled the passing of the *Uyghur Human Rights Policy Act* (UHRPA) in 2020, which was later signed by President Trump, and the introduction of the *Uyghur Genocide Accountability and Sanctions Act* of 2024 by the co-chairs of the Congressional Uyghur Caucus.

In the spring of 2019, Mujeeb Ijaz, a visionary Silicon Valley engineer with a deep sense of justice, reached out to me with a profound offer of support. He wanted to help amplify my voice and further the cause of raising awareness about the horrific atrocities facing the Uyghur people. He was committed to making a real, tangible difference. Later that summer, Mujeeb extended an invitation that would prove to be both transformative and deeply impactful, shaping the course of our efforts and leaving an indelible mark on this journey. He asked me to speak at a large Muslim gathering in Pennsylvania. This opportunity was born from one young woman. Mujeeb's daughter, Shazia, who had learned about the Uyghurs suffering at her school and, she asked her father to help amplify our voices. Because of one girl's persistence and her father's kindness, a door was opened. A connection was forged that would help bring a critical story to life. It was a reminder that sometimes it takes just one person, one voice, to spark a ripple of change.

I gave a speech on the main stage, and Jawad Mir, an award-winning producer and director from Canada, happened to hear my talk on a screen in another room. He was taken aback—this was the first time he had ever heard anything about the Uyghur people, and he immediately thought it would make a great documentary. However, he was already committed to another project at the time and didn't think much more about it.

A few months later, Mujeeb invited us again, this time to London, for another major event. Jawad was present as well, and when Mujeeb saw him, he called him over and introduced us. Mujeeb urged Jawad to consider making the documentary. Jawad responded with surprise, recalling that he had listened to my speech a few months earlier and had already thought it was an important story.

By October 2019, we had returned to Washington, and shortly afterward, Jawad reached out. He conducted his first interview with me, and from that moment on, he was deeply committed to telling the story. That was when the journey to create the documentary truly began. Eventually, we decided to work together on the documentary film that, through storytelling about my sister, her disappearance, and my efforts to find her—would cover the broader plight of the Uyghurs, their history, culture, and struggle for freedom. This documentary came to be called *In Search of My Sister*. My husband and I both agreed to be interviewed to tell the whole story, from start to finish. My niece Ziba also spoke in the film about her mother's disappearance.

On May 2, 2022, during an Eid al-Fitr celebration at the White House, President Joe Biden met with Ziba. In their brief but poignant exchange, President Biden listened intently as Ziba shared the heartbreaking reality of her mother's unjust detention. His response carried a deep sense of empathy, acknowledging the suffering endured by Uyghur families like hers. Ziba also spoke with First Lady Jill Biden, who was visibly moved by her story, reacting with profound emotion as she learned of Dr. Gulshan Abbas's plight. The moment underscored the human toll of China's persecution of the Uyghur people, bringing the crisis directly to the highest levels of the US government.

Nury Turkel, an Uyghur-American attorney and human rights advocate, was also present at the reception with President Biden. At the time, he was serving as the Chair of the US Commission on International Religious Freedom and has worked to raise awareness about the ongoing Uyghur atrocities; he was also interviewed for the film.

In addition to our testimonies, the film includes insight from Dr. Adrian Zenz. Dr. Adrian Zenz was among the first to expose the true scale and horrifying scope of the Uyghur concentration camps in 2018.

His research, grounded in open-source data, government documents, satellite imagery, and witness testimony, has systematically dismantled the CCP's disinformation campaigns. He was among the first to expose the mass internment camps in the Uyghur region, revealing the vast scale of extrajudicial detentions through his analysis of leaked Chinese government

CHAPTER TEN

documents and procurement records for surveillance equipment. He also uncovered the Chinese government's systematic use of forced sterilizations on Uyghur women, revealing how state-mandated birth-control policies, including involuntary IUD insertions, sterilization procedures, and forced abortions, were being used to suppress Uyghur birth rates. He also developed the term State Imposed Forced Labor to describe the coercive labor transfer programs constructed by the CCP. The term was adopted by the International Labour Organization (ILO) in its updated guidelines on forced labor, reinforcing global recognition of the CCP's exploitative systems. His research has provided the empirical foundation for global policy responses, including sanctions by the United States, the European Union, and other democratic nations.

Through a commitment to truth, he has shattered the CCP's web of lies, empowered policymakers to take action, and given voice to the countless Uyghurs suffering in silence. He has been more than an ally. Dr. Zenz has been a banner for the Uyghur people, standing resolute in the face of threats and pressure, ensuring that the undeniable evidence of the CCP's crimes can never be ignored.

The film covers the conditions of the occupation and my quest to rally support and solidarity among the Uyghurs in the diaspora. It also records my attempts to extract any information at all from the opaque regime as to the whereabouts of my sister. The film contains moving testimony from survivors of China's mass concentration camps, leaders within the Uyghur diaspora, prominent scholars, and researchers to paint a picture of China's genocidal policies and their effect upon Uyghur lives.

The director of the film believed it was important to provide the CCP's perspective in the film in order to present both sides of the story and allow viewers to draw their own conclusions. I made no secret of my vehement disagreement with him on this approach. To me, Beijing has all the stages and platforms it needs to spread its disinformation and false narratives to whitewash the genocide, but we Uyghur people had only this one 80-minute documentary film, and in my opinion, we should not have wasted any airtime repeating the CCP's lies. Nonetheless, the film also features a rogue

CGTN[21] columnist who provides the CCP's perspective. In order to include this propagandist, and other fabricated videos from the Chinese state media, crucial footages, key interviews, and essential voices that played a vital role in exposing the CCP's crimes were excluded from the film, removed from the final cut, and left out of the narrative. At one point, I was so incensed that I told Jawad if the film continued on this track with so much CCP propaganda and false footage, I would boycott it upon its release. He very calmly responded that it was fine, and that I would not be the first protagonist to boycott a film about them.

This gave me pause. I tried to bring some clarity to my thinking and ultimately decided to let it go. But I vocalized my feelings about this dispute whenever we hosted private screenings of the film with question-and-answer sessions at the end. Uyghurs have such a lack of resources to raise awareness of what we have gone through, and I knew a film like this would serve as a tool and an asset even if it only exposed people to what it means to be an Uyghur and the oppression we face under China's rule. And so, production continued. I am grateful for the film and all it does to highlight the situation Uyghurs face all over the world, even though I maintain my disagreement with its director about the decision to platform Chinese propaganda. My hope is merely that viewers are wise enough to recognize it for what it is when drawing their own conclusions.

I know why Jawad did this and he aimed for objectivity in his film to secure a strong platform for distribution. However, due to appeasement and self-censorship, even human rights festivals like the One World International Human Rights Documentary Film Festival rejected it. The documentary has been recognized by several festivals, including the Morehouse College Human Rights Film Festival, the Muslim Film Festival, and This Human World Festival. Despite this recognition and overwhelmingly positive feedback from reviewers, streaming platforms such as Netflix, Hulu, PBS, and Al Jazeera declined to distribute the film. Initial responses from these platforms when the film was first submitted were highly encouraging, with reviewers describing the film as "very powerful," "informative," and one that "the world

---

21. CGTN is the English-language news channel of the state-run China Global Television, based in Beijing, China.

CHAPTER TEN

community must see to understand what is happening to the Uyghurs." Yet, when it goes up to the management level, none were willing to proceed with streaming the film. While no official reason was provided, we are certain the subject matter—exposing the Chinese regime's atrocities—was deemed too sensitive, reflecting the chilling effect of China's influence on global media platforms, preemptive and fear-driven restraint of these platforms.

It's striking how the other film about former Guantánamo Uyghur detainees—one in which I was one of the interviewees—was readily accepted by many of these same festivals. Why? Because that film focused on US policies in Guantánamo Bay during the early 2000s. Criticizing the United States comes without fear of retaliation—there are no economic consequences, no threats to businesses or platforms. That is the beauty of democracy, the strength of the free world. Yet, when it comes to exposing China's atrocities, the same festivals hesitate, platforms retreat, and decision-makers engage in self-censorship out of fear. This is precisely why we fight—to protect the freedom and democracy that China's expanding influence seeks to erode. What troubles me most is that the very leaders, CEOs, and decision-makers who are surrendering their freedom of speech today fail to see the long-term cost. What they are sacrificing isn't just a film—it's the very principles their countries, their heroes, and their ancestors fought to uphold. And in doing so, they are shaping a world where their own children and grandchildren may one day inherit a reality devoid of basic rights, dignity, and the very liberties they now take for granted. I will continue to fight to defend those liberties.

In Search of My Sister was released on Human Rights Day, December 10, 2022, on platforms like Vimeo and Amazon Prime. Even before it was released online, private screenings hosted by the US State Department at numerous embassies, including those in Germany, Austria, Australia, Czech Republic, Germany, Finland, Kazakhstan, Jordan, Israel, Malaysia, Norway, Türkiye, and Switzerland, spanning a total of thirty-four countries. Most screenings were organized by US embassies and consulates, while others were hosted by local universities. In 2022, a screening took place in Brussels ahead of the Beijing Winter Olympics, at a time when Campaign for Uyghurs was already staunchly advocating for the boycott of those games. In 2023, the film was scheduled to be shown at the Jana Cekara Film Festival in Almaty,

Kazakhstan, alongside other films featuring Uyghur stories. However, following visits from Chinese diplomats to the festival's venue, the screening was mysteriously canceled—an alarming example of China's transnational repression silencing Uyghur voices beyond its borders.

On January 1, 2023, at China's 81st Press Conference on the Xinjiang Uygur Autonomous Region, Xu Guixiang, spokesperson of the People's Government of the Xinjiang Uyghur Autonomous Region, attacked me and villainized Gulshan by saying:

> Actually, the anti-Xinjiang propaganda film *In Search of My Sister* was shot by the ringleader of Uygur activists, Rushan Abbas, in collusion with a Canadian film-making team. Rushan Abbas is the ringleader of the so-called "Campaign for Uygurs (sic)" and the former vice president of the "Uygur (sic) American Association (UAA)." For a long time, as a frequent visitor of anti-China and Xinjiang-related campaign, she has been running around to collude with Western politicians and MPs. She denigrates China's policies on Xinjiang , and hypes up topics such as "genocide" and "human rights infringement." Her sister, Gulshan Abbas, was sentenced to 20 years' imprisonment in accordance with law in March, 2019 by people's court due to "participating in terrorist organizations, helping terrorists activities and gathering crowds to disturb the public order." She is serving a sentence with all legitimate rights guaranteed. In the film, Rushan Abbas cried foul for her sister by fabricating a flood of fake contents. She catered to the intent of the US and anti-China forces to contain China by Xinjiang-related issues. This farce of trading up is not worth seeing. It must be pointed out that China is a country with rule of law, where criminals must be held accountable. Based on facts and laws, Xinjiang people's court made sentences on her sister Gulshan Abbas, which stands the test of fact and history.

CHAPTER TEN

Despite the CCP's relentless denials, coverups, disinformation, and false narratives to obscure the truth of the Uyghur genocide, multiple leaks of the Chinese government's own documents in recent years have exposed the brutal reality. These leaks reveal disturbing details about mass surveillance, repression, and the systemic targeting of Uyghurs and other ethnic groups in our homeland. Whatever brave man or woman leaked these documents did so in the hopes that their actions would be a catalyst for significant change: A wake-up call to open people's eyes. Among the most significant of the leaks are the following:

1. "The China Cables." Leaked by the International Consortium of Investigative Journalists (ICIJ) in 2019, these classified documents revealed how China ran its mass internment camps in the Uyghur region, detailing detainee management, indoctrination, and movement restrictions.
2. "The Xinjiang Papers." Obtained in 2019 by *The New York Times*, this leak included more than four hundred pages of internal government documents, justifying China's crackdown in the Uyghur region, with speeches from Xi Jinping calling for "absolutely no mercy" against the Uyghurs.
3. "The Karakax List." Leaked in 2020, this government registry details three hundred and eleven Uyghurs sent to camps, with personal information and reasons for internment, including religious practices and family ties abroad.
4. "The Xinjiang Police Files." Leaked in 2022 to Dr. Adrian Zenz and the Victims of Communism Memorial Foundation and published by the BBC and other media. Contains more than 2,800 photographs of Uyghur detainees and classified speeches by officials about the repressive policies. Includes direct orders to "shoot to kill" those trying to escape camps.
5. "The Police Files" (2023). New evidence exposed the use of facial recognition technology and AI to track and detain Uyghurs based on race and religious activities.

Each leak provides undeniable proof of China's systemic repression and genocidal policies, debunking claims of "counterterrorism" or "poverty alleviation," which I highlighted during the Q&A session after the screening of *In Search of My Sister*. In late 2021, before the film's official release, we organized special screenings in the Czech Republic—Olomouc, Plzeň, Ústí nad Labem, and Prague. These events were made possible through the collaboration of our dear friend, scholar Ondřej Klimeš, whose expertise and dedication enriched the discussions. He moderated screenings, engaged with audiences, and, along with Katerina Procházková in Prague, has been instrumental in raising awareness and mobilizing international support for the Uyghur cause, especially within academic and policy circles.

In October 2019, Mudassar Ahmed, founder of the Concordia Forum, invited me to give a keynote speech near Toronto, Canada. There, I met many supportive individuals from various fields—politicians, artists, professors, and more—who have played key roles in our advocacy, organizing film screenings, and speaking engagements, and providing vital platforms. Abdulhakim and I have participated in several Concordia Forum events on human rights issues affecting Uyghur Muslims. Most recently, we attended the November 2024 forum in Atlanta, where I joined a panel on "Human Rights and Foreign Policy: Lessons from the Uyghur and Rohingya Struggles." Our collaboration with the Forum continues.

During our advocacy trips and film screenings in Canada, Tuyghun Abduweli and his wife, Gulnur, have been invaluable allies, offering transportation and opening their home to us to provide us with a place to stay. Their continuous support reminds us that we're not alone. I'm also grateful for friends like Rahima Mahmut, a prominent Uyghur advocate from London, the UK, whose powerful advocacy and beautiful singing of Uyghur folk songs help me momentarily forget the difficult situation while reminding us of the wonderful culture we must fight to preserve.

Campaign for Uyghurs continues to organize screenings of *In Search of My Sister* and in September 2024 alone, organized international screenings across sixteen cities in nine different countries—Australia, Canada, Germany, Ireland, Japan, Norway, Türkiye, the United States, and Uzbekistan—to mark the six-year anniversary of Gulshan's disappearance. Most recently, it was

CHAPTER TEN

screened in Geneva, miles away from the United Nations, with attendance from multiple member states. With immense pride, we can say that, since 2021, we have brought this powerful film to audiences in more than fifty countries. The majority are hosted by US embassies, consulates, and universities around the world. Each screening has been a platform for awareness, a catalyst for dialogue, and a step towards justice. Through these global screenings, we have amplified the voices of the oppressed, sparked critical conversations, and built an international network of solidarity that continues to grow.

In 2022, the film was hosted by Representative Chris Smith and Representative Tom Suozzi, co-chairs of the Congressional Uyghur Caucus at the Capitol Hill, in Washington, DC.

These screenings would not have been possible without the strong support of our partners and allies around the world. I take pride that, through the worldwide screenings of *In Search of My Sister*, we sent a powerful and united message that the case of my sister, Gulshan Abbas, and the plight of the Uyghur people will not be forgotten or abandoned. Behind every condemnation and every rally is a mother, daughter, son, or father whose life has been stolen by the Chinese Communist Party's ongoing genocide. When viewing the film, audiences understand the harsh realities of CCP oppression and deeply empathize with our pain. The sentiment warms me and renews my determination. We must channel this powerful emotion into action to end the Chinese regime's human rights abuses once and for all.

* * *

Abduqadir Jalalidin is a distinguished Uyghur writer, poet, and scholar, widely regarded as one of the most influential Uyghur intellectuals of the twenty-first century. As a Professor of Literature at Xinjiang Pedagogical University, his contributions to Uyghur literature and academia were profound. In 2018, the Chinese government unjustly detained him amid its broader persecution of Uyghur intellectuals. Since his arrest, no updates on his condition or whereabouts have emerged. His powerful poem, "No Way Back Home," believed to have been written during his detention, surfaced in December 2020, offering a rare and haunting glimpse into the silenced voices of those imprisoned.

As I speak about my sister's detention and the documentary that sheds light on her story, I feel compelled to share Abduqadir Jalalidin's powerful poem with my readers—a poignant testament to the suffering of the innocent Uyghur people in prison. Joshua Freeman, who translated the poem, is a specialist in Uyghur history and literature at the Institute of Modern History, Academia Sinica, and completed PhD in Inner Asian and Altaic Studies at Harvard University.

NO ROAD BACK HOME
Translated into English by Joshua L. Freeman

In this forgotten place I have no lover's touch
Each night brings darker dreams, I have no amulet
My life is all I ask, I have no other thirst
These silent thoughts torment, I have no way to hope

Who I once was, what I've become, I cannot know
Who could I tell my heart's desires, I cannot say
My love, the temper of the fates I cannot guess
I long to go to you, I have no strength to move

Through cracks and crevices I've watched the seasons change
For news of you I've looked in vain to buds and flowers
To the marrow of my bones I've ached to be with you
What road led here, why do I have no road back home

— ABDUQADIR JALALIDIN

CHAPTER ELEVEN
ECONOMIC COLONIALISM AND THE VOICE OF REGRET

Deng Xiaoping famously advised China to "hide your strength and bide your time" (韬光养晦, 决不当头), a strategic directive that shaped China's foreign policy for decades but was kept under the radar from the West and the United States. Deng's full quote encapsulates the essence of this approach: "Observe calmly, secure our position, cope with affairs calmly, hide our capabilities and bide our time, be good at maintaining a low profile, and never claim leadership." This strategy, crafted in the aftermath of Mao's turbulent rule and the Tiananmen Square Massacre in 1989, was intended to ensure China's rise without alarming the world, particularly the West. It was a doctrine of patience, calculated restraint, and strategic deception. The idea was simple: China needed time to rebuild, modernize, and strengthen itself economically and militarily before stepping onto the global stage and replacing the United States as a dominant power.

And for decades, it worked.

China enjoyed uninterrupted economic expansion by relying on the research and development of the West while stealing its technologies and cheating it of trade and business. It became the world's manufacturing hub, embedding itself deeply into global supply chains while using Uyghur forced labor. Western nations, eager to profit from China's cheap labor and vast market potential, largely overlooked its human rights abuses, censorship, and political repression. Meanwhile, China systematically expanded its influence—securing energy resources, developing military capabilities, and extending its economic reach through projects like the Belt and Road Initiative (BRI).

By the time the world started paying attention, China had already become an economic and technological powerhouse in some areas. While its foreign policy still hides behind a façade of somewhat non-intrusiveness, the ultimate goal has been clear—it is global dominance, achieved not through traditional military conquest, but through economic entanglement, political leverage, and ideological expansion.

The world is now waking up to the fact that China did not simply rise—it maneuvered, outpaced, and, in many ways, deceived those who believed it would integrate peacefully into the existing world order. The question now is whether the rest of the world has allowed this to go on for too long.

To those who pay attention to international politics, economics, and history, China's desire for global economic domination and so-called "Superpower" status is nakedly apparent. In its modern iteration, this ambition takes the form of the Belt and Road Initiative (BRI), styled as a push to reestablish under the Chinese Communist Party the prosperity enjoyed through the dominance of the Silk Road.[22] In practice, the BRI is Xi Jinping's blueprint for global domination through debt traps, land grabs, settler colonization, and slave labor.

And then, seemingly overnight, Hong Kong disappeared off the map as a free and autonomous city. As its freedoms were extinguished, the world stood by. In 2020 the CCP imposed the *National Security Law* without warning, a sweeping measure that criminalized secession, subversion, terrorism, and collusion with foreign forces. Overnight, protesters became prisoners, journalists became exiles, and democratic institutions were hollowed out. The world watched in silence, paralyzed by economic interests and unwilling to challenge Beijing's relentless march towards total control. When Hong Kongers protested the new measures, they carried signs that said, "We don't want to become the second Xinjiang."

What I fear many may not understand is the centrality of the Uyghur genocide to this global initiative. Our homeland is not only of vital strategic

---

22. The ancient Silk Road was a network of trade routes that connected China to the Mediterranean, facilitating the exchange of goods, culture, and ideas. The route passing through Xinjiang was a central corridor that linked China to Central Asia, Persia, and beyond.

CHAPTER ELEVEN

importance to Xi Jinping's blueprint, it continues to be the testing ground for the methods of imperial dominance China seeks to export within its sphere of control around the world. This began with the establishment of the Xinjiang Production and Construction Corps (XPCC), also called Bingtuan, under Mao in 1954. Reminiscent of the East India Trading Company, the Bingtuan initiative navigates the line between being a public and private corporation, at once a paramilitary group and a colonial construction company. In its early iteration in 1951, it deployed some 20,865 political detainees and prisoners in advance of 100,000 Han Chinese settlers volunteering to help develop Western China. There they established labor camps in the style of the Soviets, where the number of prisoners working the land was soon in excess of 160,000. Forty thousand women from Hunan and Shandong were sent ostensibly as soldiers but were soon forced into marriage with the soldiers there to begin establishing the foothold of Chinese families in the region. Then came the campaign to draw young people into settling in Bingtuan. Within a year of the Cultural Revolution, the population of Bingtuan exceeded two million.

Bingtuan's growing status was as a quasi-governmental para-military-state, a sort of state within a state. As it grew in prominence under Deng, it entered joint ventures with the World Bank and countries like Japan, Germany, Türkiye, Italy, Singapore, Denmark, Thailand, and the United States. Its wealth was built on cotton and oil, the major resources in East Turkistan. These two commodities form the basis of our homeland's economy. China is second in the world in cotton production and 84 percent of the cotton is from our homeland handpicked by Uyghur slaves. Its wealth is also built on the backs of widespread slave labor camps, long predating the concentration camps of recent years.

In my advocacy, I always try to make a clear distinction between the government of the CCP and the Chinese people. Despite decades of propaganda and government incentives to continue the occupation and takeover of my homeland, the citizens of China are also victims of the CCP's policies and their wildly authoritarian interpretation of communism. What I hope people will come to understand is that in more ways than one, the colonization of East Turkistan and the Uyghur people serve as a testing ground for Chinese colonization all over the world.

Xi Jinping, son of Mao's comrade Xi Zhongxun, rose to prominence in the CCP, becoming secretary general in 2012 and president in 2013. That year, he announced the Belt and Road Initiative, a statement of China's ambition to become the world's dominant economic superpower within the first half of the twenty-first century. Despite its global scope, the key to this initiative would be to bring Xinjiang, the New Territory, under the control of Beijing once and for all. When Xi Jinping visited the region in the early days of his presidency, upon seeing the mosques there full of active worshippers he scolded his officials. "What have you done so far? Are these people still here?" In May of that year, he organized a work conference regarding Xinjiang, where he gave a speech indicating the strategic importance of the region to the BRI and China's future ambitions in energy, transportation, and the Great Western Development Strategy, which was initiated in 2000. Full control of this strategic location and its natural resources had been an ongoing dream for some sixty years. Xi was determined to take the final steps to achieve it. Xinjiang would have to be fully integrated into the mainland of China.

Beginning in 2012, the Chinese government implemented a "punishment on the spot" (shoot-to-kill) policy, permitting any member of the armed forces to kill you if they think you are not following their orders. For example, a traffic policeman can kill you if you resist arrest. Radio Free Asia reported that an Uyghur teenager was shot to death by a traffic police officer when he ran a red light on his motorcycle. Special forces and armed police can raid Uyghur homes at any time and search and arrest as they wish. A high-level Chinese government official, Hu Lianhe, told a UN panel in the summer of 2018, "Xinjiang citizens including the Uyghurs enjoy equal freedoms and rights," but it was also him who told the government in 2012 that "the Uyghur problem must be taken to the final solution stage" as the Nazis did in an attempt to exterminate European Jews.

These actions brought with them, in May 2014, a series of policies known as the Strike Hard Campaign. This took the shape of bloody crackdowns across the region, increased security and police action, and a reinvigoration of the propaganda narrative that all Uyghurs are extremists, terrorists, and dangerously backward in our way of life. An initiative was put in place to

A treasured snapshot of Rushan Abbas as a baby with her nuclear family, father Abbas Borhan, mother Mariye Abliz, sister Gulshan Abbas, and her brothers Rishat Abbas and Nijat Abbas. 1968, Urumchi.

A family photo of Rushan with her beloved parents, siblings, and grandfather, Abliz Niyaz. This is the only photo with her grandfather that Rushan has in her possession in the United States, and the last photo taken of him before he passed away just days later, in January 1981, in Urumchi.

A rare photo of Nobel Laureate Dr. Abdus Salam in Kashgar, pictured with Rushan's parents at the Mahmud Kashgari's mausoleum in Upal, in 1989, a moment that reflects the rich intellectual and cultural legacy of the region before the current era of repression.

Taken in 1995, when Rushan returned from the United States to visit her family in Urumchi. Rushan is shown with her parents, sister Gulshan, brothers Nijat and Rishat, and sisters-in-law Nuriman and Hamra.

Rushan sitting with her father, Abbas Borhan, sharing a quiet, heartfelt moment during her university years. 1985, Urumchi.

Rushan with her son, Misron (Ronny), in 1992. Ronny was born prematurely, at 24 weeks, 100 days early, and was the second-smallest baby born in Washington State, with a birth weight of 820 g (1 lb 13 oz).

A family photo with Abbas Boras, Rushan's father, taken during his final trip to the United States, from October 2004 to May 2005, following the passing of his wife. In this period, he wrote his memoir—words he could never have written freely in Urumchi—and entrusted it to Rishat. Pictured are Rushan, Rishat, Hamra, his granddaughter Zerina, and grandsons Tilman and Davron.

Rushan and Abdulhakim with their sons Bugrahan and Forkan. Herndon, VA, 2010.

Rushan with her children Ronny, Shad, and Shireen, her niece Ziba, and her nephew Tilman. California, 2006.

LEFT: Gulshan with Rushan's daughter Shireen, Abdulhakim, and Rushan in 2016, when Gulshan visited the United States for the birth of her first granddaughter, Zelilah.

BELOW: With Richard Gere in the US Congress, alongside Ilshat Hasan, Shahrezad Ghayrat, Rushan, Mehliya Cetinkaya, Aysu Cetinkaya, Selami Cetinkaya, and Abdulhakim Idris. March 5, 2018.

Rushan with Abdulhakim, the late Ablikim Baki Iltebir, and his wife Dilber Iltebir. As Rushan's middle-school teacher Ablikim Baki Iltebir was one of the individuals who profoundly shaped her political perspective from a young age. November 2018.

Rushan speaking at a 2019 event hosted by the Ahmadiyya Muslim Congressional Caucus, joined by Dr. Sophie Richardson, Ambassador Sam Brownback, Amjad Khan, and Imam Azhar Haneef.

Rushan receiving an appreciation plaque after speaking at the Islamic Society of South Australia in Adelaide, Australia. Also pictured is Nurmemet Turkistani, president of the Eastern Turkistan Australian Association. December 2019.

Uyghur women in Southern Australia welcoming Rushan in Adelaide, Australia. December 2019.

Rushan at her first US Senate testimony in April 2019, with Senator Ed Markey, Bhuchung K. Tsering, VP of the International Campaign for Tibet, Gulshan's daughter, Ziba Murat, and Dr. Rishat Abbas.

Uyghur leader Mr. Erkin Alptekin in the center, together with Abdulhakim, Rushan, Dolkun Isa, Perhat Muhammed, Ekrem Hezim, and Erkin Zunun in Munich. October 2021.

Rushan and Dr. Rishat Abbas at the White House in 2019. A powerful moment of sibling unity in advocacy for the Uyghur people and their sister, Dr. Gulshan Abbas.

Rushan with then-Senator Marco Rubio at the 2020 State of the Union Address, which she attended as his guest, an invitation that underscored his steadfast support for the Uyghur cause and the fight for justice.

US National Prayer Breakfast. Rushan was recognized on the screen before an audience that included President Trump, Vice President Pence, Speaker Pelosi, Secretary Pompeo, and many dignitaries, diplomats, and human rights advocates. February 6, 2020.

In 2021, Rushan with former US Secretary of State Mike Pompeo, who made the historic US determination of genocide in relation to China's atrocities in the Uyghur homeland. Uyghurs honor him with the name "Polat," meaning "Steel," a symbol of his strength and principled leadership in standing up for justice.

Rushan with members of the Portuguese Parliament after Abdulhakim and Rushan delivered their testimony on the Uyghur genocide. September 2022.

Rushan and Abdulhakim in Malaysia in 2022 conducting critical meetings with MPs Dr. Rusnah Aluai, Dr. Hassan Baharom, and Tengku Razaleigh Hamzah about the Uyghur cause. Also pictured: Mr. Mohd Khairul Anwar Ismail, President of Global Peace Mission, Malaysia, and Ahmad Fahmi Mohd Samsudin, President of ABIM.

Rushan and Abdulhakim at the US Ambassador's residence in Italy in 2022, meeting with Italian lawmakers and diplomats, including Sen. Giorgio Fede, Sen. Lucio Malan, and MPs Paolo Formentini and Piero Fassino, to strengthen international advocacy efforts and raise awareness about the ongoing Uyghur genocide.

Rushan and Ziba Murat with then-US Secretary of State Antony Blinken at the State Department Eid Event in May 2022. Blinkin publicly acknowledged Campaign for Uyghurs during his remarks on the 2023 International Religious Freedom Report, underscoring CFU's impact on the fight for Uyghur rights.

At a historic press conference in Taiwan attended by several members of the Legislative Yuan, where Rushan delivered a presentation on the Uyghur plight. Abdulhakim Idris and Rushan are pictured with Wuer Kaixi, MP Chiao-Hui Su, , MP Wang Tingyu, then-MP Claire Wang, and Taiwan East Turkistan Association President Ho Chao-tung. February 2023.

State of the Union address, 2023. Rushan was invited as a guest of Congressman Raja Krishnamoorthi, Ranking Member of the House Select Committee on China, and greeted by Minority Leader Hakeem Jeffries. Pictured: Rushan sharing a photo of her sister, Dr. Gulshan Abbas. February 2023.

Film screening at the University of Melbourne, May 2024. Rushan, Wuer Kaixi, Sabrina Sohail, CFU Director of Advocacy and Communications, Mukerrem Kurban, Director at CFU, Nuria Khasim (great-granddaughter of East Turkistan leader Ehmetjan Qasim) with students, and members of the Uyghur community.

Türkiye, 2023. Rushan, Abdulhakim Idris, and Abdulkadir Uygur met with MP Ms. Derya Yanık, Chairperson of the Turkish Parliament's Human Rights Commission, to discuss collaborative efforts in advocating for Uyghur human rights.

Rushan on Dr. Phil. Rushan was in the episode, titled "China's Economic Takeover of America: Who Owns Our Land?" which explored China's growing influence in the United States and its human rights abuses in China. Recorded February 14, 2024, in Texas.

At the launch of the Congressional Uyghur Caucus, leaders from Campaign for Uyghurs (CFU), Uyghur Academy, Center for Uyghur Studies, Uyghur American Association, Uyghur Human Rights Project and World Uyghur Congress came together to honor the co-chairs, Congressman Chris Smith and Congressman Tom Suozzi. Pictured: Nury Turkel, Dr. Rishat Abbas, Rep. Chris Smith, Elfidar Iltebir, Rushan Abbas, Rep. Tom Suozzi, Omar Kanat, Dolkun Isa, and Abdulhakim Idris. April 16, 2024.

To Rushan Abbas and Abdulhakim Idris
With best wishes,

Rushan and her husband, Abdulhakim, with President George W. Bush and First Lady Laura Bush following the Bush Center's Forum on Leadership. April 18, 2024.

Rushan with National Security Council Advisor (then Congressman) Mike Waltz at the 2024 State of the Union Address, where she was hosted by Rep. Chris Smith.

Rushan with Evgenia Kara-Murza, Advocacy Director of the Free Russia Foundation, and Vladimir Kara-Murza, Russian-British activist, journalist, author, filmmaker, and former political prisoner in Prague, at the Forum 2000 Conference, October 2024.

Rushan and Abdulhakim Idris were welcomed to Istanbul in December 2024 by prominent Uyghur community members Jelil Turan, Jemilegul Turan, Mustafa Turan, Mehmet Ali Hafiz, and Mehmetcan Kashgarli.

Rushan with Uyghur delegates from around the world at the State Department round-table discussion providing an update on the current persecution of the Uyghur people in the Uyghur homeland, after attending a conference hosted by the Uyghur Academy International. December 2024.

CHAPTER ELEVEN

change the nature of education to better dissolve any sense of Islamic identity in the Uyghurs living there.

July of 2015 saw the passing of a new security bill that gave the government and the police broad powers to follow and monitor suspected dissidents in the region. In September 2015, a document titled "Testimony to Ethnic Equality, Unity and Development in Xinjiang" was published, further casting Muslims as terrorists and extremists, and outlawing public officials from even setting foot within a Muslim place of worship. To do so risked accusations of being involved with "religious extremism."

In August 2016, the CCP Committee's previous Secretary of the Tibet Autonomous Region, Chen Quanguo, was assigned as Committee Secretary of the XUAR. The politburo considered him a good fit for the job because of his five years of policies that had been effective in growing the GDP of Tibet—and in controlling the population. During his tenure in Tibet, he instituted many policies that increased surveillance, mass arrests and disappearances, and labor camps styled as reeducation camps. He was also the author of a policy known as the "Double-Linked Household Management System," which encouraged more than three million neighbors to spy on one another and report on each other to authorities. His time there also saw an influx of 280,000 Han Chinese settlers migrating to the region to marginalize Tibetans within their own region. These policies would serve as a blueprint for the CCP's approach to controlling Uyghurs in the XUAR. They also saw a sudden rise in protests and self-immolations by Tibetan monks and nuns, who were the primary targets of these policies.

After Chen Quanguo came to power, he began his ruthless cultural and ethnic subjugations with the arrest of the members of the Uyghur textbook development committee and abolished the Uyghur literature textbooks. A leaked internal document quoted him saying the party "must first break their (Uyghurs) lineage, break their roots, break their connections and break their origins." These chilling words only point to Beijing's harshest policies towards the Uyghurs.

In 2022, Dr. Adrian Zenz and the Victims of the Communism Memorial Foundation obtained a massive cache of leaked documents. Dating back to 2018, they contained more than three hundred thousand personal records, thousands of records and images of detainees, speeches, and the explicit instructions given to camp police. These documents were published in May of that year as a joint effort by fourteen separate media groups and came to be known as the Xinjiang Police Files. They detail the Shoot-to-Kill policy implemented by Chen Quanguo in 2018 for any attempted escapees, and his order that officials "exercise firm control over religious believers." They detail the machine gun nests and sniper towers employed within the camps. They include mugshots of the detainees with evidence they are used to harvest biometric data. Photos of interrogations show Uyghurs in shackles, and spreadsheets within the documents for the camps in Konasheher County listed eight thousand detainees and ten thousand more recommended for detainment or closer examination by the Integrated Joint Operations Platform (IJOP). These include not only lists of the detained, but separate lists of their relatives as well. They list detainees subject to solitary confinement. Another spreadsheet titled "Persons Subjected to Strike Hard Because of Religion" lists those individuals detained for studying the Qur'an, and other religious activities.

These files contradict and refute the long-standing narrative that these camps exist for voluntary reeducation or vocational training. They are prisons, highly militarized and rife with surveillance, abuse, and torture. These documents also illustrate the guilt-by-association policy of the Chinese state, and the extent to which religious practice and expression continues to be criminalized as extremist behavior. This was the first time in years that we had pictures of the victims. It was chilling to see their faces.

In much the same way that China's action in Tibet served as a blueprint for the crackdown in the Uyghur region, the apparatus of oppression used by a police state, i.e., technologies enhanced with artificial intelligence, has been a blueprint for controlling the lives of people throughout China. By now, much has been revealed about the widespread use of facial recognition and motion tracking data to build ongoing profiles of everyday citizens. The state's implementation of a social credit score to keep the masses in line similarly seems inspired by some science fiction dystopia one would never dare to imagine might take shape in the real world. What I hope readers understand is that, just as these technologies and their invasive use did not stay contained within Xinjiang, they will not remain confined to the borders of China. In fact, the state has already begun to export their model of a surveillance state to countries willing to impose this data-driven authoritarianism.

The Kampala police in Uganda have recently procured AI surveillance systems valued at $126 million from the Chinese manufacturer Huawei. In Kenya, downtown Nairobi saw the implementation of a network of two thousand cameras routed through a centralized IC3 Integrated Control and Communication Center, courtesy of Huawei. Zimbabwe has similarly partnered with an AI startup in Guangdong called Cloudwalk for access to facial recognition systems. In total, twenty-two African countries have contracted Chinese firms for the public security systems employed in China—with the support of Beijing in the form of training programs and law-enforcement cooperation programs.

Across Africa, this has been the shape of China's approach to economic colonization. Those countries that do not submit to China's seeming benevolence in exporting their invasive security practices find themselves on the business end of a debt trap. Angola, which has been borrowing from China since 1983, owes China $25 billion dollars to date—about $754 per Angolan. To pay this debt, all the oil produced by Angola is paid to China. China also invests heavily in Egypt for proximity to the Suez Canal, claims 75 percent of the oil produced in Sudan, and has made significant investments in rail travel and transportation infrastructure in Djibouti, Ethiopia, Kenya, and Zambia. In the Democratic Republic of the Congo (DRC), where 80 percent of the world's cobalt metals are mined, China controls 80 percent of the output, a figure that accounts for 67.5 percent of the cobalt refined by China, which in turn is responsible for between 60 percent and 90 percent of the world's supply. This metal is essential for everything from smartphones to advanced batteries and solar power, and China has very quickly cornered the market. Of the ten largest cobalt mines in the DRC, China controls half. Between investments in infrastructure, energy, mining, communication, and other sectors, the total debt owed by African nations to China is almost $150 billion.

Under the Belt and Road Initiative, China presents these investments and lending deals as a win-win scenario. These offers are often enticing, as Chinese money comes quicker than investments from anywhere else, if at a premium. Often, these deals also come with the promise of imported Chinese goods. In reality, the imbalance of imports to exports from these countries results in local workshops quickly becoming unable to compete with a sudden influx of products made in China. Meanwhile, they are called upon to repay debts for projects that have yet to be completed. The Overseas Development Institute estimates that 40 percent of sub-Saharan African countries now face a major debt crisis.

The cost of these countries maintaining their relationships with China also creates a cost for Uyghurs living in them. In 2017 there were raids of many Uyghur homes in Egypt. Most of those arrested were then deported back to China at the request of the government there. The rest were held for sixty days and had their passports confiscated. Most of them were students. Nigeria, which is the largest Muslim country on the continent of Africa, maintains its silence on the genocide and supports China in the UN due to its ongoing trade relationship. Despite this compliance, China continues to list Nigeria as one of those countries that are criminal for Uyghurs to visit. Uyghurs who set foot in Nigeria are sent to concentration camps upon this basis.

The curtain of silence extends into the Muslim countries of the Middle East through trade agreements with Iran, Saudi Arabia, the United Arab Emirates (UAE), and other Gulf countries, including Qatar, Bahrain, and Oman. In Iran, a $400 billion deal following the nuclear agreement of 2016 has secured cheap oil for Beijing for twenty-five years. The deal also brought with it the implementation of surveillance and digital firewall systems based on those used in China, and the promise of Iran's support of China's digital yuan, the e-CNY, in lieu of participation in American and European finance systems. Despite its status as an Islamic Republic, Iran's government continues to maintain silence about China's treatment of Muslims within its own borders. The UAE, which China regards as a trade gateway into both Europe and the Middle East/North Africa region, writes off these genocidal practices as China's own internal affairs, agreeing not to interfere. Since Xi Jinping came to power, China's thirty-five-year relationship with Saudi Arabia has grown, with China, the country that openly regards Islam as a virus to be removed and destroyed, building a high-speed rail between two of the Muslim world's

CHAPTER ELEVEN

holiest sites, Mecca and Medina. In all these countries, initiatives have also been established to teach Chinese to students in schools, alongside an uptick in Chinese immigrants moving into these countries to conduct business. All have been effectively incentivized to remain quiet about how China treats Uyghur Muslims in East Turkistan.

The CCP demands to establish itself as the only authority in the lives of its people in order to expand their brutal colonialism across the world. The genocidal policies and oppression used against the Uyghurs will only expand. Look at Tibet and Southern Mongolia. Look at Hong Kong, and Chinese dissidents. Look at how the Belt and Road Initiative is being used to manipulate countries as the CCP fights to control the narrative globally with its blood money.

Dictatorships will not allow people to live in freedom. They would rather put them in concentration camps to "reeducate" them. In August 2022, the Chinese Ambassador to France, Lu Shaye, vowed that "after reunification of Taiwan, we will do reeducation." As I tell my friends in Taiwan, please look at these pictures from Xinjiang Police Files, look at the innocent Uyghurs in the concentration camps and imagine what kind of future will be waiting for the Taiwanese people if they do not defend their freedom from the CCP's imminent threat.

China is attempting to export their worldview and authoritarian system globally. What China is doing to my people, and to Tibetans & Hong Kongers, is a preview of what we will see, should we allow China to continue their crimes. If we allow China to continue on this path, the world that has been built on the foundations of freedom, democracy, and human rights will be dismantled before our very eyes. It will be your children, and grandchildren, that will deal with the consequences of an illiberal world. When learning about the genocide, Americans will often ask, "Why don't the Muslim countries support you?" It is not enough to say that China has bought their silence. China has bought their loyalty as well. When we go to them for help, the Muslim countries ask us, "Why are you letting America use you to contain China?" The result is that in the wake of China's economic expansion and this form of extortion disguised as mutually beneficial business, the Uyghurs of my homeland are entirely isolated on the world stage, without an ally that is sufficiently independently positioned to speak on our behalf.

America is far from immune to these colonial endeavors. Through its shell corporations, China has bought an incredible amount of land on US soil, driving up real estate costs for local farmers and businesses. Some of these plots of land are in strategic proximity to eight military bases and installations. Among them, Dugway Proving Ground in Utah houses military equipment and biological and chemical weapon defense systems. In addition to missile and drone operations, Whiteman Air Force Base houses the entirety of the air force's bomber force, as well as Nuclear Command, Control, and Communications (NC3) systems. Three full wings of intercontinental ballistic missiles are also kept there. Naval Station Norfolk berths a variety of naval vessels, including aircraft carriers, destroyers, submarines, and amphibious assault ships. China has purchased land in close proximity to each of these, in some cases constructing windmills and turbines tall enough to gain a line of sight into these bases with mounted cameras. These turbines also grant them access to the American electrical grid, leaving an opening for them to upload malware to directly target our power systems.

When it comes to imports, it is not merely consumer goods manufactured in China that we rely on. America relies on China and other nations for its health care as well. The vast majority of active pharmaceutical ingredients and prescription drugs alike are manufactured overseas, and China is by far the largest provider. Together, China and India account for 91 percent of the medications prescribed to American patients. Direct conflict with China could deal a devastating blow to the availability of common pharmaceuticals and prescription drugs, a cost that would inevitably be paid in human lives. Due to ongoing drug shortages, which have increased every year, as many as sixty million Americans are currently going without the medication they need.

This growing dependency on China for manufacturing across all sectors has become an issue facing the governments of all nations, no matter what their size or strength. Be they democracies or authoritarian regimes, the trade deals and infrastructure development offered by the Belt and Road Initiative often appear too good to pass up, and even in the West this has led to a general attitude of appeasement to maintain relations with China.

CHAPTER ELEVEN

Based on the evidence, it is becoming increasingly clear that continuing this tack will only yield inevitable consequences down the line.

While China has successfully bought the silence of governments, businesses, and institutions around the world, there have been rare individuals willing to speak out, even at great personal cost. One of them is Richard Gere, a renowned American actor. I first met him in 2008 during a protest in San Francisco against the Beijing Olympic torch relay. Uyghurs, Tibetans, and Chinese democracy activists stood together in defiance of China's growing influence. When I spoke to him about the Uyghur atrocities and asked for his support, he responded without hesitation:

"We are all together in this fight."

Richard Gere was one of the few in Hollywood who bravely refused to kowtow to China's power. During the 1993 Academy Awards ceremony, he spoke about the human rights abuses in Tibet inflicted by China. The CCP banned him from the country. For years, Richard Gere spoke out against the CCP's brutal repression in Tibet and its broader human rights abuses. But in an industry desperate for access to China's massive box office market, his heroic actions made him a pariah. He was quietly blacklisted from major roles, no longer appearing in big-budget Hollywood films. His career suffered because he had the courage to call out China's crimes.

This is how China operates—not only through economic entanglement and coercion, but through erasing, punishing, and silencing voices that challenge its narrative. Today, many corporations, media outlets, and celebrities choose self-censorship over justice, fearful of losing access to China's lucrative market. How many others saw what happened to Richard Gere and decided that silence was safer?

The reality is that Uyghurs, Tibetans, Hong Kongers, and dissidents do not need more silent bystanders. We need leaders, advocates, and institutions willing to risk their comfort for the truth. Richard Gere made that choice.

But it is not only actors and activists who face this kind of pressure. China has mastered the art of economic coercion on a global scale—silencing not just individuals, but entire nations.

Through its vast economic leverage, trade agreements, and strategic investments, the CCP ensures that countries, corporations, and multilateral institutions stay in line, avoiding any real challenge to its atrocities. The consequences of crossing China are clear—leaders and governments who dare to speak out risk losing lucrative trade deals, economic investments, or even being targeted with direct political retaliation.

This is how China's economic colonization works. It does not need to wage war to bend nations to its will—it only needs to make them dependent.

For many Uyghurs, escaping persecution in China is a journey of immense danger and heartbreak. A tragic example is the plight of Uyghur refugees in Thailand, highlighting China's influence and global inaction. In 2014, 350 Uyghur refugees fled escalating repression, seeking safety in Thailand. Instead, they were detained in inhumane conditions for nearly eleven years. Despite relentless efforts by human rights groups and activists to prevent their forced repatriation, they remained at risk of imprisonment, torture, forced labor, or execution if they were returned to China.

In June 2015, Turkey resettled 172 refugees, though five died due to inadequate medical care, including two children. For those still in Thailand, the nightmare continued, with many detained for nearly eleven years in overcrowded cells meant for short-term stays. In July 2015, 109 Uyghur men, women, and children were forcibly deported from Thailand to China, where many disappeared into the prison system. Others remained in Thai custody, living in limbo.

On January 9, 2025, we learned that the CCP was pressuring Thailand to deport the 48 remaining Uyghurs.

On January 17, I arrived in Tokyo for the Campaign for Uyghurs' advocacy training workshop for the Uyghur community in Japan. During my time there, I learned of the imminent risk of deportation facing Uyghurs detained in Thailand. Concerned allies from various governments urged me to travel to Bangkok to meet with Thai politicians and other key stakeholders working tirelessly to save them. Before making a decision, I called my husband, Abdulhakim, for his advice. Given Thailand's close ties with Beijing and the security threats we had recently faced during the 8th General Assembly of the World Uyghur Congress (WUC) in Sarajevo, he cautioned me about the risks. He insisted that if I were to go, I should not travel alone and should keep the trip confidential until after my departure from Bangkok. I agreed.

CHAPTER ELEVEN

To ensure my safety and effectiveness, I planned to travel with Polat Sayim, Deputy Chairman of the WUC Executive Committee, and Sawut Memet, head of the WUC's Asia Affairs Committee.

On January 19, we landed in Bangkok around six in the evening after nearly eight hours in the air. While we were en route, the situation for the Uyghurs in Thailand took a dire turn. We learned that a deportation order had been issued for the early hours of January 20. The timing was strategic: the United States was observing Martin Luther King Jr. Day and preparing for President-elect Donald Trump's inauguration, and Thailand's pro-Beijing Prime Minister, Paetongtarn Shinawatra, was scheduled to visit China on February 4, 2025. Our phones were ringing nonstop. Allies, friends from the embassies, human rights defenders, journalists, and the families of the Uyghurs detained at the Immigration Detention Center (IDC) in Bangkok's Sathorn district were reaching out in desperation. The warning was clear: deportation was imminent, and we needed to act fast, raising the alarm in the media and contacting other stakeholders.

Thanapee, a journalist from *The Reporters*, requested a live interview. Before going public, I called my husband to discuss the risks of disclosing my location. His response was resolute: "This is a battle between freeing them and the evil CCP. Do whatever you can, but be careful. Don't leave the hotel alone, watch your surroundings, and be cautious with your food and drinks." With his blessing, I went live that night, calling for urgent action while simultaneously writing emails and making frantic calls to the US State Department, Congress, and embassies of like-minded nations. My interview with *The Reporters* sent ripples through the media, and soon after, journalists from Thai PBS, *The Guardian*, France's *Le Monde*, and The Associated Press began reaching out for interviews. The fight had begun.

Being on the ground for twenty-eight hours, we worked tirelessly to alarm the world and urge the Thai government to halt the deportations. We met with MPs, civil society leaders, diplomats, and journalists for support. After another eight-hour flight on the night of January 20, I landed in Japan on January 21 and, just four hours later, addressed the Uyghur Friendship Group at the Japanese Parliament. I said:

> Today marks the 11th day of their hunger strike, a desperate attempt to avoid deportation and torture in China. Despite international outcry, a 2023 recommendation from Thailand's Human Rights Commission, and UN experts' inquiries, Thailand has refused to release or resettle these men. The UN High Commissioner for Refugees, under China's influence, has denied them refugee status. Thailand's inaction shows how China manipulates global institutions and international law. I urge you to take action—issue a statement, demand their immediate release, and press Thailand to honor its obligations under the Convention Against Torture.

The Uyghurs in detention went on an eighteen-day hunger strike, drawing global media attention and condemnation from human rights organizations, US officials, governments, and legal experts.

Despite pressure and offers of resettlement from countries like the United States, Canada, and Sweden, Thailand deported forty Uyghurs back to China. They were sent back to active genocide. On February 27, 2025, Thailand caved to Beijing's pressure. Just one day after the deportation, Thailand announced a new deal for TikTok to invest $8.8 billion in data centers over the next five years, highlighting the economic interests overshadowing human rights. This is yet another example of how China weaponizes its economic influence to coerce nations into complicity with its human rights abuses. By leveraging trade deals, investments, and political pressure, Beijing ensures that authoritarian control extends far beyond its borders, silencing opposition and reinforcing its grip over those who dare to resist.

What I hope readers will understand from all of this is that the exploitation and genocide of the Uyghur people is not some minor, isolated issue without ramifications for the rest of the world. It is, in fact, the central issue upon which China's threat to all people is built. This genocide is not only eradicating my people and breaking our culture under the yoke of homogeneity. It is enacted precisely to build the wealth and strategic positioning necessary to establish global domination for China, through international

CHAPTER ELEVEN

extortion and economic practices with which most countries are unable to compete.

Through these practices of economic colonization, China buys the silence of governments globally. They would prefer that we remained silent about it. If we do not use our voice today, the only voice we will have to speak with tomorrow will be the voice of regret. Understand that this regret will not be solely for the loss of the Uyghur people and our way of life. That loss is profound and is felt by my people every day. It will take generations to begin to heal what has been done to us. Beyond this, the nations of the world will inevitably regret the onslaught of Chinese economic colonization built upon the wealth extracted via this genocide. China goes out of its way to incentivize silence, whether it is from those countries over which it holds its economic sway or from the United Nations itself. Oftentimes, we have seen that these incentives appear too good to refuse. If China is able to establish the global economic dominance it seeks through the BRI and its modern form of imperialism, silence will no longer be in the best interest of these entities. The regret of my people will surely be shared in all corners of the globe. I fear that by then it will be too late.

The civilized societies of the world must demonstrate the integrity to take concrete action to address these horrors. The soul of humanity is being tested: will we have the moral courage to pass this test?

CHAPTER TWELVE
THE GENOCIDE OLYMPIC GAMES AND OUR GENOCIDE REPORT

On October 19, 2018, shortly after my sister's detention, I wrote my first op-ed telling my sister's story and published it in *The Washington Post*. In May 2019, I wrote an article for *USA Today*, sharing the long history of Uyghur repression—from my grandfather's imprisonment to my father's time in reeducation camps. I described parents banned from giving children Muslim names, men forced to shave their beards, mosques bulldozed, and crematoriums rising in a region where traditional burials are sacred. I detailed the worsening crisis and the reality we faced.

By May 2019, US Deputy Secretary of Defense Randal Schriver estimated that up to three million Uyghurs—out of just eleven million—were imprisoned in newly built camps. Former camp survivors testified to brutal conditions, including forced renunciation of religion and identity, torture, and rape. Meanwhile, thousands of Uyghur children were separated from their parents and placed in state-run orphanages to be indoctrinated into abandoning their heritage.

Like many before it, this piece concluded with a call for the United States to employ targeted sanctions under the *Magnitsky Act* against the high-level Chinese officials most responsible for these policies. I wrote,

> Time is running out. . . . Despite the horrendous atrocities the Uyghurs are facing, including my own family, we are confronted by a muted world. Is an entire ethnic and vulnerable religious group becoming collateral damage to short-term

CHAPTER TWELVE

politics? Or will the United States take a stand for its highest ideals of human dignity and freedom?

The article was titled: "I've Fought China's Slow-Motion Genocide of Uyghur Muslims. Now, My Family Are Victims." I noticed that when it was published, the words "slow-motion" had been added. It made me think. The terminology surrounding accusations of genocide are fraught, and when identifying genocide there is a tendency to split hairs. By this point we had contended for years with the qualification of China's treatment of Uyghurs as a *cultural* genocide—a term that tends to create in people's minds an unwarranted distinction between it and a "real" genocide. Calling something a cultural genocide serves to soften the accusation. After that, I asked myself, is this a slow-motion genocide, or is it just genocide?

In August 2019, I was invited to give a speech in London for some researchers, experts, advocates and human rights defenders. I began my speech by stating, "What is happening today to the Uyghurs is common knowledge by now. We have been crying out for help for years. But no action. Right now, the Chinese Communist Party is setting the stage to alter the course of history and change the world as we know it." The rest of my remarks were as follows:

> Will we be able to uphold the vow "NEVER AGAIN" with real actions to follow or shall we sadly witness a repeat of the 1938 Munich Agreement as countries around the world avoided acknowledging Nazi Germany's human rights abuses for the sake of economic trade, at the cost of millions of lives? At the beginning of the Holocaust, countries around the world continued to do business with Germany including the United Kingdom, enabling their economies while millions of innocent people were being detained and held in concentration camps. The United Kingdom paid the price of economic cooperation with Nazi Germany, with bombs blowing up over their heads. The countries and leaders said that access to information was slow, and they hid behind claims of ignorance. Now, it is the 21st century. Ignorance

is not an excuse anymore. China's first concentration camp was built under the "Strike Hard Campaign" in 2014 in Lopnur.[23] It has been five years. According to media reports, the size of the camps has grown 465 percent in the past eighteen months alone. China is a growing economic power. Its growth potential is limitless. And right now, millions of Uyghurs are becoming collateral damage to international trade policies that are enabling China to continue to murder my people. Enabling them to continue their Orwellian police state in my homeland. Enabling China to continue to threaten our freedoms around the world. But it's not just about the freedom of religion to the millions incarcerated in my homeland right now. It's about the freedom to live. It is about survival. It is no secret that China created militarized islands on top of coral reef reserves in the South China Sea. This land grab effectively extended their sea territory and increased tensions over disputed waters. Keep that in mind when looking at the Belt and Road Initiative (BRI)'s projected path so you are not surprised. Control over key sea passages will choke out economic competition in the area and enhance China's authority in the Indo-Pacific region. From North to South, and East to West, China's growth and thirst for power is ceaseless. Bullying and manipulation of the United Nations should not go unchallenged. The model and the technology underpinning mass repression in our homeland is already being rolled out to other parts of China and being actively exported to more than a dozen countries around the world. This is a warning that our freedoms are in danger if we do not act. On July 10th a joint statement signed by twenty-two, later increased to twenty-four, mostly western democratic countries were issued to the United Nations condemning China's so-called "Uyghur Detention Centers." As a response thirty-seven countries released a letter defend-

---

23.   A county in Xinjiang

ing China's treatment of the Uyghurs. Then, the numbers increased to fifty currently. What if those countries are 100 or 150? China is spreading its communist ideologies around the world. This threatens all of us. This challenges everything we have worked for in the past 100 years. We must act now. We are running out of time. Continuing to do business as normal with China today is being complicit with genocide and supporting the spread of communism to the world. If we fail to challenge Communist China on this terrible atrocity with the determination to stop it, it would be the beginning of darkness for accountable democracies as a totalitarian government effectively utilizes mass surveillance and repression to instill fear at home and abroad. If the free world does not act soon, China's debt trap tactics, expansion of its BRI, manipulation in the United Nations, and provision of 5G technology to the West will position China to threaten the entire world's population.

What the PRC is doing to the Uyghurs is effectively killing four birds with one stone:

1. Forcing millions of Uyghurs into slavery.
2. Dislocating Uyghurs from their homes, neighborhoods, towns, and counties to make room for Han Chinese settlers and opening the land for the Belt and Road Initiative.
3. Jailing Uyghur men in camps and prisons and forcing unwed and abandoned Uyghur women to marry Han Chinese and assimilate.
4. Orchestrating organ farms, where millions are forced to undergo DNA tests and prepped for slaughter. The human rights organizations of the world need to pay attention and take the lead against the PRC's organ slavery trade practice.

China has already won in linking anything, whether money from trade or fear of retaliation, to the West's ability to stand up independently against evident evil. I do not know what it takes to get the attention of world leaders to realize that now is the time to stand up. Do not wait for mass executions and gas chambers. Act now, and act bravely.

In March 2020, I was invited to speak on a panel at the United States Holocaust Memorial Museum in Washington, DC. Before the event, the museum staff led us on a tour through the exhibits, chronicling the slow and deliberate march towards genocide in Nazi Germany. As I walked past images and testimonies detailing the systematic persecution of Jews, an unsettling familiarity settled in my chest. I thought to myself, *This is how it started. This is how it is continuing right now. This is genocide.*

The event, organized by Naomi Kikoler, Executive Director of the Simon-Skjodt Center for the Prevention of Genocide, along with Andrea Gittleman and Hans Hogrefe, brought together experts to discuss the atrocities facing Uyghurs in China. Among the panelists were Dr. Adrian Zenz, Alim Seytoff, Director of the Uyghur Service at Radio Free Asia, and Jessica Batke, Senior Editor at ChinaFile. Each speaker laid bare the horrors unfolding in East Turkistan: mass internment camps, forced labor, and the relentless erasure of Uyghur culture.

I had worked with Alim Seytoff at Radio Free Asia in 1999 and later served with him on the Uyghur Association Board in 2009. His decades-long commitment to exposing China's repression—first as a founding member and president of the Uyghur American Association, and later in leadership roles within the World Uyghur Congress—had been instrumental in shining a light on the plight of our people.

As the discussion unfolded, I listened to Naomi Kikoler speak about her family's connection to the Holocaust. Her words, carrying the weight of history, only deepened my sense of urgency. The parallels between the past and present were undeniable. The systematic dehumanization, the forced disappearances, the state-sponsored cultural destruction—these were not just echoes of the past, they were unfolding in real-time.

CHAPTER TWELVE

The gravity of this moment stayed with me throughout the event. Even as I spoke, I felt an unshakable conviction growing within me. It was no longer enough to bear witness; action was imperative.

In the days that followed, I made a decision: Campaign for Uyghurs would compile a report systematically detailing how the situation in East Turkistan met every qualification of a genocide. We were a small team with limited resources, but the moral imperative was clear. We had to document the truth. We had to push for recognition.

Because history had already shown us what happens when the world looks away.

Abdulhakim Idris and I started to work on this genocide report with my team at Campaign for Uyghurs. Assembling this report was an ongoing and involved process that represented several months of research, gathering testimony and evidence, as well as constructing a cohesive list of proposed action from the UN, governments, NGOs, corporations, and individuals alike. This report, titled *Genocide in East Turkistan: The Genocide of Uyghurs by Definition of the United Nations Convention on Genocide Prevention*, was completed and published in 2020. It was first published in English and then translated to Turkish, Arabic, Mandarin, and Japanese.

I began looking into the Geneva Convention's descriptions of genocide and the ways in which it is identified and classified by the United Nations. The term came into use in 1944 after being coined by Raphael Lemkin. A year later, during the Nuremberg trials of Nazi officials in Germany, it was used as a descriptive term for the charges of crimes against humanity. It was not until January 12, 1951, that an official description of genocide as a crime was adopted in the United Nations, in the form of a nineteen-article contract in Resolution 260 (III), the "Convention on the Prevention and Punishment of the Crime of Genocide."

This document, in its definition of the crime found in article 2, lists five actions that constitute crimes of genocide, as follows:

- killing members of the group,
- causing serious bodily or mental harm to members of the group,

- deliberately inflicting on the group conditions of life calculated to bring about its physical destruction in whole or in part,
- imposing measures intended to prevent births within the group, and,
- forcibly transferring children of the group to another group.

It states that any act aimed at eliminating a national, ethnic, racial, or religious group constitutes genocide. This struck me—just one act is enough, and there was ample evidence for most, if not all. A strong case existed for four out of five, with mass killing being the only exception—though this likely reflected the government's ability to cover its tracks. With millions missing, survival numbers remain unknown. The rise in crematoriums near camps and past mass burials after violent crackdowns suggest a grim reality, underscoring the low value of Uyghur lives in China.

In a speech to the People's Liberation Army, Chinese military official Chi Haotian stated that China should learn from the failures of the Germans and Japanese in World War II by closely studying why they lost. In his opinion, they lost the war because they fought on too many fronts at once instead of dismantling their enemies one by one. He went on to say, "China should keep other enemies in its heart while getting rid of the primary enemy."

The Nazis kept records of their concentration camps, and of how many were sent to the gas chambers. China destroys all evidence. In the aftermath of the Urumchi Massacre in 2009, Human Rights Watch reported that 40,000 Uyghurs had disappeared. Disappeared to where? How many were jailed or executed? How many perished that night? There is no official record to prove the actions of the state in the past fifteen years. How many people need to die to make the case that the Uyghur people are being systematically eradicated?

The report confirmed that Uyghurs qualify as a targeted group, defined by their national, ethnic, racial, and religious traits. With a history of being distinct from China, then occupied, and now part of the Xinjiang Uyghur Autonomous Region, Uyghurs have a unique nationality, ethnic heritage, and shared religious culture. Each of these identities has been systematically repressed. The CCP is waging a war on religion. Through the banning of Islamic practices, the razing of our places of worship, and the burning of

CHAPTER TWELVE

our holy book; by forcing us to eat pork and denying even the right to lay our dead to rest as our tradition calls for, the Uyghur Islamic identity is not only erased, but criminalized. Through forced abortion and state-imposed sterilization, and by taking the right from Uyghur women to choose who to marry and raise families with, the state targets the Uyghur ethnic identity for destruction as well.

The "Pair Up and Become Family" program forces Uyghur households to host Han Chinese officials for surveillance and control. Uyghur girls are also coerced into marrying Han Chinese men in mass ceremonies, with government officers monitoring the marriages. Those who object face detention in camps. The government offers incentives for these forced marriages, including money, housing, and jobs, while using propaganda and a state-sponsored "dating app" to commodify Uyghur women. When their sons and husbands disappear into the camps, they are often shipped to various factories and forced labor facilities within the mainland to work as slave labor. A report by the Australian Strategic Policy Institute titled "Uyghurs for Sale" revealed that more than eighty thousand Uyghurs were taken from concentration camps to be sent to factories for the manufacture of goods from a wide array of renowned Western brands: GAP, Nike, Apple, and Volkswagen to name just a few. As many as five hundred such brands benefit from forced Uyghur labor.

Additionally, 84 percent of China's cotton production occurs within the Uyghur region. It is also where the Heinz Corporation farms tomatoes for their ketchup products. In the summer of 2020, US Customs even came across and seized thirteen tons of human hair, exported as wigs from the region. Today, "Made in China" could be synonymous with "Made by Uyghur Slaves." How many lives do thirteen tons of hair represent?

Transferring these prisoners across the country is also another method of influencing the demography of East Turkistan: The region is advertised among Han Chinese as a beautiful and fertile place to move and start a life, while Uyghurs are systematically spread out across the rest of the country.

When both mother and father disappear, their children are subsumed by a network of state-run orphanages, closed-off buildings and boarding schools, where they are taught to see their cultural heritage as a viral infection to the . philosophy. Dr. Adrian Zenz has stated that "boarding schools provide the ideal environment for cultural engineering of minorities,"[24] revealing the purpose of the Chinese government in establishing these institutions. The children are dressed in traditional Chinese clothes not worn in civil society for centuries to instill a connection to Chinese history and identity. They are taught to forget their own language, religious and cultural values, and even the faces of their own parents. There are videos of those who were taken from their mothers as infants, unable to recognize them years later as children.

Forcibly transferring the children of one group to another group is explicitly listed as a recognized genocidal act as well. At the time of the report, there were an estimated more than 900,000 Uyghur children taken from their parents. According to the Human Rights Watch report, China's objective was to place all Uyghur children in state-run orphanages by 2020.[25] As stated by then-Human Rights Watch China Director Dr. Sophie Richardson, "the Chinese government's forced separation of children is perhaps the cruelest element of its oppression in Xinjiang." [26]

In the *Frontline* documentary "China Undercover" premiered on PBS on April 7, 2020, directed by Robin Barnwell and produced by Robin Barnwell and Gesbeen Mohammad, a Chinese official made the following statement about the violation of Uyghurs' human rights: "What violation of human rights? They have no rights, so there is no violation."

Together with other Uyghur organizations, activists, and coalition partners, we worked to help secure the passage of a landmark piece of legislation in the US Congress: the *Uyghur Human Rights Policy Act*. Passed by Congress in December 2019, the act affirmed that the Chinese government is violating Uyghurs' basic human rights. It was signed by President Trump and became

---

24. "China Muslims: Xinjiang schools used to separate children from families," BBC. https://www.bbc.com/news/world-asia-china-48825090
25. "China: Children Caught in Xinjiang Crackdown," Human Rights Watch. https://www.hrw.org/news/2018/10/16/china-children-caught-xinjiang-crackdown
26. "China: Xinjiang Children Separated from Families," Human Rights Watch, https://www.hrw.org/news/2019/09/15/china-xinjiang-children-separated-families

CHAPTER TWELVE

law in June 2020. Yet, there is still little understanding of how the Chinese system is intricately designed to repress Uyghur identity, strip their autonomy, and extract value before discarding us. This is not a slow-motion genocide, it is a precise, deliberate machine crushing the Uyghur spirit, with each piece working to erase our people.

***

An article in *The Washington Post* published on January 11, 2025, ahead of Rubio's confirmation hearing for the role of United States Secretary of State, states:

> *By 2018, Rubio had become convinced that his concerns about China had become reality—a view that was hardened after a fateful meeting with a woman named Rushan Abbas. . . .*
>
> *Abbas's story came to the attention of Rubio, who found parallels with the way Cubans were treated by the Castro regime and embraced her cause as a symbol of what he called China's genocide of the Uyghurs.*

***

In our genocide report, which we released in June 2020, we urged the European Parliament to enact legislation similar to both this bill and the existent *Uyghur Human Rights Protection Act*, to develop Magnitsky sanctions against all Chinese officials behind the concentration camps, and to decline participation in the 2022 Winter Olympics, which were to be hosted in Beijing. The report recommended several actions to address the situation, including stripping China of its Human Rights Council status, recognizing East Turkistan as an occupied territory, and formally acknowledging the ongoing events as genocide. We also suggested creating a joint commission to compile a report for the

International Court of Justice (ICJ), following Gambia's successful case on behalf of the Rohingya Muslims at the ICJ in November 2019.

After releasing the report in a few languages (English, Chinese, Arabic, Turkish, and Japanese), we traveled to Türkiye to share it with Uyghur students and lawmakers. Initially, we struggled to gain attention from the media, as we were a small, newly formed organization. However, as other reports were published, including Dr. Adrian Zenz's and another by Newline Media, the issue began to attract more attention.

On the final day of the first Trump administration, Secretary of State Mike Pompeo declared China's treatment of Uyghurs a genocide. Though delayed until early 2021, this move placed the administration on the right side of history. Mary Kissel, a senior adviser to Pompeo, and Kelley Currie, US Ambassador-at-Large for Global Women's Issues, played key roles in securing the designation. Announced on January 19, 2021, it condemned mass internment, forced labor, sterilizations, and cultural erasure as genocide and crimes against humanity.

Upon taking up office under President Joe Biden, Secretary of State Antony Blinken reaffirmed this statement, making it one of only a few issues agreed upon by both administrations.

Also in 2021, the passing of the *Uyghur Forced Labor Prevention Act* made it US policy to assume any and all goods manufactured in the Uyghur region to be made using forced labor. It called as well for the president to impose sanctions on those companies and individuals engaging in forced labor. Nike, Apple, and Coca-Cola all lobbied Congress to weaken the bill. China's Foreign Affairs Committee issued a statement threatening retaliation, saying "The U.S. act fabricates the so-called 'forced labor' issue in China's Xinjiang and grossly interferes in China's internal affairs under the pretext of human rights. Should the United States choose to go down the wrong path, China will take resolute and forceful countermeasures."

I wrote an article in December 2021 for *Haaretz* with Sami Steigmann, a Holocaust survivor based in New York, calling for Israel to boycott the Olympics. Despite the obvious parallels, Israeli officials showed no intention of abstaining from the games, with one official going so far as to call the boycott "bizarre." We wrote,

CHAPTER TWELVE

The Holocaust revealed that genocide is too much for a single group to bear. Instead, it is up to the world to recognize the shared humanity between all people, and demand that no single group be deemed unworthy of basic human dignity. However, that lesson comes with tests. We are facing one right now, in East Turkistan. If we seek to honor the memory of the Holocaust, we must behave differently when we see, again, atrocities aimed at wiping out a people. We must act now, in this moment, for these people. We cannot be indifferent to this fight, or we continue to dishonor those we have failed in the past.

Concurrently, the Uyghur Tribunal in the United Kingdom affirmed in December 2021 that China was committing genocide, crimes against humanity, and torture, to which both my husband Abdulhakim Idris and I testified, he as an expert witness and I as a fact witness. This tribunal judgement levied what it referred to as "allegations of the gravest human rights violations and international crimes." The conclusion of that document reads as follows:

> Maybe the public, whom the Tribunal serves—better informed of world affairs if less experienced in the realities of war than the drafters of the 1948 documents—would have more concern for victims in far-off lands than their leaders might expect. Maybe they could see sense in having a document easier to apply than the Genocide Convention, such as a convention to prevent crimes against humanity, to drive their own countries to act without delay when a million and more are interned in order for their minds, born free, to be trained to follow a single line of thinking, their bodies to be at the disposal of those who would rape or torture, their rights to bring new life into the world curtailed not just in the genocidal way identified but by effective separation of the sexes though forced labour, by their children created in human relationships lost not through death but through non-human

alienation achieved by being entered into a model making machine. Maybe they, more than their political leaders and international bodies, know that wherever and whenever gross human suffering occurs, action must follow. From the needless suffering of fellow citizens anywhere in the world it can never be right to look away.

I began to have a sense of hope. Surely, with bipartisan support and an official recognition of the crimes of genocide, the world would begin to take action. The Beijing Winter Olympics to be held in February of 2022 became a rallying point for our movement.

Since 2018, Campaign for Uyghurs and many other advocacy groups have been urging the International Olympic Committee to reconsider holding the Olympics in Beijing at all. As early as October 2018, the US Congressional-Executive Commission on China called for those hosting rights to be revoked due to the "dire human rights situation." Both the president and vice president of the IOC issued statements discouraging a boycott, with Vice President John Coates claiming it was "not within the IOC's remit" to challenge the Chinese government over the genocide. Over two-hundred human rights organizations disagreed, calling for a boycott of what soon became known as the "Genocide Games."

That the IOC had been unwilling to revoke Beijing's host status for these games came as a great disappointment to us. The Olympic Games represent a celebration among people of all nations and ethnic groups, people who speak different languages and believe in different religions, coming together in the name of friendly competition and the celebration of those differences. How in the world can a country actively conducting the genocide of one of its own ethnic groups, erasing its culture and language, whittling away its population while banning its religious traditions, be allowed to host such an event? To us, it rang of the Berlin Olympics of 1936, hosted by Adolf Hitler's regime. At the time, the official Nazi newspaper wrote that in those games, black and Jewish athletes should be barred from competing. It was not until the threat of a boycott from other nations that these bans were lifted.

CHAPTER TWELVE

A survey showed 49 percent of Americans and 54 percent of Canadians believed China's human rights abuses should bar it from hosting the Winter Olympics. Ahead of the games, several countries declared diplomatic boycotts. The United States announced its boycott on December 6, 2021, followed by Australia on December 7, and the United Kingdom and Canada on December 8.

In addition to those four countries, the diplomatic boycott grew to include India, Belgium, Lithuania, Estonia, Denmark, and Kosovo. While athletes competed, no diplomatic representatives or dignitaries of the boycotting countries attended. The Beijing Winter Olympics became the least-viewed games in history.

The diplomatic boycott did not extend, however, to the myriad corporate sponsorships entangled with the Olympics. This was a victory, though if I am honest, it felt very much like a pyrrhic one. On the heels of a bipartisan willingness to recognize China's genocide, the disappointment over a return to business as usual was palpable. The lesson in this disappointment was that the political will to call out genocide for what it is, despite all the effort taken to reach that point, would not be enough on its own. The words themselves are meaningless without the willingness to take decisive action to back them up.

Why was there such resistance to taking the strongest possible measures to revoke Beijing's host status at these Olympics? Several factors were at play. Despite an increasing number of countries willing to call out China's actions as torture, repression, crimes against humanity, and even genocide, very little action was taken in the United Nations. China holds an inordinate amount of influence there, through its financial support and positions on the Security Council and Human Rights Council, ironic as this position may be.

For governments and corporations alike, the thought of jeopardizing economic relations with China is distasteful. As already stated, the cost of forgoing the profit margins made possible by Uyghur slave labor is more than many widely recognized brands are willing to pay. To them, abiding by the sanctions designed to penalize these practices is a direct inconvenience to their bottom line. This is not solely found in manufacturing or agriculture. While information about the camps, forced labor, and other atrocities was coming to light, the Disney Corporation filmed portions of its live-action adaptation of the movie *Mulan* in the region. Despite the controversy, and our own attempts to reach out to Disney to ask them not to support this oppressive regime, scenes were filmed mere miles from the sites of some of the concentration camps. When the film was released in July 2020, at the government's request, the credits gave special thanks to the Xinjiang Public Security Bureau. This is the same organization responsible for the arrest of millions of Uyghurs and their deportation to the concentration camps that now litter my homeland.

Under the Biden administration, having both affirmed the reality of the genocide and passed legislation to sanction it, there was no cohesive China policy to untangle the decades of appeasement we have become accustomed to. As Biden's climate czar, John Kerry advocated for a soft approach to China, in the hopes that it would encourage them to assist in reaching the global benchmarks of the Paris Climate Accords. Those who understand that the Uyghur region carries strategic value to the Chinese government's Belt and Road initiative for its rich natural resources will also understand that China is unlikely to make good on any promises of carbon neutrality. This will be especially true if they are allowed to continue exploiting my homeland and its people.

On February 4, 2022, the opening day of the Beijing Olympics, Campaign for Uyghurs and the Uyghur Human Rights Project were nominated for the Nobel Peace Prize by US Representatives Tom Suozzi and Chris Smith, co-chairs of the bipartisan Congressional Uyghur Caucus, who have been steadfast champions of the Uyghur people. Their unwavering support, standing against genocide when so many have chosen complicity, has been a lifeline for our cause. In this fight for justice, dignity, and the survival of a people, we are honored to count them not only as allies but as beacons of hope in the struggle for Uyghur human rights. Congressman Suozzi marked the nomination with this statement:

> Put simply, the Chinese Communist Party has committed genocide against the Uyghur people. For years, these atrocities went unnoticed by the public eye. But through the heroic work of the Uyghur Human Rights Project and Campaign for Uyghurs, and countless others, they brought

CHAPTER TWELVE

this genocide front and center for the world to see. Let us never forget the words spoken by Dr. Martin Luther King "the greatest tragedy is not the brutality of evil people, but rather the silence of the good people."

Heartfelt and touching as these words were, the fight is far from over. If it is true that our work has seen some success in bringing the Uyghur genocide to the attention of the world—with the nomination of a Nobel Prize representing an opportunity and a platform to further inform the good people of this world—what will it take for them to break their silence, and help us bring this genocide to an end?

That same day, just as the Nazis used the 1936 Olympics to project unity, Beijing exploited the games to whitewash its crimes. The CCP meticulously staged every spectacle to push its propaganda. In a brazen move, China chose a young Uyghur athlete, Yilamujiang, from Altay, Xinjiang, as one of the final torchbearers. Her presence was a calculated stunt—a hollow attempt to deny genocide by showcasing a token Uyghur while countless others languished in camps, prisons, and forced labor factories.

The International Olympic Committee, ever willing to toe Beijing's line, insisted there was no political significance to Yilamujiang's selection. But to anyone paying attention, the message was clear. This was a regime that did not merely deny its crimes—it forced the victims to participate in their erasure.

Standing up to a genocidal regime comes at a cost, one many corporations, nations, and institutions refuse to pay. Too often, they turn a blind eye for economic gain. It is disappointing and painful, but it fuels my determination to educate the public, hoping more voices will rise to pressure them to do what is right. The scale of this atrocity—the systematic erasure of an ethnic identity—is laid bare for those willing to see. Despite denials and cover-ups, the truth is clear: this is a genocide unfolding in plain sight. The question is: What will the world do about it?

When discussing the Genocide Games and the atrocities of the genocidal regime, I also want to highlight another critical issue: how China infiltrates our educational institutions through Confucius Institutes, using them as tools for propaganda and control. While infrastructure projects and economic entanglements are the backbone of the CCP's global ambitions, there is also a war for narratives and minds , fought through education and cultural diplomacy under the guise of academic exchange and mutual understanding. At the heart of this effort is the Confucius Institute (CI) program, a global network of state-sponsored educational centers designed to spread the CCP's ideology and control over international discourse. CIs are marketed as language and cultural programs but serve as tools of China's broader geopolitical strategy. These institutes are established in partnership with universities and educational institutions around the world and are overseen by the Office of the Chinese Language Council International, known as "Hanban," which is directly affiliated with the CCP's propaganda apparatus. Through Confucius Institutes, the Chinese government embeds its influence into foreign academic institutions, setting the terms of engagement for discussions about China while suppressing viewpoints that challenge its authoritarian rule. CIs operate with the same intent as Beijing's infrastructure investments: to project China's power in a way that appears benign while consolidating control over how the world perceives China's history, policies, and expansionist ambitions—just as the BRI projects bind nations through economic dependencies. Universities hosting these programs often face pressure to avoid sensitive topics like the Uyghur genocide, Tibet, Hong Kong, and Taiwan. Scholars risk censorship, funding loss, or threats for speaking out. Chinese students are coerced into monitoring peers. Recognizing the threat, the United States, designated the Confucius Institute US Center as a foreign mission in 2020, acknowledging its role as an arm of the CCP.

Multiple universities across the United States, Canada, Australia, and Europe have severed ties with Confucius Institutes, citing concerns over academic freedom and national security. Yet, in regions where China wields significant economic leverage through the BRI, such as Africa, the Middle East, and Southeast Asia, CIs continue to proliferate, embedding Beijing's ideological footprint in educational systems that are already susceptible to external influence. The marriage between the Belt and Road Initiative and Confucius Institutes reflects China's dual strategy for global dominance. While infrastructure projects secure an economic foothold globally, Confucius Institutes shape minds and narratives in a way that serves the interests of the

CHAPTER TWELVE

CCP. These institutes serve as Trojan horses for CCP propaganda, weakening the very institutions that should stand as bastions of free thought and resistance against authoritarianism.

In 2019, I was invited to speak at Columbia University with Tibetan, Hongkonger, and Chinese dissident activists. Yet, on the event day, after I arrived in New York, the panel was abruptly canceled due to pressure from the Chinese Students and Scholars Association (CSSA), which often suppresses discussions challenging Beijing's narratives. The organizers searched for alternative venues, but each time, the university canceled. For the first time in my advocacy, I felt as if I were in Beijing, not America, with censorship enforced without question. The CCP's influence reaches far, even shaping discussions in American institutions. In October 2024, thanks to brave students and faculty at Columbia, I was able to speak, albeit virtually. It marked a hard-won victory against Beijing's censorship. The five-year delay serves as a warning that academic institutions are not immune to the pressures of authoritarian regimes.

In February 2022, I was a visiting fellow at Duke University, where I participated in briefings, discussions, and private meetings. Among those, I met with some Chinese international students who were deeply concerned for their family members' safety. They took extreme caution, wearing masks, ensuring no other Chinese students saw them meeting with me, and lowering their voices, fully aware of the CCP's transnational repression.

During the visit, I also gave a presentation titled "Uyghurs: China's Genocide in a Mute World." It was then brought to my attention that Duke University operates a campus in Kunshan, China, in cooperation with the Chinese government.

When I raised concerns about this partnership with Duke's President Vincent Price, Provost Kornbluth, and Dean Ashby, their response was dismissive. They assured me that students at Duke Kunshan University (DKU) enjoyed complete academic freedom and could openly discuss topics such as Xinjiang and Tibet without interference.

I knew this was a lie. I told them so.

Before leaving, I left a letter outlining the threats to academic freedom, Duke's ethical responsibilities, and the dangers of collaboration with China.

I have seen firsthand how Chinese partnerships infiltrate institutions, how discussions about Uyghurs and Tibetans are systematically silenced, and how even American students at Chinese university campuses are subject to surveillance and self-censorship. The idea that DKU students were freely discussing these issues in China without repercussions defied everything I knew about the CCP's iron grip over its people.

A few days later, I received a letter from President Vincent Price, thanking me for my visit. He wrote:

> We appreciate your interest in Duke and recognize with gratitude your commitment to human rights.... I will share your letter with my Duke and DKU senior leadership colleagues as well as our subject matter experts. Please know that we take these issues seriously and will take your concerns in mind as we make plans for the future of our engagement with China.

In my response to President Price, I stated:

> It is much appreciated that Duke University has joined with other universities to keep Xinjiang cotton and Xinjiang-based forced labor from contributing to Duke-branded merchandise. However, this is not enough, and Duke University is risking remaining complicit in the Uyghur genocide. Duke still has a campus in Kunshan in cooperation with China. To continue working with China to have a Kunshan campus is akin to Duke being complicit with German universities and their policies of expelling Jewish faculty and contributing to the Nazi ideology of violence and antisemitism in the 1930s.

Genocide is not a single event—it is a calculated, systematic process. As I reflect on my conversation with Duke University's President Price, I feel an urgent need to lay bare the full scope of the CCP's genocide against the Uyghurs. Below, I outline the ten stages of this atrocity as identified by

CHAPTER TWELVE

Gregory Stanton of Genocide Watch. These expose the deliberate steps taken to erase an entire people:

1. CLASSIFICATION

Uyghurs are systematically labeled as *potential terrorists* and *separatists*. The Chinese government has cultivated an *us vs. them* mentality among the Han Chinese population, reinforcing the idea that Uyghurs are a threat to national stability.

2. SYMBOLIZATION

Uyghurs are visibly distinct from Han Chinese, making them easy targets for state surveillance. They are routinely stopped and forced to show identification at checkpoints, while Han Chinese citizens move about freely. Their religious and cultural attire further marks them as *others* in their own homeland.

3. DISCRIMINATION

Uyghurs are treated as criminals by default, subjected to severe restrictions on employment, travel, and daily life. They are denied stable jobs, barred from purchasing transportation tickets, and prevented from staying in hotels. Even within East Turkistan (Xinjiang), Uyghurs are unable to move freely without state permission.

4. DEHUMANIZATION

The Chinese government openly portrays Uyghurs as *abnormal and in need of reform*. In a CNN interview, Chinese Ambassador to the United States Cui Tiankai stated, "We want to turn Uyghurs into normal persons," implying that their very existence, beliefs, and culture are deviations that must be corrected.

5. ORGANIZATION

The genocide is meticulously planned and executed. Neighborhood watch committees, special forces, and mass surveillance programs monitor and control Uyghur communities. The Chinese government purchases massive quantities of handcuffs, pepper spray, and riot-control equipment to facilitate mass detentions and the operation of internment camps.

6. POLARIZATION

The Chinese government stokes public fear by broadcasting selective, manipulated footage of violent incidents to paint Uyghurs as dangerous extremists. This manufactured fear justifies sweeping crackdowns, even though the mass incarceration of millions is a wildly disproportionate response.

7. PREPARATION

Under the guise of "preventing extremism," Uyghurs are forcibly removed from their homes and relocated to internment camps. Government officials and military personnel facilitate mass arrests, with entire families disappearing overnight.

8. PERSECUTION

Millions of Uyghurs vanish into the camp system, leaving families in despair. Some receive cryptic notices that their loved ones have died in detention, while others are left in agonizing uncertainty, never knowing their relatives' fate. Uyghur homes, businesses, and property are confiscated and handed over to Han Chinese settlers under the "Double Relative" assimilation program. Under this initiative, Han Chinese officials are embedded in Uyghur homes as "relatives," spying and indoctrinating their hosts. As Uyghur families lose their homes and livelihoods, Han settlers receive government benefits, deepening Beijing's campaign of ethnic erasure.

9. EXTERMINATION

Crematoriums are built adjacent to the internment camps—a chilling indication of mass deaths occurring inside. Reports emerge of forced sterilization, forced abortions, medical experiments, and organ harvesting. Uyghur birth rates plummet as the CCP methodically eliminates future generations.

10. DENIAL

The Chinese government categorically denies committing genocide, framing its actions as necessary for "stability" and "reeducation." CCP officials justify these crimes with chilling language, arguing that "sacrificing a generation" is necessary to maintain control. Meanwhile, state propaganda floods social

CHAPTER TWELVE

media with staged videos of Uyghurs praising the government, reinforcing the false narrative that they are thriving under CCP rule.

The world has seen this before. Each time, people said *Never Again*. But *Never Again* means nothing if we allow history to repeat itself.

CHAPTER THIRTEEN
THE LIGHT OF HOPE

The genocide of my people has become China's dark, open secret in recent years. The Chinese government continuously generates false narratives that ensure disinformation is ever present. It offers incentives for silence to those who will accept them, and to those who will not, it leverages the threat of harm upon them and their loved ones. The Uyghurs in the diaspora, hundreds of thousands strong, remain tethered to our homeland by love of our families and our traditions. Through the levers of transnational repression, the CCP pressures us to see our family members back home as hostages of the state, the first targets of reprisal if we should speak up.

I was at the Interparliamentary Task Force on Human Trafficking conference under Anne Basham's leadership, when I spoke with Piero Tozzi, Staff Director at the Congressional Executive-Commission on China (CECC), and Scott Flipse, Director of Communications & Policy at the CECC, about the CCP's strong transnational repression against Uyghur-Americans and Uyghurs in the European Union. I urged them to take action, and in response, they organized a hearing on September 12, 2023, titled "Countering China's Global Transnational Repression Campaign," chaired by Representative Chris Smith and Senator Jeff Merkley. The week before the hearing, Abdulhakim and I traveled to Almaty, Kazakhstan, with the assistance of the US Consulate in Almaty for a screening of *In Search of My Sister*, only for it to be canceled due to CCP pressure. Feeling defeated, I arrived home at night, only six hours before I testified at the CECC hearing the next day.

At the CECC hearing, looking around the room, there were only two Uyghurs in attendance—Elfidar Iltebir and Tahir Imin Uyghurian. I thought back to 2019 and 2020, when hearings like this would be packed—standing

CHAPTER THIRTEEN

room only, filled with Uyghurs carrying pictures of their missing family members who wanted to bear witness and show their support. But not anymore. The CCP had intensified its threats against those who spoke out and participated at political events, targeting their families back home with harassment, imprisonment, or worse. For many Uyghurs in the diaspora, even the faint hope of hearing their loved ones' voices again had become a weapon used against them. Who could know for sure what the cost of being here might be?

Most recently, in another example of an unprecedented act of judicial harassment and transnational repression, the Chinese Embassy in France sued Dilnur Reyhan, sociologist and president of the Uyghur Institute of Europe. Her trial on March 12, 2025, at the Evry court in Paris, is seen as an attempt to silence a leading advocate for Uyghur rights. Scholars and human rights activists condemn the case as lawfare, part of a broader CCP strategy to suppress dissent.

We have hope. We are making strong impacts. Our efforts are producing significant results, and the CCP's escalating acts of transnational repression are a direct response to the powerful influence of our work. Every action they take against us only underscores the strength and effectiveness of our advocacy and the growing global recognition of our cause. The CCP wants to take our hope or make us believe there is none. They are wrong. Day by day, the world is changing. People in every nation are beginning to see the truth of the Chinese occupation of my homeland, and the policies that serve to destroy our freedoms, our families, our ways of life, and our very population. Despite desperate attempts to secure complete compliance from the world, the number of informed individuals willing to speak out against the genocide slowly but surely continues to grow. That is why we will not stop our work, nor give up our hope for a better future.

At the February 6, 2020, US National Prayer Breakfast that Abdulhakim and I were attending, I was unexpectedly recognized on the big screen among several other freedom fighters in a room filled with the world's most powerful leaders—President Trump, Vice President Pence, Speaker Pelosi, Secretary of State Pompeo, along with statesmen, politicians, diplomats, journalists, and experts as well as human rights defenders. It was a moment honoring tireless advocacy, speaking truth to power, and sacrificing my sister's freedom. I imagined seeing her face there, her quiet strength radiating through a soft, knowing smile. The way she would lift her head ever so slightly, a look of pride in her eyes, for love. The love we have for each other. A love for life we should be experiencing together. And the very love that has been leading me to fight onwards. Instead, she remained unseen, locked away in a prison cell for a crime she did not commit, to silence my voice by the regime I stood up to condemn. That absence was a stark reminder: no accolade, no grand stage could ever erase the pain of knowing she is suffering while I stand free. But at that moment, I made a silent vow. This fight, this sacrifice, would never be in vain. Until she is free, until all of our people are free, until world democracy and human dignity are fully defended, I will not stop.

Progress remains slow, but we have not been without our victories. As of January 2025, since the implementation of the *Uyghur Forced Labor Prevention Act* (UFLPA) in June 2022, the Forced Labor Enforcement Task Force has added 144 entities to the UFLPA Entity List. This means these companies are barred from exporting goods to the United States—a significant step in holding businesses accountable and cutting off profits that fuel the Uyghur genocide.

While many corporate entities continue to benefit from the exploitation of forced Uyghur labor, exposing their complicity is not without effect. In September 2024, an audit report exposing the Volkswagen corporation's cover-up of forced labor in their Urumchi factory was widely reported. Volkswagen had made claims in December 2023 that an audit conducted by Guangdong Liangma Law and overseen by Berlin-based consultancy Löning GmbH[27] had found "no indication of forced labor" under SA8000 standards. Markus Löning was initially hired for his prominent reputation in Germany's human rights field and was a respected figure. However, his reputation has been severely tarnished due to his involvement in Volkswagen's controversial and ultimately misleading audit, which undermined his credibility, and the trust placed in his work. Following this audit, global index provider Morgan

---

27. Markus Löning is Germany's former Commissioner for Human Rights. Löning – Human Rights & Responsible Business GmbH is a Berlin-based international management consultancy specializing in human rights.

CHAPTER THIRTEEN

Stanley Capital International removed the "red-flag" preventing investors from buying Volkswagen shares due to forced-labor concerns. The sham audit report was mailed to the Washington, DC office of Campaign for Uyghurs from an anonymous source in June 2024.

We shared this leaked report with Dr. Adrian Zenz, who conducted a meticulous analysis of the document, revealing the methodological flaws in how the audit was conducted under SA8000 standards. Dr. Zenz highlighted how the audit had failed to operate thorough due diligence, ignored key indicators of coercion, and relied on interviews conducted under duress.

SA8000, the international standard for Social Accountability management systems, has been set by the global organization Social Accountability International since 1997. Dr. Zenz discovered that the audit in question ignored crucial elements of the standard, including worker confidentiality and comprehensive interviews. Instead, interviews were livestreamed to law offices in Shenzhen, directly enabling China's state surveillance. The report also shows that only managers were questioned about forced labor. None of the workers at the plant, nearly a quarter of whom are Uyghur, were asked to be interviewed at all.

This came as somewhat of a surprise, however, as neither of the two entities involved in Volkswagen's audit were accredited to carry out SA8000 audits in the first place. In fact, Liangma Law's chief compliance officer was Clive Greenwood, an eccentric figure who only months before the audit reinvented himself as a compliance officer after a long career as a chef and pub owner. Greenwood had published a post only a year earlier with the question "What's the value of an SA8000 audit in China?" beside a photo of a pile of peanuts. Meanwhile, another report revealed that Liangma staff celebrated the CCP's 103rd anniversary with the same songs Uyghurs are forced to sing in the internment camps: "Without the Communist Party, There Would Be No New China." This is the same song that Uyghurs in "reeducation" camps were forced to sing.

The audit's claim to clear Volkswagen of forced labor practices was not merely misleading, it was a deliberate cover-up implicating the German auto manufacturer in one of the world's worst human rights atrocities. Despite citing contractual confidentiality obligations to avoid public response to this revelation, Volkswagen sold the plant and exited the region in November 2024. This was a small victory, but one that proved that stakeholders in such companies still hold sway when it comes to upholding international standards for human rights—when they are willing to apply pressure.

In 2024, China's Universal Periodic Review (UPR) was conducted at the United Nations. Campaign for Uyghurs submitted recommendations carefully articulated to include the term "genocide." We were the only organization to do so. Our submission to the UPR stakeholder summary report was cited six times in the resulting document. These were the sole references to the word "genocide."

At the UPR session, Beijing manipulated the UN system and made requests to many countries under the influence of China's Belt and Road Initiative to praise China. As a result, a record number of 163 countries requested to speak during the interactive dialogue between Member States, and each was granted just forty-five seconds to deliver their remarks. Of these, more than 130 countries either chose to ignore China's dark record or to commend its so-called progress. This included nations that, by their own account, should stand against repression, not endorse it. It was jarring how sharply this orchestrated praise contradicted the realities of the PRC rule that put marginalized groups under an indefensible persecution in so-called reeducation camps and called Uyghur forced labor poverty alleviation.

At this point, I want to applaud US Ambassador Michele Taylor for her resolute stance among the twenty-eight countries that spoke against human rights atrocities. In just forty-five seconds, Ambassador Taylor delivered a statement describing in detail the crimes of the CCP and eight recommendations on the ongoing Uyghur genocide and violations in Tibet, Hong Kong, Macao, and mainland China.

On February 1, 2024, I testified at a hearing before the Congressional-Executive Commission on China, titled "The PRC's Universal Periodic Review and the Real State of Human Rights in China". It covered the PRC's efforts to intimidate and spy on human rights activists during the session and to manipulate and undermine international mechanisms such as the UPR as if the UN were their playground. The occurrences in Geneva at China's UPR revealed an obvious gap in the international frameworks meant to hold the

CHAPTER THIRTEEN

CCP accountable. I remain proud of the United States for its active efforts to fill this gap. Following the UPR, Campaign for Uyghurs organized a side event at the UN addressing Islamophobia in Asia and the persecution of Uyghur Muslims. It was attended by diplomats from fifteen countries, including two Muslim-majority countries.

With the strong support of Representatives Chris Smith and Tom Suozzi leading as the co-chairs, we also coordinated the relaunch of the US Uyghur Congressional Caucus in April 2024, first founded in 2021. Current National Security Advisor Mike Waltz (a member of the House of Representative at the time) attended the launch and delivered powerful remarks:

> Cultural genocide, mass rape, and sterilization. We need to say these terms out loud. We shouldn't be shy about it. This is happening right now, and it is unacceptable. It should be just as unacceptable to you as it is to me—to all the American CEOs who bend the knee to Chairman Xi, pay $25,000 to $50,000, and listen to the ridiculous propaganda from a dictator who tells us that America is in decline, democracy is in decline, and all of it will be replaced with socialism with Chinese characteristics.

Mike Waltz has relentlessly advocated for Gulshan's release over the past four years and led several letters to Biden and former secretary Blinken demanding the administration to push for Gulshan's release.

In collaboration with UN Watch, we exposed the biases present in the reporting by UN Special Rapporteur Alena Douhan, which claimed that the sanctions targeting China for its human rights abuses, including forced labor, were crimes against humanity. From 2020 to 2023, she and her office had accepted $560,000 from China before publishing a report that entirely supported China's official, false narrative. When I delivered remarks at the United Nations exposing this, the chair reprimanded me instead of investigating her.

Through our coalition building, we united groups that worked towards passing the TikTok bill into law. The bill, officially known as the Protecting

Americans from Foreign Adversary Controlled Applications Act seeks to address national security concerns by requiring TikTok's Chinese parent company, ByteDance, to divest its ownership or face a nationwide ban in the United States. During congressional debates, TikTok leveraged its platform to mobilize teenagers, urging them to flood lawmakers with calls to oppose the bill. This orchestrated campaign exemplifies how the Chinese government can manipulate US democracy through its control over digital platforms.

Additionally, a visa-restriction amendment targeting the officials responsible for the detention of Gulshan Abbas in the Senate was passed unanimously.

In March 2023, the UN Working Group on Arbitrary Detention released an opinion determining that Gulshan's detention was indeed arbitrary and calling for her release without delay. In September 2024, I was very proud to witness my niece Ziba lead an advocacy mission with the International Service for Human Rights before the UN Human Rights Council. In her statement, she spoke of the absurdity of Gulshan's imprisonment, saying,

> My mother is a medical professional who devoted her life to helping people and saving lives. She is a non-political, warm-hearted and loving mother. The charges against her are preposterous and baseless. My mother is suffering the consequences because her family in the United States spoke out against the Chinese government's unfair treatment of Uyghurs. This is a clear example of kin punishment and transnational repression.

The mission and Ziba's relentless advocacy at the European Union quickly led to discussion in the European Parliament, resulting in a resolution to immediately and unconditionally release Gulshan Abbas and Ilham Tohti. The resolution was adopted by 540 of 610 voting members of the European Parliament, an overwhelming majority. The motion strongly condemned the PRC for ignoring the recommendations of the Office of the High Commissioner for Human Rights (OHCHR), called for independent access for the OHCHR to the Uyghur region and pledged to produce a comprehensive situational update and action plan to hold the PRC accountable.

CHAPTER THIRTEEN

It further called for EU member states to suspend extradition treaties with China and Hong Kong and to address transnational repression enacted within their territories. "This resolution reflects a growing global consensus and the mounting diplomatic pressure on China to release all wrongfully imprisoned individuals in the Uyghur region, like my mother," Ziba said.

In 2023, upon the formation of the Axel Springer Freedom Foundation in Germany, I was appointed as Chair of its advisory board alongside many distinguished advocates for human rights from around the world.

The 8th World Uyghur Congress General Assembly congregated in Sarajevo, Bosnia and Herzegovina, on October 26, 2024. There were several attempts to disrupt the process through methods such as libel, harassment, and death threats. A few weeks before the Congress, Chinese officials called the hotel where all the delegates were going to stay and tried to book every hotel room in the building at three times the rate the World Uyghur Congress was paying. However, the hotel rejected their offer and informed us about the incident. The Bosnian government was also made aware of this act of transnational repression.

Right before we left for Sarajevo, armed men in masks released a video with photos of me, my husband Abdulhakim, Dolkun Isa, and Omer Kanat, calling for our execution. Just prior to the election, an email was sent with a picture of the venue along with firearms in various colors, asking what color rifle I'd like to be murdered with. Thankfully, despite all these attempts to stop the process, the elections went forward. I was honored to be elected to the role of Chairperson of the Executive Committee at the World Uyghur Congress.

It has been a profound honor to attend the US President's State of the Union Address three times—in 2020, 2023, and 2024—each time as the guest of a lawmaker who has played a pivotal role in advancing the fight for justice for the Uyghur people. Their steadfast commitment to human rights has been transformative.

In 2020, I attended as the guest of then-Senator Marco Rubio, one of the earliest and most vocal champions for Uyghur rights. At a time when many lawmakers had yet to grasp the full extent of the CCP's atrocities, Senator Rubio was already pushing forward landmark legislation, unrelenting in his pursuit of justice. Still, most of the time I met someone, I had to repeat my explanation of who we were, what the CCP was doing to my people, and why I was there. It was a reminder of how invisible our suffering remained.

By 2023, when I attended as the guest of Ranking Member Raja Krishnamoorthi, the conversation around China had expanded beyond human rights—it had become a national security priority. As a leader on the Select Committee on the CCP, he has worked to make clear that countering China's authoritarian influence is both a strategic imperative and a moral obligation. His ability to bridge human rights and national security has made a tangible difference in bipartisan engagement, ensuring that justice for Uyghurs remains central to US policy on China.

In 2024, I was invited by Representative Chris Smith, a true giant in the fight for human rights. With a record number of human rights-focused laws to his name, he has set the standard for moral leadership in Congress. That night, as he introduced me, I could see how far we had come. Every single person I spoke to responded not with confusion, but with recognition. "I am deeply sorry for what is happening to your people," they said. Knowledge had replaced anonymity.

Through their actions, these leaders have shown what true leadership looks like—standing up for the voiceless and ensuring justice is pursued. Their solidarity continues to be a beacon of hope in this fight.

That shift has been one of the greatest victories of our advocacy and is also a testament to work members of Congress have done to amplify the Uyghur issue. But recognition alone is not enough. The voices of those suffering in the camps and prisons of China must be amplified until the world does more than acknowledge their pain—it must act to end it.

Campaign for Uyghurs was awarded the World Democracy Courage Tribute in 2021 by the National Endowment for Democracy, and the Freedom Impact Award in 2023, by Freedom House. In 2024, I was recognized with the Huntington Her Hero Lifetime Achievement Award by the New York State Bar Association.

On April 18, 2024, Abdulhakim and I participated in the Bush Center's Forum on Leadership: Protecting Religious Liberties event, where we had the honor of talking about the plight of the Uyghur people with former president G.W. Bush and former first lady Laura Bush. I had previously met them in

CHAPTER THIRTEEN

2007 at the Prague Democracy and Security Summit and later that summer had a meeting with Laura Bush in her office at the White House speaking to her about China's oppression of the Uyghurs and forced transfer of Uyghur girls to China proper. These distinctions have each represented an opportunity to ensure that the Uyghur plight remains central to critical global discussions. I hardly see them as distinctions of my own—rather, they highlight the impact of collective action and sustained support for the Uyghur people.

As 2025 came in, with it came new life and hope. My niece Zamira welcomed her newborn baby—the very same day, years ago, that my sister, Gulshan Abbas, gave birth to her. February 7. A poignant full circle of life. During this deeply personal time for my family, we received a momentous announcement: Campaign for Uyghurs had been nominated for the 2025 Nobel Peace Prize—its second nomination since 2022, when it was nominated by Representatives Tom Suozzi and Chris Smith, the co-chairs of the Congressional Uyghur Caucus. The 2025 nomination was by Representatives John Moolenaar and Raja Krishnamoorthi, Chair and Ranking Member of the United States House Select Committee on Strategic Competition between the United States and the CCP.

This humbling recognition came with a painful reminder of an unbearable cost as I looked into my nieces' eyes as their children grow up without being able to know their grandmother.

These words ring especially true today. Only through action in the service of justice do we have a real chance at peace. And I have witnessed so many noble actions. The dedication and tangible efforts of those who stand with me in this struggle—our team at Campaign for Uyghurs, our advisers, our board members, our allies, and all who work tirelessly to expose and counter the Chinese government's crimes against humanity and its genocide. You inspire me, and together, we empower each other to honor the promise of *Never Again*.

The true impact of this recognition is not the honor itself but the awareness and further action it inspires, and the hope and courage that it renews. I am grateful for the strong support and recognition from Ranking Member Raja Krishnamoorthi and Chairman John Moolenaar of the Congressional Select Committee on the CCP, who have continuously stood for justice and human rights. I deeply appreciate the US representatives, as well as the public servants, Members of Parliament, and Members of the European Parliament worldwide who stand with the Uyghur people in the face of tyranny.

Ending the Uyghur genocide would mark one of humanity's most defining steps towards global justice and lasting peace. Confronting a regime that seeks to expand its authoritarian grip at the cost of human dignity—and holding it accountable—is a necessity for the future of freedom worldwide.

***

Before my sister's detention, I had built a successful career in business. From 2010 to 2016, I worked as an international Program Manager then promoted to international director at Leo A. Daly, a prestigious century-old architecture firm in Washington, DC. I later transitioned to an international consulting firm as a business development director. Had it not been for the unjust imprisonment of my sister, Gulshan, I might have continued in the corporate world, balancing advocacy for my people with my professional responsibilities—just as I had done for years before this genocide began. But everything changed on the one-year anniversary of Gulshan's detention. I walked away from my career, no longer able to treat my advocacy as something I could tend to only after work hours. I became a full-time activist, though not by choice. Sometimes, with bitter sarcasm, I call myself an "accidental full-time activist"—a path forced upon me by the Chinese Communist Party's repression.

Since my sister's disappearance in September 2018, I have devoted every waking moment to this fight. In the past eighty months, I have only stepped away twice—once when Shireen dragged me to the Chesapeake Bay area for a weekend of retreat, taking away my phone and laptop for forty-eight hours, and another time in 2023, when Shad and Shireen arranged a trip to Türkiye. Even then, I found myself slipping into virtual panels, speaking at conferences, and joining meetings amid our vacation. Yet, through it all, I make time for what matters most. At least three times a year, I fly to the West Coast to spend a week or two with my son Ronny working remotely, and I call him in the evening of every even day of the week, no matter where I am

CHAPTER THIRTEEN

in the world or what time zone. I make every effort to see Shad and Shireen as often as I can, even during the busy schedules and trips, especially with Shireen being close by in Northern Virginia. In the midst of this relentless fight, those moments with her are my most precious times. When I sit with her, even for just an hour or so, it's a chance for me to breathe, to gather my strength before stepping back into the battle. In her presence, I find a fleeting sense of normalcy, a reminder of the love and family that fuel my fight. And then, renewed, I return to the struggle—because this fight is far from over. Because while my life has become a nonstop battle for justice, love remains the anchor that keeps me going.

The fight continues.

Upon the tragic deportation of forty Uyghurs from Thailand to China, CFU worked with Secretary Rubio's office staff on the issue. Subsequently Secretary Rubio issued a statement on the forced return of forty Uyghurs to China reaffirmed the ongoing Uyghur genocide, making this the third consecutive U.S. administration to recognize it. Secretary Rubio underscored the commitment to human rights, stating, "China, under the direction and control of the Chinese Communist Party, has committed genocide and crimes against humanity targeting predominantly Muslim Uyghurs and other members of ethnic and religious minority groups in Xinjiang," and urged all nations not to forcibly return ethnic Uyghurs who are seeking safety back to China.

On March 14, Secretary Rubio announced a new visa restriction policy targeting foreign government officials complicit in the forced repatriation of Uyghurs and other persecuted groups to China, where they face torture and enforced disappearances. The policy, implemented under Section 212(a)(3)(C) of the *Immigration and Nationality Act*, was immediately applied to Thai officials responsible for the forced return of the forty Uyghurs on February 27.

The CCP will likely use the return of these Uyghurs for propaganda, releasing videos of family reunions to whitewash the genocide. Unlike the 2015 deportation, where Uyghurs were shackled and blindfolded, the CCP took extreme measures in 2025 to conceal its actions, using blacked-out trucks and blocking roads. The 109 Uyghurs deported in 2015 disappeared, and their fate remains unknown. History suggests their return is a death sentence. As the world watches, we must ask: How many more Uyghurs must die before the international community acts? How many more lies must be told until we unmask China for the criminal regime it is? The memory of those deported will live on as a testament to a government that chose self-interest over its sacred duty to protect those seeking refuge from genocide.

* * *

The past two years also saw the aggressive employment of propaganda tours in the Uyghur homeland, highly curated by the CCP to project the image of interethnic harmony in the region. The same mosques where one may face criminal penalty for entering are featured in tours to outsiders, showcasing the supposed religious diversity celebrated in China. In reality, the ability to manufacture such an image speaks to just how much control the government exerts over the region. Even as the party projects this image, May of 2024 saw the Secretary of the Central Political and Legal Affairs Commission, Chen Wenqing, visit my homeland and order local officials to prioritize "maintaining social stability" and "accurately prevent and crack down on violent terrorist crimes," doubling down on the old and tired narrative that the widespread human rights abuses endured by my people are justified in the name of counterterrorism. In fact, these statements are a blatant admission that the CCP intends to perpetuate a permanent campaign of genocide against Uyghurs. Instead of addressing international scrutiny, they have intensified their efforts. It is up to the international community to continue to see through this euphemistic propaganda.

Most Uyghurs in the diaspora, including myself and my allies at Campaign for Uyghurs, rely on international law, Western democracies, and the hope that the Islamic world will eventually recognize the Uyghur genocide. A small group, disillusioned by global inaction, believes armed struggle is the only path to reclaim our homeland. Most democratic nations prioritize economic ties with China over recognizing the genocide, and it will likely take years for the world—especially the Islamic world—to break free from China's influence and support justice. For those who wish to solve our issue through armed struggle, even if they one day have the opportunity to take up

CHAPTER THIRTEEN

arms, it will not be easy to stand against China, and they will immediately be labeled "terrorists" and eliminated. They are well aware of this.

The work of advocating for Uyghur rights today, of raising awareness of the very real genocide playing out in real time and trying to coax some shred of sympathy or action from those entities capable of holding China's government to account is a near-constant battle against convenient counternarratives. Where it becomes politically inconvenient to support us, we face an endless deluge of excuses and What-About-isms[28] that only serve to muddy the waters. A great deal of Campaign for Uyghurs' work has been merely to make the case that genocide is in fact occurring, with little assurance that anything can be done about it, even when those governmental and international bodies whose purview it is to prevent such atrocity recognize it as such. Uyghurs deserve justice and freedom

From the 1950s, after China's colonization of our homeland in 1949, through the land reforms, the "Hundred Flowers Campaign," the "Great Leap Forward," and the political campaigns of the 1960s and '70s, including the Cultural Revolution, Uyghurs endured more than twenty-five years of immense tragedy. Under these movements, China executed Uyghur religious and intellectual leaders, imprisoned them, and sought to assimilate the population while suppressing their religious beliefs. The world remained largely unaware of these horrors. I hope my father's account in Chapter Four "What My Father Witnessed," provides a firsthand perspective of this painful history.

The "Elimination of Counter-Revolutionaries" in China during the 1960s and 1970s was a series of campaigns led by the CCP under Mao Zedong to target and persecute those seen as enemies of the Communist revolution. The term "counter-revolutionary" was used broadly to label anyone opposed to socialism or the Communist Party. These campaigns aimed to consolidate power and enforce ideological purity, especially during the Cultural Revolution (1966–1976), when intellectuals, officials, and artists suspected of capitalist or traditionalist views were targeted.

---

28. Whataboutism is a rhetorical tactic used to deflect criticism or avoid addressing an issue by pointing to a different, often unrelated, wrongdoing. Instead of engaging with the original argument, the person using whataboutism responds with "But what about X?" to shift the focus.

Until August 2001, as Beijing eagerly sought entry into the World Trade Organization (WTO)[29] China's state media flooded the world with propaganda videos that painted Xinjiang as a land of "peaceful harmony" and "happy, friendly Uyghurs" and inviting Western investment in the region. But everything changed overnight after the horrific September 11 attacks in the United States. Exploiting global fears, China swiftly rebranded itself as a "victim of terrorism" and launched a ruthless "counterterrorism" campaign. From that moment on, any peaceful protest, religious gathering, or social activity by Uyghurs was criminalized under the false label of "terrorism" and "illegal religious activities." What the world saw as legitimate expressions of dissent or faith became punishable by death, life imprisonment, or enforced disappearances, laying the groundwork for the brutal genocide that continues today.

After generations of oppression, there is no quick solution. It will take time and global unity to heal the wounds of my people and rebuild our right to self-determination under China's occupation. The journey will be long and difficult, and as China faces increasing scrutiny, sacrifices will be required. Those who speak out against injustice face retaliation, and this will likely continue. However, we must not let this deter us or dim our hope for a better future.

The struggle for basic human rights and dignities for Uyghurs is a life-or-death fight, one that, in my own way, I have been fighting all my life. The high cost of awareness, assistance, or even sympathy has often meant that we Uyghurs have had to rely on each other to survive, even in the most unlikely settings. Today, Campaign for Uyghurs and other Uyghur organizations are working to train and empower a new generation of young activists to continue raising the alarm, holding whoever will listen to account, and pushing for a brighter future. They will need hope, and so I continue to hold out for it. I hope that my people will be free to live, worship, and marry as they choose. I hope that one day I will rejoice together with Gulshan and my husband's relatives. For them, I must keep fighting, keep speaking out, and educating the world about our people and what they endure. I owe it to the victims, to my family, and to our shared humanity to hold onto that hope.

---

29. China became a member of the World Trade Organization (WTO) on 11 December 2001.

CHAPTER THIRTEEN

Despite the immense challenges, I have witnessed firsthand how a lone voice can shatter indifference, and how truth, relentlessly spoken, can move mountains. Over the last five years, my husband Abdulhakim and I have traveled across almost forty countries, standing before world leaders, politicians, policymakers, interfaith leaders, journalists, students, and everyday citizens, urging them to confront the undeniable reality of China's genocide. I have raised my people's voice on the global stage, frequently speaking at major institutions, ensuring their suffering is heard where it matters most. I have testified and delivered remarks before the US Congress, the European Union, and parliaments and senates across the world—including France, Italy, the Czech Republic, Luxembourg, Portugal, Japan, Germany, Romania, Malaysia, Indonesia, Spain, Poland, and Türkiye. I have briefed politicians, policymakers, and diplomats in Austria, Belgium, Croatia, Israel, Slovakia, Switzerland, Jordan, and Greece, bringing the truth of my people's oppression to those in power. With every speech, every testimony, and every meeting, I carry the weight of their silenced cries, determined to turn their unheard agony into undeniable action. Even during the Covid crisis 2020 and 2021, while the world was in lockdown and many remained in the safety of their homes, we refused to pause our fight. Amid the uncertainty of the pandemic, we traveled to Türkiye and the United Kingdom, undeterred by the risks to our health and safety. We carried on our advocacy without hesitation, knowing that the oppression of our people did not stop—and neither could we. During the pandemic, we met with, advised, and supported the "Where is My Family" movement in Türkiye organized by Jewlan Shirmemet and his friends. They launched a daily protest in front of the Chinese consulate in Istanbul—a grassroots campaign seeking information about their missing relatives, which lasted over a year.

I have spoken at more than fifty universities worldwide, and more than thirty Holocaust Museums, World Affairs Councils, Amnesty Chapter groups and interfaith communities, not only sharing the stories of my people and warning them of the CCP's totalitarian threat to freedom and democracy and to their very future but also equipping people with the knowledge and responsibility to act. Through our advocacy-training workshops held with Uyghur diaspora communities in more than a dozen countries, including Australia, Austria,

Germany, the Netherlands, Canada, Türkiye, the United Kingdom, and Japan, we have helped train more than four hundred Uyghurs to become advocates, and we galvanized many impactful activists, ensuring that this movement does not end with us but grows stronger with each new voice.

What gives me the greatest hope is not the speeches or the policies, but the next generation of Uyghur advocates. Young men and women, born into exile, refuse to let our history be erased. I remember when I was a student, driven only by the fire in my heart and sustained by the hope of a better future for my people. I remember the early days of Campaign for Uyghurs when resources were scarce and every advocacy trip depended on the generosity of Uyghur community members or, sometimes, complete strangers, just for the chance to speak with someone who might make a difference. Now, I have the privilege of passing on everything I have learned. Every hard-won battle and every lesson carved from struggle has prepared me to teach those who will carry this fight forward.

These numbers are proof that the world is listening. Proof that, despite the CCP's efforts to silence us, our voices ring louder than ever. Every speech given, every student trained, every person moved to action is another step towards the day when we will no longer have to fight for the basic dignity of our people. Until then, I will keep speaking, keep fighting, and keep standing.

Because silence is not an option. Because hope is not a choice, it is a necessity. And because, one day, we will see justice.

The repercussions of China's genocide extend far beyond the Uyghur homeland, and Uyghur community. As all criminals do, the CCP wants us to be complicit in its crimes to silence us—from the tomatoes we eat to the clothes we wear and to the cars we drive. The CCP taints them with the blood, sweat, and tears of Uyghurs, sugarcoating the poisoned pill so we fall prey to its designs—knowingly and blissfully. You are what stands between this darkness and human dignity. Yes, the path ahead remains daunting. Yet, we fight. We fight so we may live in peace and liberty. We fight to leave a better world to our next generations. We fight, because we have to.

I love my sister with every fiber of my being. That love is my fuel, the force that drives me forward each day. But my fight is not only for her. It is for my people. It is for every soul crushed under the weight of tyranny. It is

CHAPTER THIRTEEN

for the sacred ideals of freedom and democracy, not just for Uyghurs, but for the future of all humanity.

That is why I will never stop. For the millions of Uyghurs imprisoned in concentration camps, their voices smothered, their identities stripped away. For the women robbed of control over their own bodies, denied the right to choose how to live, whom to love and marry, and how to raise their children. For the little ones torn from their parents, reshaped into instruments of the very regime that stole them away.

When I was growing up as a child, my father used to explain the meaning of my name as light and brightness. He used to tell me that a lighthouse stands tall against the fiercest storms, unshaken by crashing waves and howling winds. It does not waver in the darkness, nor does it bow to the raging sea. Instead, it shines—a beacon of hope for those lost in the vastness, guiding them safely to shore. Therefore, without thinking much of anything, I developed an unconditional love of lighthouses. I take pictures of lighthouses and collect them as my hobby. Now, I feel that the Uyghur people are that lighthouse.

Through decades of oppression, forced disappearances, and an attempt to erase our very existence, the Uyghurs have refused to be extinguished. Like the lighthouse, we remain steadfast, illuminating the truth even when surrounded by darkness. Our culture, our faith, our language—though under relentless attack—stand resilient, refusing to fade. A lighthouse does not beg the storm for mercy; it simply endures, its light cutting through even the blackest night. The Uyghur spirit, unbroken and defiant, continues to shine despite the forces that seek to silence it. And like sailors finding hope in the distance, the world must see that light and answer its call—to stand with the Uyghurs, to fight for justice, to defend our democracy, and to ensure that Uyghurs' resilience is met with action. Because no matter how fierce the storm is, the light of truth will never be extinguished.

I fight for my mother and father, for the horrors they witnessed, for the wounds left by the Cultural Revolution and all that came after. I fight for my people, for all we have lost, for all that has been stolen from us. I fight for my family swallowed by the camps, those whose fate remains unknown, whose voices have been silenced but never forgotten. I fight for the future of democracy and the free world. Like all Uyghurs in exile, I fight because I refuse to surrender to despair. Because, despite the darkness, I still cling to hope. Hope that one day, I will see them again. Hope that one day, we will all be free.

I left my homeland thirty-six years ago, leaving behind my parents, my family, my friends—everything I knew—in search of something we were denied. I came to the United States seeking freedom and democracy, believing that these were the unshakable pillars of a just society. But today, those very ideals are at risk, threatened by the rising tide of authoritarianism led by the Chinese regime.

The Uyghur struggle is at the front and center of the fate of freedom and democracy worldwide. When the world turns a blind eye to the CCP's manipulation of global leaders and allows Beijing's unchecked assault on democracy to persist, it does more than embolden an authoritarian regime—it endangers the very foundation of the free world. Every concession to Beijing's influence chips away at the principles of liberty, justice, and human dignity that bind us together. If we fail to act, we risk eroding the values that define our shared humanity. Original thought and religious beliefs are a danger to any authoritarian regime. The individual freedom to choose—what we believe, how we believe, and why we believe—is one of the major achievements of the modern world. It defines our sense of liberty, of freedom of conscience. Yet now this foundation of our freedom has come under attack. This disturbing trend is clearly visible in the persecution of the Uyghur Muslims, Tibetans, Falun gong practitioners, Southern Mongolians, and Hong Kongers today. These blatant violations of human rights by the Chinese communist regime is only one part of a rising tide of intolerance that is rapidly suffocating the world with the totalitarian ideology of the CCP and Xi Jinping. Our struggle should be the concern of everyone who values the basic human rights of dignity, respect, and freedom of belief for all people. These rights are a fundamental part of the human legacy, our legacy, that is increasingly under attack from a new tyrannical threat.

The future is being shaped today. The question is whether we will allow it to be shaped by oppression or by justice. To turn away now is to surrender not just the Uyghurs, but the very ideals that define free societies.

CHAPTER THIRTEEN

This is why I will never stop. Not just for my people, but for all people who believe in human dignity, for the right to worship freely, to speak without fear, to raise families without the shadow of a totalitarian regime looming over them. I fight because the world cannot afford to look away. Because silence is complicity, hope is our weapon, and freedom is worth fighting for.

The battle we are fighting is the battle for all of us. And if we fail to fight, the cost will be paid by all of us.

I have never forgotten my sister, my in-laws, or the millions of innocent souls suffering in my homeland—and I never will. Their pain fuels my resolve, their resilience courses through my veins, giving me the strength to fight on. They are the heartbeat of my struggle, the unwavering force behind every word I speak and every action I take.

To be their voice is my life's calling, a noble cause I will carry until justice prevails.

A LETTER TO THE UYGHUR DIASPORA

To My Beloved Uyghur Diaspora,

I could not end this book before speaking directly to you.
The Uyghur people.

The keepers of our past, the guardians of our present,
and the architects of our future.
You are the thread that weaves our story through time.
It is you who will carry our spirit forward, keeping us alive against all odds.

There are nights when the weight of our shared sorrow feels unbearable,
when the silence of the world becomes deafening.
When the pain of missing our loved ones is too much to bear.
I find myself gripped with regret and despair;
with frustration
a flame that roars within me, demanding justice for the countless
lives shattered,
for the stolen freedoms, and for the dreams extinguished before they
could bloom.
For the lies, for the complicity, and for the opportunists.

But in the stillness that follows the storm,
I am reminded of the strength of our ancestors—
those who endured so that we might rise.

A LETTER TO THE UYGHUR DIASPORA

I see your faces, spread across the world,
Each of you carrying a piece of home in your hearts.
Your brilliance and resilience humble me;
Your courage reminds me that while anger may ignite a fire,
It is unity that rebuilds what has been broken.

Our struggle must not consume us,
Instead, let it fuel our determination,
Sharpen our voices,

Speak boldly, with the truth in our heart and the passion of our soul,
and be a voice for those who cannot speak.

Focus people's minds and hearts when we tell the stories,
So, when they hear, they cannot turn away

Rise above the disagreements of the past and do not let them become chains
    that bind you. Together, we are unbreakable.
Build bridges with those who may not understand our struggle,
Change begins with understanding.

Seek and cherish allies;
Wisdom and beauty bloom where differences meet.

Give generously, offering your time, your voice,
and your heart whenever and wherever you can.

Seek knowledge,
learn, grow, and teach,
Education empowers us all.
Support the women who have carried the burden of our survival;
Their strength is our legacy.

Celebrate.

UNBROKEN

Celebrate our culture, our dance, our music, our poetry, and our art—
Carry on our religion, language and heritage,
let it flow like a river to the next generation.

Remain agents of peace, lean on each other when we are in need,
speaking truth to power, lifting each other as we climb,
showing the world that even in our pain,
we will not forsake our principles.

Honor our people with a vision of a better world
where freedom and dignity are not dreams but promises kept.
And no matter how dark it gets,
hold onto hope, for it is the light that will guide us through.

Carry this torch together—
not to burn, but to illuminate the path ahead.

With steadfast hope and unyielding love,

RUSHAN ABBAS

AFTERWORD

The fight for justice does not end with the turning of these pages.

Though decades have passed since I first found myself entangled in this struggle, the weight of it remains—etched into my heart, carried in every breath, in every memory of those who have suffered and those who continue to suffer. The Uyghur diaspora is scattered across the world, living in exile, torn from the land that once rooted us. Their freedom came at a cost—a life of displacement, a longing for home that may never be fulfilled. And for those who remain behind, in the shadow of oppression, freedom is still a distant dream.

My sister remains imprisoned. Her future, uncertain. Her grandchildren are growing up without her, robbed of her warmth, her stories, her love. They are left with silence where her voice should be. And my people—our people—continue to endure under the crushing machinery of a regime that seeks to erase them.

But we remain unbroken.

History has shown us that no regime, no matter how brutal, can silence the truth forever. The world may turn away, governments may falter, but voices raised together can shake the walls of even the strongest prisons. I have seen it.

This journey has tested me in ways I never could have imagined. I have felt despair so deep it nearly swallowed me. I have felt frustration, helplessness, grief that has no words. But I have also witnessed extraordinary resilience. I have seen courage shine in the face of hopelessness, kindness emerge in the most unexpected places. I have learned that even in the darkest of times, a single voice—unyielding, unwavering—can become a lifeline.

This book is a record of pain, but also of love. Love for my people, love for justice, love for the truth, and love for freedom. It is a testament to what it means to refuse to be erased. To the sacrifices made in the pursuit of justice. To the unbreakable bonds that sustain us, no matter the distance, no matter the walls that separate us.

The Uyghur genocide is not just a tragedy—it is a test of our collective conscience. What we allow to happen to the Uyghurs today will set a precedent for how authoritarian regimes treat vulnerable communities in the future. This fight is about more than one people; it is about defending human dignity, freedom, and justice worldwide. You have the power to take a stand.

To those who want to do something to work towards a more just world, continue to educate yourself about the Uyghur genocide, the Uyghur people, their culture, and their heritage. Share what you learn with friends and family. Awareness matters, and it is the first step to impactful advocacy.

Let your lawmakers know you support holding China accountable for the abuse of Uyghurs. Demand stronger sanctions against those responsible for genocide, forced sterilization, transnational repression, forced labor, and mass surveillance. Advocate for policies that protect Uyghur asylum seekers and ensure they are not turned away but welcomed and given the opportunity to rebuild their communities. Governments must take a firm stance against religious persecution and family separation, but they will only act if we demand it.

The Uyghur issue must be included in global conversations about surveillance, artificial intelligence, women's reproductive rights, and data privacy. These discussions are incomplete without addressing how China is using these tools to erase an entire people. The world cannot claim to uphold human rights while ignoring one of the greatest human rights crises of our time.

Your choices as a consumer can drive real change. Refer to the comprehensive database provided by Jewish World Watch[30] and the Coalition to End Forced Labour in the Uyghur Region website[31] to find out if your favorite brand is being complicit. Companies pay attention when their customers demand accountability. Contact them. Make your voice heard. Boycott products tied to Uyghur forced labor, including clothing, agricultural goods, solar panels, and electric vehicle components. If you live in a country that does not have an import ban, encourage your government to eradicate Uyghur forced labor and Chinese forced labor from their supply chains. This will help impact the global standard for countering modern slavery.

If you have a platform—whether large or small—use it to uplift Uyghur stories. Invite Uyghur speakers, share their testimonies, and counter disinformation. Organize community events, sign petitions, connect with allies, and help spread the truth. Every action, no matter how small, contributes to the fight for justice.

---

30. Uyghur Forced Labor Database, https://jww.org/site/uyghur-china-forced-labor-database/
31. Coalition to End Forced Labour in the Uyghur Region, https://enduyghurforcedlabour.org/

AFTERWORD

Uyghur-led organizations like Campaign for Uyghurs are on the frontlines of this battle. Supporting our work through donations, attending events, or even hosting them in your university or community allows us to keep fighting. Visit the Campaign for Uyghurs' website, https://campaignforuyghurs.org, to stay informed, take action, and learn more about the Uyghur cause. Every ounce of support fuels our advocacy, strengthens our movement, and brings us closer to justice.

This is not just about the Uyghurs. It is about the future of freedom itself and future for our children. This is not just about one people or one region—this is about the fundamental values of freedom and democracy that shape our world. This is a fight between right and wrong. Good and evil. The fight for justice is a fight for the future, where human rights, dignity, and truth prevail over oppression. What happens to the Uyghurs is a test for all who believe in democracy, the rule of law, and a just global order. If we fail to stand against authoritarianism today, we risk a future where freedom is no longer guaranteed for anyone. The choice is ours. The choice is yours.

The fight is not over. . . .

But neither is our hope. Neither is our resolve.

To those who are still waiting for freedom—who are still waiting to be heard—I promise, we are still fighting. I am still fighting.

And we will never stop!

Rushan, with her eldest son Ronny, bowling in the Pacific Northwest on the final day of authoring *Unbroken: One Uyghur's Fight for Freedom*. April 2025.

INDEX

Note: Page numbers followed by "*n*" refer to notes.

Ababekri, Waris, 73, 74–75, 77, 80
Abaq, Qali, 42
Abbas Borhan, 28–29, 31, 70–71, 90–91, 93, 100
    Abdus Salam International Centre for Theoretical Physics (Trieste) visit, 58
    articles about, 138–144
    as Chairman of the Xinjiang Science and Technology Society, 52
    death of, 137
    detention and release, 47–49
    and "The Hope of Tengritagh Association", 74–77
    Janabil and, 94–95
    legacy of, 138
    as "local nationalist", 33–34, 39
    meeting with Faulkner, 81–82
    meeting with Iminov, 42, 44
    paper hats enforcement, 33–35
    rebels at home, 38, 40
    and Salam relationship, 58–59
    as the "Scholar for Life Science", 138
    struggle sessions, 50–51
    trip to the United States, 81
    "What I Witnessed" (Abbas Borhan), 31, 32–51, 123
Abbas, Gulshan, 16–18, 20, 60, 124, 131, 204, 208, 212
    China's Ministry of Foreign Affairs' press conference, 147–148
    health concerns, 147
    In Search of My Sister (documentary), 152–159, 198
    kin punishment, 148
    sentenced to jail, 147
    villainizing, 156
Abdulhakim Idris, 5–6, 13, 25, 59, 187, 198, 205, 206, 212, 213
    background and marriage, 145
    letters to his missing mother, 148–150
Abduqadir, Erkin, 140–141

INDEX

Abduqadir, Gulshen, 101
Abdus Salam International Centre for Theoretical Physics (Trieste), 58
Abliz Niyaz, 28, 42–43, 50, 123–124, 128
Afghanistan, 109, 112
Ahmed, Mudassar, 158
Aksu Prefecture, 56
Alptekin, Erkin, 101–102
al-Qaeda, 104, 112
Amat, Ismail, 61
Amnesty International, 133
Angola, 167
artificial intelligence surveillance systems, 166–167
Artush, 91–93, 124
Ashby, Dean, 193
atomic bomb testing, 60
Australian Strategic Policy Institute, 183
Australian Uyghur Tangritagh Women's Association (AUTWA), 10
Axel Springer Freedom Foundation, 205
Azizi, Saifuddin, 55–57

Barin Massacre (1990), 99–100
Batke, Jessica, 180
Bawudun, Medinay, 144
Bay County, 55–56
Beg, Helil, 65
Beijing Winter Olympics (2022), 185, 186, 191
diplomatic boycotts, 188, 189
Belt and Road Initiative (BRI), xxiv, 13, 13n2, 14, 54–55, 161, 162, 164, 167–168, 169, 170, 175, 192, 202
Berlin Olympics (1936), 188, 191
Bermuda, 116–118
Biden, Jill, 152
Biden, Joe, 152, 190
Bitter Winter (magazine), 11
Bitterwinter. org, 149
Blinken, Antony, 186
Brown, Eric, 12, 13, 23
Brown, Premier Ewart, 117, 118
Brownback, Sam, 20–21
Bugrahan, 145–146
Bunin, Gene, 21
Bush Center's Forum on Leadership, 206–207
Bush, Laura, 206–207
ByteDance, 204

"Caged Bird" (Angelou), xxviii
Campaign for Uyghurs (CFU), xx, 5, 188, 203, 206, 212, 214
board members, 23
CCP against, 25–26
cyberattack on, 21–22
genocide report, 181–186
In Search of My Sister, screenings of, 158–159
NED support for, 22
Nobel Peace Prize, nomination of, 190–191, 207
camps and the detentions, 4–5, 10, 11, 13–15, 152–153

Canada, 8, 158
Capitol Hill, 7, 151
Center for Constitutional Rights, 114, 115
"Century of Humiliation", 53
Cetinkaya, Aysu, 8
Cetinkaya, Mehliya, 8
Cetinkaya, Selami, 8
Chaqmaq River, 40–41
Chen Quanguo, 3, 165, 166
Chen Wenqing, 210
Chi Haotian, 182
Children of a Lesser God (movie), xxii
"China Undercover" (documentary), 184
Chinese Central Committee, 32
Chinese communist party (CCP), xix, xx, xxiv, 12, 53, 54, 121, 138, 177–180
    "Hundred Flowers Campaign", 27, 211
    Mao's "land reform" campaign, 27
    mass detentions of the Uyghurs, 4–5, 10, 11, 13–15, 152–153
    National Security Law (2020), 162
    transnational repression, xxiv, 16, 22, 147–60, 193, 199
    web of lies, 152–154
    see also Great Cultural Revolution (1966)
Chinese Language Council International ("Hanban"), 192
Chinese Students and Scholars Association (CSSA), 193
Clarke, Michael, 13
Cloudwalk, 167
Coates, John, 188
Columbia University, 193
concentration camps, xxiii, 5, 169
Concordia Forum, 158
Confucius Institutes, 191–193
Congressional Executive-Commission on China (CECC), 147, 198–199
cotton production, 183
Covid crisis, 213
Craig, Greg, 116, 117
cultural genocide, 177
Cultural Revolution (1966), xxii, 27–31, 32, 138, 215
    beginning of, 32
    detentions and release, 46–50
    forced labor, 35–36, 41
    "Great Wall Newspapers", 33
    humiliating signs or placards, 36, 38
    leadership of, 32–33
    newspapers role, 36–37, 41–42
    paper hats enforcement, 33–35
    rebels, division of, 38, 42
    Uyghur intellectuals, targeting of, 27–31
    Uyghurs, dividing of, 35
Currie, Kelley, 186

Dawamat, Tömür, 100

INDEX

Dawut, Rahila, 2
debt trap, 167
"December 12th Riot Incident", 62–73
Democratic Republic of the Congo (DRC), 167
Deng Xiaoping, 52, 161
Disney Corporation, 189–190
"Double Relative" assimilation program, 196
"Double-Linked Household Management System", 165
Douhan, Alena, 203
Dugway Proving Ground (Utah), 170
Duke University, 193–194
Dunleavy, Michael, 108, 109–110

East Turkistan Islamic Movement (ETIM), 113
East Turkistan Islamic Republic, 53
East Turkistan Union, 145
East Turkistan, 27, 54, 169
    colonization of, 163
    Han Chinese settlement, 61
Egypt, 167, 168
Eli, Ablimit, 58
Eliyev, Tiyipjan, 41, 41n7
Emet, Mijit, 61, 62–64, 144
Ezizi, Saifuddin, 61

facial recognition systems, 166, 167
Faulkner, Brent, 96, 97, 98–99
Faulkner, Ed, 96, 97, 98–99
Faulkner, Jenni, 96, 98–99
Faulkner, Lin, 81–82, 96–97
Faulkner, Lois, 96–97
First August Agricultural Institute, 82–84, 85, 87, 88, 95
Flipse, Scott, 198
Forced Labor Enforcement Task Force, 200
forced marriages, 3, 4
Forkan, 145–146
Fort Benning, 106
Fried, Daniel, 117, 121

Genocide in East Turkistan report, 181–186
genocide, ten stages of, 194–197
Gere, Richard, 171
Germany, 181
    Mihrihan Anilar ("Caring Mothers") initiative, 10
Ghulja Massacre (1997), 24, 24n3, 44, 111
Ghulja protest (Feb 5, 1997), 100–101
Gittleman, Andrea, 180
Global Times, 147
Great Chinese Famine (1959–1961), 55–56
Great Leap Forward, 55
Great Western Development Strategy, 164
Greenwood, Clive, 201
Greve, Louisa, 12
Guangdong Liangma Law, 200, 201
Guantanamo Bay detention camp (Cuba), 105–122
    after 9/11 attacks, 107

Camp Delta, 107
Camp X-Ray, 107
Chinese interrogators in, 113
habeas corpus, 114
resettlement of Uyghurs, 116–118, 121
Uyghur detainees, interrogation of, 108–114
Uyghurs: Prisoners of the Absurd (film), 120–121, 155
Gulf countries, 168
Guterres, Antonio, 9

Hamra (wife of Rishat), 25
Han Chinese, 3, 4, 119–120, 163, 165, 183, 195, 196
Hanliang, Song, 83–85, 87, 89, 90
Harri, Halmurat, 147
Hasan, Ilshat, 7
He Jingnian, 56–57
He Rui, 56–57
Heinz Corporation, 183
Henríquez, Patricio, 120–121
Hogrefe, Hans, 180
Holocaust Memorial Museum (Washington, DC), 180
Hong Kong, 54, 162, 169, 205
"The Hope of Tengritagh Association", 73–76
protest, 78–80
Students Drenched in Joy", 77
into "Students Science and Cultural Association", 76–77
Hu Lianhe, 164
Huawei, 167

Hudson Institute, 19
panel on "China's 'War on Terrorism' and the Xinjiang Emergency", 12–16
Human Rights Watch (HRW), 1, 120, 133, 182, 184
"Hundred Flowers Campaign", 27, 211

Idris, Abdurehim, 15
Ijaz, Mujeeb, 151–152
Ilham, Jewher, 2
Iltebir, Ablikim Baki, 6, 139–140
Iminov, Hebibe, 43–44, 45–46
Iminov, Muhammed Imin, 32, 42, 43, 44–45
Immigration and Nationality Act, 209
Immigration Detention Center (IDC) (Bangkok), 173
imports, 170
In Search of My Sister (documentary), 152–159, 198
leaks, 157–158
official release, 158
Integrated Joint Operations Platform (IJOP), 166
International Court of Justice (ICJ), 186
International Labour Organization (ILO), 153
International Olympic Committee (IOC), 188, 191
International Religious Freedom Summit, 20

INDEX

internment camps. *See* camps and the detentions
Interparliamentary Task Force on Human Trafficking conference, 198
Iran, 168
Isa, Dolkun, 73, 74–75, 77, 79, 205
"Islamic terrorism", 14

Jalalidin, Abduqadir, 159–160
Jana Cekara Film Festival, 155
Japan, 172, 173–174
Jappar, Abdulhakim, 34, 79
Jin Shuren, 53

Kaiser, Walter J., 81
Kaixi, Wuer, 23
Kampala police (Uganda), 167
Kanat, Omer, 205
Kashgar, 58
Kashgary, Sureyya, 6
Kathy, 133
Kenya, 167
Kerry, John, 190
Kikoler, Naomi, 180
Kissel, Mary, 186
Klimeš, Ondřej, 158
Knowledge Is Power (journal), 143–144
Konasheher County, 166
Kornbluth, Provost, 193
Krishnamoorthi, Raja, 206, 207
Kurban, Mukerrem, 6, 8–9
Kyrgyzstan, 112

Letip, Abdurehim, 42
Little Red Book (Mao Zedong), 37
Long Shoujin, 49
Löning GmbH, 200
Löning, Markus, 200
Lu Shaye, 169

Magnitsky Act, 176–177, 185
Mahmud al-Kashgari, 58
Manchu dynasty, xx
Mao Zedong Quotes, 48, 49, 51
Mao Zedong, 27, 28, 30, 36, 37, 38, 55
  "May 16th Manifesto", 32
  print newspapers of, 41–42
  see also Great Cultural Revolution (1966)
Mariye Abliz, 28, 29–30, 33, 34, 35, 37, 40, 45, 46, 47, 49
  background, 123–124
  belief in kindness, 126
  calla lily, 129–130
  death of, 123, 129
  devotion to her children, 125–126
  forced harvest labor, 50
  locked up in a house at the General Administration, 51
  medical expertise, 127
  medical practice, forcibly removed from, 128–129
  meeting with Iminov, 42, 44
  professional journey, 124, 125

her resilience, 128
retirement, 127
sense of compassion, 128
Shireen Sweets (bakery), 117
her students, 126–127
Uyghur women empowerment, 127–128
work ethic, 124–125
mass detentions, 4–5, 10, 11, 13–15, 152–153
Menace: China's Colonization of the Islamic World & Uyghur Genocide (Abdulhakim), 5, 149–150
Merkley, Jeff, 198
Mihrihan Anilar ("Caring Mothers") initiative, 10
Mir, Jawad, 151–152, 154
Misron (Ronny), xxi, 130–131, 132, 133, 134, 137, 208
Momin, Yusuf, 42, 42
Moolenaar, John, 207–208
Morgan Stanley Capital International, 201
Morrison, Sid, 100
MREs (Meals Ready-to-Eat), 111n18
Muhammetimin, Abdushukur, 47, 48
Mulan (movie), 190

National Endowment for Democracy (NED), 22
National Security Law (2020), 162
Naval Station Norfolk, 170
Nazi concentration camps, 182

Nazi Germany, 180
"The New Colossus" (Lazarus), xxvii
New York Times, The, 18
New York, 7, 8
Nigeria, 168
Nijat, 20, 37, 60, 124, 126
9/11 attacks, 104–105, 108, 212
 interrogation, 108–110
"No Way Back Home" (Jalalidin), 159–160
nuclear test (Lop Nur), 54
Nuremberg trials, 181

Office of the High Commissioner for Human Rights (OHCHR), 204
"One Voice, One Step" initiative, 6–10, 12
Operation Enduring Freedom, 107
Opium War I (1839–1842), 53
Ordu-Baliq, xix
Orwell, George, xxiii
Osmanof, Mirsultan, 47
Overseas Development Institute, 168

"Pair Up and Become Family" program, 3, 183
Pakistan, 109, 112–113
Palau, 120
Paris Climate Accords, 190
People's Liberation Army, 182
Platt Amendment, 107
Polat (son of Iminov), 44, 45
Pompeo, Mike, 186
Price, Vincent, 193, 194

INDEX

Pride (*Ghururname*) (Abduqadir), 140–141
Pulati, Akeda, 2
"punishment on the spot" policy, 164, 166

Qasim, Abu Bakr, 111–113, 114–115
Qing dynasty, 53

Radio Free Asia Uyghur Service, 15, 24, 72, 103, 109, 131, 180
Red Army, 27
Red Guards, 28, 29–30, 36–37–40
  in Tiananmen Square, 37
  "struggle sessions", 38, 41n8
  see also Cultural Revolution (1966)
"reeducation" camps, xxiii, 3, 12, 13, 165, 166, 169
Reporters, The, 173
Reyhan (wife of Iminov), 43
Reyhan, Dilnur, 199
Richardson, Sophie, 184
Rishat Abbas, 20, 22, 23–25, 26, 50, 103, 124, 143–144
Roberts, Sean, 13, 113
Rozi, Yalqun, 2
Rubio, Marco, 205, 209

SA8000 standards, 201
Salam, Abdus, 58
Salam, Ahmad, 59
Saudi Arabia, 168–169
Sayim, Polat, 173–174

Schriver, Randal, 176
September 11 attacks, 104–105, 108, 212
Seytoff, Alim, 180
Seyyid (Yarkent) Kingdom, xx
Shad (Shadman), 99, 105, 121, 131, 132, 134–135, 137, 208
Shahidi, Borhan, 35, 35n5, 36
Shahidi, Nusrat, 35, 36
Shahidi, Suyum, 35, 36
Shamseden, Zubeyra, 6
Shanghai Cooperation Organization (SCO), 109, 112
Shawdun, Abdurehim, 33
Shawn Zhang, 10
Sheng Shicai, 53
Shireen Sweets (bakery), 117
Shireen, 105, 121, 131, 132, 133, 135–136, 137, 145, 208
Shoot-to-Kill policy, 164, 166
Sidik, Erkin, 103
Simahuli, Janabil, 83, 94–95
Small, Andrew, 13
Smith, Chris, 147, 151, 159, 190, 198, 203, 206, 207
Staley, Jamie, 7
State Imposed Forced Labor, 153
Steigmann, Sami, 186
sterilization, 4, 153
Strike Hard Campaign, 164–165, 178
"Students Drenched in Joy", 77
Sulaiman, Eset, 57
Suozzi, Tom, 147, 151, 159, 190–191, 203, 207

Taiwan, 169
Taliban, 112
Talip, Selime, 42, 45
Tang Dynasty, xix
Taylor, Michele, 202
Tengritagh Uyghur Overseas Student and Scholars Association, 103
"Testimony to Ethnic Equality, Unity and Development in Xinjiang", 165
Teyip, Nur, 88–89
Thailand, 172–173, 174
Tiananmen Square Massacre, 62, 97–98, 119, 161
Tiankai, 195
Tibet, 54, 165, 166, 171
TikTok bill, 203–204
TikTok, 174
Tohti, Ilham, 2, 204
Tora Bora mountains, 112
Toribiong, Johnson, 120
Toyan Prairie, 40–41
Tozzi, Piero, 198
transnational repression, xxiv, 16, 22, 147–60, 193, 199
Trump, Donald, 151, 185
Turkel, Nury, 152
Turkey, 172
Twitter (now X), 4, 10, 19

Ulughchat County, 40–41
UN Committee on the Elimination of Racial Discrimination (CERD), 11–12
UN Watch, 203
UN Working Group on Arbitrary Detention, 204
United Nations Human Rights Council (UNHRC), 9, 11
United Nations Security Council (UNSC), 9
United Nations, 7, 8, 181, 189
United States (US), 170
    airstrikes in Afghanistan, 112
    Beijing Winter Olympics, diplomatic boycott, 189
    Chinese Embassy, 4, 5
    free speech, 121
    freedom and democracy, xxiii, 26
    Iraq war, 113, 114
Universal Periodic Review (UPR), 202–203
Unrepresented Nations and Peoples Organization (UNPO), 101
Urbina, Ricardo M., 115, 116, 121
Urumchi City Police Department, 96
Urumchi Massacre (2009), 119–120, 132, 182
Urumchi, 1, 24, 28, 38, 56
    American scholars' visit to, 81
    Shaoguan attack (2009), 119–120
US National Prayer Breakfast, 199–200
US Senate Committee on Foreign Relations (SFRC), 21
USA Today, 176
Uyghur Academy, 24, 25, 143

INDEX

Uyghur American Association (UAA), 24, 103
Uyghur Association Board, 180
Uyghur Cultural and Education Association, 10
Uyghur cultural event (Capitol Hill), 7
Uyghur Forced Labor Prevention Act (UFLPA), 186, 200
Uyghur Friendship Group, 173–174
Uyghur Genocide Accountability and Sanctions Act (2024), 151
Uyghur Human Rights Policy Act (UHRPA), 25, 151, 184–185
Uyghur Human Rights Project, 190
Uyghur intellectuals
    arrest of, 1–2
    articles about Abbas Borhan, 138–144
    forced to wear paper hats, 33–35
    Mao's regime targeted, 27
    organizing, 25
    Red Guards' target, 29–31
    Uyghur student protests (1988), 62–80
Uyghur Khaganate, xix
Uyghur student protests (1988, Urumchi), 62–80
    December 11 meeting, 62–65, 71, 72
    December 12 movement, 65–67
    interrogation, 67–72
    Students Science and Cultural Association, 78–80
    thirty-seventh anniversary of, 72
Uyghur Tribunal (2021, London), 25, 187–188
Uyghur women
    campaign of mass rape, 3
    injustice against, xxiii
    Mihrihan Anilar ("Caring Mothers") initiative, 10
    "*One Voice, One Step*" initiative, 6–10, 12
    sexual abuse, xxiii, 3
Uyghurian, Tahir Imin, 198
Uyghurs: Prisoners of the Absurd (film), 120–121
Uyghurs
    DNA collection, 1
    as extremists, xxiii
    forced sterilizations, 4, 153
    homeland, xix–xx, xxiv
    hope and resilience, xxv
    monitoring and surveillance, 3
    passport, obtaining, 95–96
    policy of destruction against Uyghur officials, 61–62
    restrictions on religious studies, 109, 109n17, 182–183
    suppression of Uyghur birth rates, 3–4
    unemployment, 61
    violation of privacy, 1

"vocational training", 18
Volkswagen, 200–202

Waltz, Mike, 203
Wang Enmao, 37, 42
The War on the Uyghurs (Roberts), 113
Washington Post, The, 18, 176, 185
Washington State University, 81, 82, 88, 96, 100
Water Margin, xxiv
Weinstein, Ken, 12, 19
Western Train Station, 48
"What I Witnessed" (Abbas Borhan), 31, 32–51, 123
WhatsApp, 6
"Where is My Family" movement, 213
Willett, Sabin, 114–115, 116, 117, 121, 134
World Bank, 163
World Uyghur Congress (WUC), 101, 172, 205
World Uyghur Youth Congress, 145
World War II, 182

Xi Jinping, 9, 54, 162, 163, 164, 216
Xinjiang Daily News, 59
Xinjiang Education Ministry, 84–88, 96
   Red Head File, 86–90
Xinjiang Famine, 55–56
Xinjiang Medical Institute (Urumchi), 124
Xinjiang Police Files, 166, 169

Xinjiang Production and Construction Corps (XPCC) (Bingtuan), 163
Xinjiang Public Security Bureau, 190
Xinjiang University, xxii, 3, 29–30, 31, 32–33
   Biology Department, 60
   criticism event, 36, 39–40
   Cultural Revolution task force at, 32–33
   forced labor, 35–36, 50
   humiliating signs or placards, 36, 38, 39–40
   paper hats enforcement, 33–35
   rebels, division of, 38, 42
   "Red Building", 29–30
   students sent to military farms, 51
   Uyghur intellectuals, targeting of, 28–31
   Uyghurs, dividing of, 35
   see also Uyghur student protests (1988, Urumchi)
Xinjiang Uyghur Autonomous Region" (XUAR)
   criminals sent to, 60–61
   Famine (1959–1961), 55–56
   Students Science and Cultural Association student protest, 78–80
   surveillance state, 167
Xinjiang Victims Database (Shahit.biz), 21

INDEX

"Xinjiang" (New Territory), xx, 1, 12, 53
   Xi Jinping visit, 164
Xu Guixiang, 156

Yaglakar Dynasty, xix
Yalqun, Kamalturk, 2, 23
Yalqun, Tumaris, 2
Yang Zengxing, 53
Yasin, Dolqun, 43, 45–46
Yasin, Ihtibar, 20
Yilamujiang, 191

Zamira (daughter of Gulshan Abbas), 16, 207
Zenz, Adrian, 4, 152–153, 165–166, 180, 183–184, 186, 201
Zhang Yang, 84–85, 87
Zhao Lijuan, 121
Ziba (daughter of Gulshan Abbas), 16, 152, 204, 205
Zimbabwe, 167